Sociological
Theory:
Historical and Formal

Sociological Theory:
Historical and Formal

Neil J. Smelser
University of California,
Berkeley

R. Stephen Warner
Yale University

GENERAL LEARNING PRESS
250 James Street
Morristown, N.J. 07960

Manufactured in the United States of America

Published simultaneously in Canada

Library of Congress Catalog Card Number 76-4716

ISBN 0-382-26018-X

ACKNOWLEDGMENTS

DOUBLEDAY & COMPANY, INC.: *The Old Regime and the French Revolution* by
Alexis de Tocqueville. Translated by Stuart Gilbert. Excerpts from pages 30, 136–137,
140, and 176–177. Copyright ©, 1955, by Doubleday & Company, Inc.

INTERNATIONAL PUBLISHERS CO., INC.: *The German Ideology* (Parts I and III)
by Karl Marx and Frederick Engels. Edited by R. Pascal. Excerpts from pages 2, 22,
197, 198, and 199. Copyright, 1947, by International Publishers Co., Inc.

OXFORD UNIVERSITY PRESS: From *From Max Weber: Essays in Sociology*, tr. and ed.
by H. H. Gerth and C. Wright Mills. Copyright 1946 by Oxford University Press, Inc.
Renewed 1973 by Dr. Hans H. Gerth. Reprinted by permission of the publisher.
Excerpts from pages 55, 71, 78, 82, 121, 128, 140, 147, 151, 271, 276–277, 280, and
294.

CHARLES SCRIBNER'S SONS: *The Protestant Ethic and the Spirit of Capitalism* by
Max Weber. Translated by Talcott Parsons. Excerpts from pages 35, 48, 115, 171,
181–182, and 229. By permission of Charles Scribner's Sons. Copyright 1930 Charles
Scribner's Sons.

THE FREE PRESS: *Suicide* by Emile Durkheim. Translated by John A. Spaulding and
George Simpson. Excerpts from pages 89, 210, 246–254, 315, 383, and 390. Copyright 1951 by The Free Press, a Corporation. Reprinted by permission of the publisher.

MACMILLAN PUBLISHING CO., INC.: Excerpts from pages 5, 26, 27, 28, 69, 81,
106, 213–214, 262, 267, and 404–405. Reprinted with permission of Macmillan
Publishing Co., Inc. from *The Division of Labor in Society* by Emile Durkheim. Translated by George Simpson. Copyright 1947 by The Free Press. Excerpts from pages
xxxvii, 5–6, 49, 56, 95, 96, 97, and 101–102. Reprinted by permission of Macmillan
Publishing Co., Inc. from *The Rules of Sociological Method* by Emile Durkheim. Translated by S. A. Solovay and J. H. Mueller. Copyright 1938 by George E. G. Catlin,
renewed 1966 by Sarah A. Solovay, John H. Mueller, and George E. G. Catlin.

Preface

In the Introduction that follows, we describe the ways in which the two essays in this book complement one another. We regard this complementarity as hardly accidental, as a brief review of our academic histories will document.

Before his arrival at the University of California, Berkeley, in the fall of 1958, Neil J. Smelser spent several months working out a one-semester undergraduate "theory course" in sociology. He decided to combine the conventionally separated spheres of classical theory and contemporary theory into a single course to show better the continuity of the sociological enterprise. The result was Sociology 109, a course required for sociology majors but increasingly elected by scores of others over a seven-year period. The course underwent a number of revisions before Smelser set down the essay presented here.

R. Stephen Warner enrolled as an undergraduate in Smelser's Sociology 109 in 1963 and acted as a teaching assistant for it in 1965.

Along with his fellow students and teaching assistants, he was impressed by the power of the theories that Smelser explicated and stunned by Smelser's exposure of their logical and empirical flaws. He was especially concerned, however, with a problem raised by Smelser at the outset of the course but never (in Warner's view) satisfactorily resolved: How is derivation of hypotheses possible if we fail to identify the basic axioms or postulates that link one concept to another? (The essay presented here by Smelser devotes some additional attention to this issue.) Over a period of time, Warner became convinced that the understanding of a theory must begin with the explication of its domain assumptions. When he was asked to teach courses in sociological theory at Sonoma State College (1967–1968), at the University of California, Berkeley (1969–1970), and at Yale University (currently), his ideas gradually evolved into the approach represented in this book. For several years, his graduate course in the "History of Sociological Thought" has been presented along these lines (with the additional treatments of Simmel, Freud, and others).

Each essay is, therefore, deeply rooted in our individual teaching experiences, and we welcome this opportunity to bring our ideas together. We wish to acknowledge our sources of assistance, support, and helpful criticism. Warner is plainly and deeply indebted to Smelser; to Barclay Johnson, who was a fellow teaching assistant in the original Sociology 109; and to the oral and written reactions of the many students who participated in his theory courses. For fellowship support during part of the writing of his essay, Warner is grateful to Yale University and to the John Simon Guggenheim Memorial Foundation; and for their hospitality, he thanks the Department of Sociology at the University of California, San Diego. Finally, Warner has benefited from the manuscript comments made by Jeffrey L. Berlant, Bliss Cartwright, Mary E. Curran, Bruce C. Johnson, Ellen Langer, Leon Mayhew, Ronnie Steinberg Ratner, and Jonathan Rieder. Smelser's debts are somewhat more diffuse. He would like to thank the graduate students who served as teaching assistants for Sociology 109 in the years he offered it, and, in particular, Warner, whose association over many years has constituted an important learning experience and friendship. The hundreds of undergraduates who took the course should also be mentioned; their response to the course was always gratifying, and many of their questions and comments continue to shape Smelser's reflections about sociological theory.

RSW

NJS

Contents

PART TWO
Sociological Theory: A Contemporary View

CONTENTS

CHAPTER **9**
Issues That Arise in Theorizing in the Social Sciences:

CHAPTER **10**
Emile Durkheim's Theory of Suicide   161

CHAPTER **11**
Talcott Parsons' Theory of Deviance and Social Control   179

CHAPTER **12**
Karl Marx's Theory of Economic Organization and
  Class Conflict   205

x

Introduction

This book brings together two different but complementary treatises on sociological theory. Though each is self-contained, the two essays show certain affinities. In these opening pages we shall indicate briefly their points of agreement and their analytical differences.

In Part I, Warner focuses on the theories of Tocqueville, Marx, Durkheim, and Weber. In Part II, Smelser discusses Durkheim, Parsons, Marx, and Michels. An obvious point of agreement, then, is the treatment in both essays of the works of Durkheim and Marx. Beyond the fact that we are in basic agreement about the identity of the sociological classics, there are three notable convictions that we share.

First, we—and the theorists whom we analyze—endorse the enterprise of studying society scientifically. Whether or not the methods of social science are identical to those of other sciences, we affirm the possibility and the necessity of regarding social life as an area of existence amenable to disciplined, clear-sighted analysis. In Part I, Warner outlines the process of the "discovery of society," in which the nucleus of the sociological viewpoint triumphed over earlier, nonsociological and non-scientific, approaches. In Part II, Smelser spells out a set of criteria by which the scientific adequacy of any sociological theory can be judged. These two frameworks complement each other nicely.

Second, both of us take theories as our object of analysis. Though we reconstruct theories differently, we take them seriously as intellectual productions, attempting sympathetically but critically to move through a process of reasoning as the theorist himself might have done. We accept provisionally the theorist's own grounds as legitimate; we explicate his ideas in a way that he did not but in a way that does not do violence to his project. We each assess the theory's internal consistency and then evaluate the theory according to other criteria, whether empirical, methodological, or philosophical.

Third, we each reject as false the dichotomy between the "history of sociological thought" and "contemporary sociological theory." Although only one of our protagonists (Talcott Parsons) is contemporary, we regard the theories of all of these men as alive and useful today. Smelser uses one set of criteria to analyze four theories formulated in 1867, 1897, 1911, and 1951. The historical scope of the works treated by Warner extends from about 1760 to 1920. The issues that he outlines can be used to illuminate contemporary theories as well.

Notwithstanding these common orientations, our two essays employ different approaches, as the reader will immediately perceive. The most evident difference between the two contributions to this volume is that although we both chose Durkheim and Marx, Smelser does not consider Tocqueville or Weber and Warner does not discuss Michels or Parsons. Since each of us aimed to be selective rather than exhaustive, however, that difference is of little consequence. Each of us could have chosen a number of other theorists (for example, Freud or Radcliffe-Brown) to support the analytic points made about theory. Indeed, in other writings, we have done so: Smelser has developed an exposition and critique of Tocqueville as a comparative analyst,[1] and Warner has subjected Parson's theoretical formulations on money, on power, and on other "generalized media" to a critical evaluation and elaboration.[2] The important point about the essays in this volume does not concern which theorists we choose to analyze as much as it concerns *what the respective theorists tell us about theorizing.*

There are several important nuances of difference in *how* we analyze the theorists. These differences may be summarized by noting that Warner's emphasis tends to be more *substantive* and Smelser's more *methodological.* This contrast, moreover, has several facets.

First, Warner tends to approach the systems of ideas that constitute a theory by asking how they are grounded in more general *philosophical and metaphysical assumptions*. He outlines, for example, the historical development of a set of ideas about human nature and about the social order, ideas that are distinctively sociological in substance. He focuses on fundamental assumptions about human nature and social order, about the nature of conflict, and about the relations between knowledge and action, using these as dimensions for distinguishing theorists from one another. Smelser, while acknowledging the importance of general assumptions in the structure of a theory, tends to approach systems of ideas by asking how they are grounded in *scientific norms and procedures*. He is more interested in whether a theoretical framework is logically consistent, in whether it is capable of generating hypotheses through derivation, and in whether those hypotheses are testable.

This point of contrast is best seen in our respective critical remarks on Marx's assertions about the nature of capitalism and on his derivation of predictions for its revolutionary demise. In asking why Marx's predictions appear not to have been fulfilled for advanced capitalist societies, Warner suggests that some of Marx's substantive *assumptions* appear to have been oversimplifications or otherwise in error. These include Marx's assumption of bourgeois rigidity, his assumption of worker homogeneity, and his assumption of the progressive polarization of society and the progressive immiseration of the workers under capitalism. Smelser's assessment of Marx's predictions agrees in part with Warner's; in particular, Smelser suggests that if Marx's assumptions concerning the workers' needs and wants were modified, many of his incorrect predictions would become more tenable. In general, however, Smelser tends to trace the unsatisfactoriness of Marx's analyses and predictions to certain *logical and methodological flaws* in his formulations— to the vagueness, logical contradiction, and immeasurability of concepts like simple average labor, surplus value, and exploitation.

Second, both of us are concerned with different facets of the empirical aspects of theory. Warner tends to be more interested in what impact a theory has upon man's purposive efforts to make and remake society. Marx not only diagnosed and explained the evils of capitalist society, but he also believed that his theory would directly inspire revolutionary action and would ultimately play a central role in the revolutionary transformation of society. Durkheim not only developed a scientific theory of modern society as perilously balanced between the forces of social integration and those of disintegration, but he also believed that through that scientific understanding people could, by purposive effort, enhance the unity and solidarity of society. Smelser tends to minimize the role of theories as instruments of social transformation. His interest in the empirical side of theories tends to be more strictly explanatory. He asks how theories, as explanatory frameworks, square with the empirical facts available to the theorist and also with data that have been recorded since. He asks whether Marx's theory gives a good account of the behavior of British workers in the early nineteenth century, but he ignores the question of whether such a theory constituted a cause for their behavior. He asks whether Durkheim's account of variations in suicide rates among many social groups is adequate, but he ignores the question of whether our scientific understanding of those rates might contribute to society's purposive efforts to modify them and their causes. In other words, Warner is concerned with the power of theories as instruments of historical change, Smelser with the validity of theories as devices to explain history.

Third, Warner is more interested in the historical and biographical contexts of theoretical development than Smelser. He often turns to the intellectual influences that were dominant in a given period—the influences of positivism or individualism, for example—and asks how they formed either a positive influence or a polemic target for a given theorist. He sometimes asks the same kind of question about a theorist's personal biography; he considers, for example, the unique pattern of individuals and ideas that influenced Marx's formulations at different phases of his career. And finally, Warner seeks to show how theorists were influenced by the very social and historical changes which they are attempting to explain; the changing fortunes of the various classes in France in the late eighteenth and early nineteenth centuries, for example, were certainly among the significant influences on Tocqueville's distinctive preoccupations with equality and liberty. To ask such contextual questions enriches our understanding of theorists. Without asking them we cannot know why they made the choices they did. Smelser's concern, again by contrast, tends to be more formal and "timeless." Recognizing that a given system of ideas is a definite product of a specific set of historical and personal circumstances, he nevertheless proceeds to consider those ideas without special reference to those circumstances. Instead, he uses a number of general and unvarying, logical and methodological criteria that are pertinent to *any* self-conscious effort to generate explanations of society, no matter at what time or in what context they might have been produced.

We regard these points of contrast as complementary rather than contradictory. Taken together, our two essays provide an analysis that is more comprehensive, more complex, and more provocative than either of us, working alone, could possibly have generated.

---

1. Neil J. Smelser, "Alexis de Tocqueville as Comparative Analyst." In Ivan Vallier, ed., *Comparative Methods in Sociology: Essays on Trends and Applications* (University of California Press, 1971).
2. Bliss C. Cartwright and R. Stephen Warner, "The Medium Is Not the Message: An Analysis of Talcott Parsons on Power and Money as Generalized Media." In J. J. Loubser et al., eds., *Explorations in General Theory in the Social Sciences* (The Free Press, forthcoming).

PART ONE

Sociological
Theory
in Historical Context

R. Stephen Warner
Yale University

CHAPTER 1

The Uses of the "Classic Tradition"

This essay introduces and endorses an activity that professional sociologists typically pursue: the study of the "classic tradition" in sociology. In the course of this discussion, I shall focus on the ideas of four men, whose works are widely recognized as part of this tradition: Alexis de Tocqueville (1805–1859), Karl Marx (1818–1883), Emile Durkheim (1858–1917), and Max Weber (1864–1920). Making the rounds of any good department of sociology, you are likely to hear students and faculty members discussing the works of or mentioning the names of such long-deceased men as Durkheim and Weber. You would probably see many people reading Durkheim's *Suicide* or Weber's *Protestant Ethic and the Spirit of Capitalism*—or, at the least, you would spot these books resting prominently on library and study shelves. Indeed, you would receive the impression that sociologists, more than practitioners of such disciplines as physics, biology, and even economics, are remarkably obsessed with the past achievements of their discipline. Why should this be so?

The Classics as Data

A sociologist can have a number of reasons for studying the work of the founders of his field. He might study the classics in pursuit of an enterprise called the *sociology of sociological thought*—a branch of the sociology of knowledge, in which the investigator seeks to unveil the social sources for or the backgrounds to specific kinds of thought. Typically, the investigator addresses such issues as the social class background of a social theorist, his career pattern, his pattern of contact with other theorists, and the predominant social issues of his day. Karl Mannheim [1936] is correctly regarded as one of the founders of this sort of investigation. The contemporary American sociologist Lewis Coser astutely employs a sociology-of-knowledge perspective in his study entitled *Masters of Sociological Thought* [1971]. Coser contributes to our understanding of certain theorists by suggesting answers to such questions as why Georg Simmel did not develop a systematic sociology and why Weber's sociology was so deeply pessimistic. Yet the practitioner of the sociology of knowledge is less interested in the *ideas* of social thinkers than in explaining *why* they said what they did. In hands less deft than Coser's, this approach too often degenerates into an attempt to *explain away* the works of social thinkers. At least by implication, this approach tends to diminish their utility for us. Many sociologists rightly persist in reading the classics not merely as sources of data about social thought but as inspirations for their own thought.

Then, a sociologist might use the founders and their activities as data for a closely related type of inquiry: the *sociology* (or *history*) *of sociology as a discipline*. Inspired by such sociologists as Edward Shils [1970], this enterprise seeks to locate the factors that have contributed to the institutionalization of sociology, especially to its incorporation into graduate training departments and to its organization into professional associations. Recently, Paul Lazarsfeld and his associates have published a series of studies on the emergence and institutionalization of sociology as an empirical science in several countries (see Oberschall 1972). These studies have contributed to our understanding of some of the classic thinkers (as Terry Clark [1973] points out, for example, Durkheim's work has to be understood in part as an attempt to make sociology fundamental to the French educational system). They have also suggested the ways in which sociology as a discipline might be better organized to carry out its tasks. Still, this branch of sociological inquiry is more interested in explaining the relative *success* of particular sociological schools than in examining the ideas themselves. Moreover, the study of the rise of sociology as a discipline frequently must concern itself with intellectual productions that most sociologists today consider outmoded and even quaint (for example, the racialist ideas of the nineteenth century).

Thus, the reading of the classics in which sociologists engage has also to be distinguished from *intellectual history*, a related enterprise which is challenging and valuable in its own right. Reading Richard Hofstadter's *Social Darwinism in American Thought* [1955] enhances our understanding of the beginnings of American sociology, and reading Carl Becker's *The Heavenly City of the Eighteenth Century Philosophers* [1932] expands our knowledge about the Enlightenment. From these books, the reader learns to appreciate how the spirit of a specific time and place is reflected in systematic social thought—how the individualistic spirit of nineteenth-century America is reflected in early American sociology and how the rationalistic spirit of eighteenth-century France is reflected in the works of the *philosophes*. Yet the sociologist's selective attention to a few great thinkers of the past strikes the historian as eclectic and as a violation of historical continuity. That Herbert Spencer (1820–1903) was in fashion among sociologists at the turn of the century, that he was declared intellectually dead three decades later, and that he has recently been partially resurrected would seem irresponsible faddism if we were to suppose that the current sociologist's interest in past sociologists is genuinely historical.

Many of the sociologists who read Durkheim and Weber, however, are seeking to *learn from* them. In this sense, there is no radical break between the study of the classics and contemporary theory. To be sure, these contemporary sociologists make use of the writings of sociologists of knowledge and those of intellectual historians, in order to understand the founders. Ideally, however, they do not regard the classics as merely data to be used or approach them merely as problems to be explained. Rather, they regard the classic authors as colleagues, and engage with them in what Robert Merton [1967] has aptly called "a dialogue between the dead and the living." In conversations with a living person, it helps to know "where he is coming from" in order to understand his observations; so also it is valuable to understand the context in which a thinker of the past wrote. If you live in a medium-sized American city and if a visitor tells you that he finds your city busy, noisy, and frightening, his statement carries different meanings if he comes from a small New England town, from New York, Chicago, or Los Angeles, or from a village in southern Italy. Similarly, to evaluate the methodological writings of Emile Durkheim and Max Weber, it is essential to appreciate the different intellectual contexts in which they participated. Therefore, our approach to the classic thinkers is facilitated by, but not identical to, the sociology of knowledge and intellectual history.

6

The Classics as Colleagues

All of the men whom we shall consider died at least a half century ago, wrote in a field in which there has been an explosion of research and publication in that half-century, and lived in times and places vastly different from our own. In what sense can we say that the works of these men are still sources for a contemporary dialogue? Many answers can be given, but we will mention three that seem to be of widely acknowledged importance.

First, the works of Tocqueville, Marx, Durkheim, and Weber are replete with propositions, interpretations, hypotheses, theories—in short, with sociological *ideas*—that we can apply to our own understanding of society. Some of these ideas lend themselves to concise restatement as discrete propositions. Examples of such propositions include Tocqueville's notion that social unrest is produced by a sharp downturn in welfare following an extended period of advance; Marx's suggestion that political predisposition can be predicted on the basis of socioeconomic position; Durkheim's correlation of religious affiliation and suicide rates; and Weber's thesis that entrepreneurial activity is likely to be found disproportionately among members of Protestant religious groups. These ideas, like other similar ones, have been tested, refined, reformulated, sometimes refuted, and sometimes affirmed by contemporary research. Because the men who posited them were brilliant social analysts, their works are rich mines of such ideas in our own search for understanding and knowledge.

And yet, if such discrete propositions can be extracted from the classics, why should we bother to read the originals? Why is it not enough to codify these propositions, to assess them in light of the current evidence, and to consign the original studies to the student of history? To be sure, there is great merit in the kind of codification that has been done by Lewis Coser in *Functions of Social Conflict* [1956] (which draws heavily on Simmel) or by Ralf Dahrendorf in *Class and Class Conflict in Industrial Society* [1959] (which was inspired by Marx and Weber). These authors have attempted to update, rather than to deify, classical works and have thus contributed to the growth of sociological understanding. Moreover, it is folly to maintain that the classic works are currently viable in all aspects. Developments in research methods and in techniques of statistical analysis have surpassed the efforts of Marx to survey workers' attitudes [Weiss 1973] and the efforts of Weber to establish a statistical correlation between Protestantism and entrepreneurship.[1] Furthermore, sociological and historical scholarship have cast doubt upon the accuracy of some of the data that classical authors presumed to be factual. In this sense, some of the nuggets from the classic mines have surely been tarnished by time.

Nonetheless, the classics remain viable on balance and still repay study. This is partly because the matrix in which the nuggets are embedded adds greatly to their appreciation and partly because the most valuable ideas in these works are not easily stated as discrete propositions. To regard Marx merely as a generator of the propositions that industrial workers are radical and that capitalists are conservative is not only to misunderstand him (for reasons that will be discussed later), but also to use him wastefully. Marx and the other theorists whom we shall explore provide a sociological world view, one that we can adapt to suit our own needs. Because of the global nature of the sociological wisdom of the classic authors, their views have not become obsolescent.

Let us explore this idea a bit further. As we shall see, Marx is a theorist of revolutionary progress. He interprets history as a progression of epochs, each of which contains internal contradictions that work to bring about a qualitative leap into the next epoch. The course of this progression culminates with a final leap into socialism. Durkheim, while also a believer in historical progress, viewed its development both as a more continuous process and as one requiring marginal adjustment. He was a reformer rather than a revolutionary. Weber, though he also wanted to explain the grand sweep of history, was less convinced than Marx or Durkheim of the usefulness of the concept of a single line of historical progress. He was ever on the watch for evidence of turns of contingency in the historical record. These are not merely or even primarily *political* differences; they are *theoretical* differences. They represent what Thomas Kuhn [1970], a contemporary historian of science, refers to as divergent *paradigms*, or what the sociologist Alvin Gouldner [1970] calls different *domain assumptions*.

Any scholarly activity is based upon certain deeply seated, affectively laden, and intellectually consequential ideas—often implicit rather than articulated—which shape research agendas and establish criteria for the relevance of findings. Because sociology has not reached agreement on a single paradigm, the rate at which systems of ideas become obsolescent is very low.[2] Accordingly, even if some of the individual propositions within the theories of Marx, Durkheim, or Weber have been refuted to the satisfaction of some sociologists, the theories as wholes remain alive. Therefore we continue to study these theories partly because they may resonate with our own fundamental beliefs about society and partly because they enable us to understand better those of our contemporaries whose fundamental beliefs differ from our own but whose theoretical articulations are inferior in scope, power, and candor to the classic authors. Reading the classics is thus an exercise in self-discovery and theoretical dialogue.

A second reason for reading the classic authors is to recapture the *sense of discovery* that they experienced. We reexperience the author's original excitement when Tocqueville tells us that it was not in the most backward and oppressed areas of Western Europe that the revolutionary ardor of the 1790s was most prevalent, but quite the opposite; when Marx warns smug and complacent Germans that his analysis of the crisis of British capitalism is about Germany's fate as well; when Durkheim triumphantly proclaims that the suicide rate is inversely proportional to the degrees of religious, domestic, and political integration; and when Weber argues that the effect of Calvin's single-mindedly God-centered theology was, paradoxically, to stimulate the worldly activity of capitalist accumulation. Each of these discoveries represents an inversion of some form of common sense, and it is fascinating to follow the authors through the processes by which the discoveries were made.

The present-day student of sociology is both helped and hindered by the increasing respectability of sociology as a discipline. He is helped because sociology has succeeded or nearly succeeded in overcoming so many older, inadequate modes of social interpretation—biological determinism, climatic determinism, theological determinism, and even psychological reductionism. And he is also helped because there is now so much good sociology to read. Yet the present-day student is hindered because so much of the sociological point of view appears to be little more than common sense. No longer is there much novelty in the ideas behind such concepts as relative deprivation, the economic foundation of social life, the social determination of individual deviant behavior, or the economic consequences of religious ideas. Indeed, the "Protestant ethic" is close to becoming a cliché. So many sociological ideas, albeit vulgarized, have become part of today's conventional wisdom that we are in danger of losing sight of the *particularity* of the sociological point of view.

To read the classics is to restore the freshness of that point of view and to relive the intellectual struggle required to attain it. This is true for the reading of each of the classic works discussed here and also for the reading of the entire sociological tradition from the time of the

Enlightenment to World War I. In each work we find the theorist engaging in a debate with some aspect of conventional wisdom. Tocqueville and Durkheim do battle with the "common sense" view that unrest is the product of a burdensome existence; Marx and Weber with the view that modern economic society is a "natural" product of eternally valid laws. Each of us today—whether we are acting as social scientists, as conscientious citizens, or as dutiful family members—continuously interprets the social events around us. In this task, we need the ability to dismiss conventional wisdom as well as the ability to employ it. The sense of judgment gleaned from the sociological classics can serve as an intellectual inspiration.

From the sociological tradition as a whole we get something more, something that is of particular relevance to those who have a deeper interest in sociology: a sense of what it is that sociologists study. In spite of all the paradigm disputes among sociologists, there is a general but powerful consensus among them that society—whether it is considered as an entity, a network, an arena, or a milieu—is the object of our study. For all the sociological wisdom contained in the writings of such diverse early thinkers as Aristotle and Thucydides, Machiavelli and Hobbes, it is only in the middle of the eighteenth century that we begin to witness the predominance of such propositions as the following, borrowed from Peter Berger and Thomas Luckmann [1966, p. 61 ff.]: that *society is man's creation* (not God's or nature's), that *man is a social product* (not an autonomous, preformed creature), and that *society is an objective reality* (not a fiction to be willed out of existence). I shall return shortly to this story of the discovery of society and consider its effect on the sociological point of view.

A third reason to read the sociological classics is somewhat more controversial. The classic authors, in this view, are or ought to be *role models* for contemporary sociologists, especially in the breadth of vision of their intellectual efforts. Marx and Weber took the whole of human history as their field of inquiry, and they sought to answer such grand questions as "what are the historical or evolutionary sources of modern society," "what will be society's fate," and "how can we help to determine that fate?" Durkheim, too, was inspired by these questions, though his erudition was geared toward the then available anthropological record rather than toward historical data. Tocqueville was only relatively more modest and directed most of his attention toward societies in Europe and North America.

If the sweep of their efforts was impressive, so also was the comprehensiveness of their sociological perspective. Marx and Durkheim, especially, insisted upon viewing society as a whole, endeavoring to understand how its various aspects fit together, whether harmoniously (in the case of Durkheim) or conflictually (in the case of Marx). Tocqueville and Weber, though less inclined to regard societies as interrelated wholes, nonetheless shared this "macroscopic" inclination, each of them interpreting vast ranges of social phenomena as reflections or representations of some overarching trend, such as equality (Tocqueville) or rationalization (Weber). All four of these authors thus labored to reduce the strangeness of numerous features of contemporary existence by subsuming these features within relatively parsimonious frameworks. In this sense they were interpreters of society as well as formulators of social scientific hypotheses.

Moreover, in each of these great thinkers there is a strong ethical or normative inclination, a bias toward scholarly issues the resolution of which would significantly enhance the quality of human life. All four of these men were not only scholars but also activists who—whatever their positions on a conventional political continuum (from Marx on the "left" through Weber and Durkheim to Tocqueville on the "right")—spoke to the burning issues of their times.

There is, in this view of the relevance of the classics, an exhortation to follow a sociological "calling," the elements of which include historical erudition, macroscopic comprehensiveness, and ethical inspiration. Not surprisingly, this exhortation has, of late, issued prominently from relatively radical members of the sociological profession and from the circles of sociology's friendly and not so friendly critics. C. Wright Mills, particularly in *The Sociological Imagination* [1959], and more recently Alvin W. Gouldner, in *The Coming Crisis of Western Sociology* [1970], have been prominent among those on the left who have exhorted their colleagues to emulate, in one way or another, the sense of vocation shown by the classic scholars. And even among centrists and conservatives, theorists such as Raymond Aron [1968, 1970], Talcott Parsons [1937], Peter Berger [1966], and Robert Nisbet [1966] have extolled the vision of the classic authors, returning themselves to the reading of the classics and urging others to do so.

The increasing professionalization of sociology—which has resulted in the necessity for a specialization of task and in the production of huge quantities of knowledge—has doubtless rendered an emulation of the achievements of a Marx or a Weber all but impossible for the contemporary social scientist. And yet the exhortation is not in vain. For one thing, each member of a task-specialized scholarly discipline can try to direct his part of the joint effort to the resolution of the "grand questions" and to persuade his colleagues to do likewise. And for another, the example of the classic authors continues to have relevance for those who teach or want to teach. Regular attention to the classic tradition helps to remind us that sociology has an important function in that general enterprise which seeks to increase our understanding of what goes on around us.

For these reasons—because their ideas are alive, because their works communicate a sense of discovery, and because their example is inspiring—the classic authors richly deserve our attention, not merely as historical phenomena but as living colleagues. It is the purpose of this essay to suggest some of the benefits to be gained by such attention.

Organization and Themes of This Essay

In the material that follows, I shall begin with an overview of the germination of the sociological point of view at the end of the eighteenth and at the beginning of the nineteenth centuries. In this period society was first designated by large and influential bodies of thought as a suitable object for sustained intellectual inquiry. Then I shall focus on the ideas of four men: Alexis de Tocqueville, Karl Marx, Emile Durkheim, and Max Weber. This selection, like any other, is limited and by no means exhausts the range and variety of the sociological classics. Other people might want to add or substitute classic authors such as Auguste Comte (1798–1857), Herbert Spencer (1820–1903), Vilfredo Pareto (1848–1923), and Georg Simmel (1858–1918). Or they might prefer to include more clearly psychological thinkers such as Sigmund Freud (1856–1939) and George Herbert Mead (1863–1931). I chose the four men discussed here because their works are "alive" today, and not simply part of the record of the development of the field, and because these authors show a certain comparability in that they speak to similar issues—especially to the problems of structure and process in modern societies. These four authors provide among themselves a wide range of convictions as to what are appropriate intellectual problems and interpretative schemes and a diversity of political stances.

Moreover, for the past several decades there has been nearly universal agreement among sociologists writing on the classic tradition that Durkheim and Weber are two of its most outstanding figures, and only slightly less agreement about the centrality of Marx.[3] Tocqueville is included partly because he was a transitional figure between the controversies surrounding the French Revolution and time of the rise of an institutionalized sociology, and partly because his thought seems to be of immediate value for our times, a conviction that is becoming widely shared [see Richter 1966 and Smelser 1971].

The ideas of each of these major theorists will be presented *in con-*

text, in several senses of this term. First is the *historical* context. The next chapter, entitled "The Discovery of Society," outlines an intellectual dialogue that centered around the English Civil War of the 1640s, the Enlightenment, the American Revolution, and the French Revolution—a dialogue that remained alive for nineteenth-century social theory (and remains alive today). In succeeding chapters, such historical processes as the rise of "bourgeois" society in the early nineteenth century and the international rivalries of the late nineteenth century will assume importance. I shall also consider the *biographical* context of each thinker, since a given work can often be understood only in the light of its place in a theorist's life. For the analysis of each theorist, it will be important to ascertain what he intended to do and thus to state our analysis of his work with sympathy, and even use his own language. Finally, the *intellectual* context will be illuminated, since it is frequently crucial to know a bit about an author's audience in order to appreciate what he was saying and why he was saying it. The four pictures that emerge from this contextual approach are rounded interpretations even though they are necessarily brief. The classics reveal more upon each reading and suggest different interpretations to different readers. Tocqueville, Marx, Durkheim, and Weber each wrote many volumes, and the secondary literature (especially on Marx) is enormous. The present treatment represents an interaction between its author and the four theorists. It is my hope that this interaction will interest you in working out your own.

Although I shall examine individually the works of each of these four authors, I shall also compare these works on a number of issues. Some of these points of comparison are *topical*, in that each author sought to come to grips with the implications of the emergence of modern industrial and political Europe. Partly, however, the comparisons are *formal*, reflecting each author's basic choices on a number of issues that confront any comprehensive social theory.

The first such issue is the relationship conceived to exist between *human nature* and *social order*. Partly for ethical purposes ("What kind of society is best for human beings?") and partly for interpretative purposes ("Given what we know about human nature, how is society possible?" or "Given that society exists, how will humans be shaped?"), each of these thinkers has definite, though not always articulated, convictions on the question of "man and society." Some of the earlier theories posited a relatively simple deduction of the nature and necessity of society from a view of human nature as fixed. Later, distinctively sociological theories recognized that what we know as humanity is as much a product as a producer of society. But if this is so, what are the limits, if any, within which human beings can be molded? Are people infinitely malleable or is there an obdurate human nature that will in time assert itself? Whether one maintains that the ultimate explanatory principles of sociology can only be principles of individual psychology (the "psychological reductionism" of George Homans [1964]) or that society is a phenomenon "of its own kind" that must have its own explanatory principles (the "emergence" thesis of Durkheim), some conception of human nature (what I shall call a "philosophic anthropology") enters any social theory for interpretative reasons no less than ethical ones.[4]

The second recurrent issue in the works of these social theorists is the *attitude toward conflict*, which I shall view as moving between the two poles of *harmony* and *tragedy*. Some theorists (Plato among them) maintain that in principle if not in current reality it is possible to have a social order within which all true values can be realized. These thinkers conceive the possibility of a single rational ordering of the social world within which conflict is unnecessary. They tend to approach social conflicts as ultimately eradicable given the right measure of social reform. I shall refer to these authors as "theorists of harmony." On the opposite side are those who insist that conflicts of values are, in principle, irreducible and who typically insist that trade-offs must be made among desirable states of existence. They do not necessarily laud conflict (Tocqueville certainly did not), nor do they hold that all conflicts are necessary and unamenable to reform. Yet they argue that choices must be made in society such that social actors must give up something desired for something else. (For example, as Tocqueville would argue, a measure of equality must be foregone in order to preserve liberty.) I shall call these thinkers "theorists of tragedy."

Third, I shall draw attention to the theorist's conviction about the relation between his theory and its potential practical uses. Many volumes have been written on this exceedingly complex problem of the relation between *science and values* or *knowledge and action* [see Sherman 1974]. Some sociologists insist that their scientific activity has no necessary connection to practical or ethical concerns. They vigorously defend their right and capacity to be "value-free." Other scholars just as vigorously insist that the "value-free" position is neither possible nor ethically desirable. Much of this debate centers on interpretations, amendments, and refutations of what Max Weber meant by "objectivity" in social science; I shall again touch on this issue when I discuss Weber.

The issue for the classic tradition is broader, however. All four of our major thinkers were passionately concerned with social problems.

The issue among them is the way in which sociological knowledge bears upon intervention in the affairs of the real world. For some, the social world is taken as a given, knowledge of which is to be sought and codified in order to effect social changes only when that knowledge has become authoritatively certain. These theorists tend to draw their methodological inspiration from physics and other "hard" sciences and to insist that social theory is impotent until it is definitively confirmed by empirical test. Such labels as "positivism" and "technical theory" have been applied to this tendency [see Warner 1970b and Wolin 1969]. As we shall see, even theorists as ethically motivated as Durkheim display it. The other tendency, sometimes called "critical theory," typically insists on a radical divergence between the methods appropriate to the natural sciences and those appropriate to social science. The crucial point of divergence is that, for the "critical" thinker, social theory can effect social changes in the very process of its formulation and not merely when it has reached the status of a finished product. Insofar as human beings act on the basis of what they consider to be true or possible, their belief in a theory can itself be consequential for action. Thus, for the "critical" theorist, the social world is not conceived solely as a given to which social theory ought to adjust. Rather, social theory is conceived as a force in itself, which, under certain circumstances, is capable of shaping the world. Marx provides the best example of this "critical" approach, though aspects of the "positivistic" tendency are also apparent in his work.

All three of these issues—man and society, harmony and tragedy, knowledge and action—are areas in which social thinkers make consequential choices, and these choices reflect the theorist's "domain assumptions." Considerable disagreement on these matters exists among our authors, although they represent only a few of the many possible combinations of such choices. Sufficient variation and dissensus will be presented, however, to demonstrate the importance for theoretical analysis of articulating the basic choices made by any theorist.

Finally, a fourth theme deserves mention. One of the great intellectual contributions of the sociological point of view is its fascination with the phenomenon of the *unanticipated consequences of social action*. All of our authors have a well-developed appreciation for the paradox that a person's actions can have important social effects that were unintended or that were even considered by him to be undesirable. For example, a shoe manufacturer may vigorously compete with other shoemakers and may himself become rich. Meanwhile, however, through what Adam Smith spoke of as the intervention of an "invisible hand," the shoemaker is, as well, contributing to the wealth of the nation. He did not anticipate this effect but it has, nonetheless, occurred. Or consider the example of a pacifist who may "turn the other cheek" when his life is threatened, but whose very passivity may encourage the greater violence that it is his desire to eliminate. Machiavelli would likely have advised him that it is often necessary to use ethically dubious means to attain such an ethically desirable end.

These examples are elementary and are subject to controversy. Turning them around, one could say (with Marx) that the shoemaker's competitiveness is part of a process that will lead to the revolutionary transformation of his social world or (with Gandhi) that the pacifist's willingness to undergo injury is the only means to eliminate violence from society in the long run. Nonetheless, the suspicion that intention and forethought are often at variance with social consequence is one of the central ideas of a sociological perspective and, as we shall see, one on which all of our authors in one fashion or another have something to say.

CHAPTER 2

The Discovery of Society

Innovations in social theory are often the result of turmoil and change. Plato's *Republic* and Aristotle's *Politics* were produced not at the height of Athenian power and culture (the fifth century B.C.) but after the defeat of Athens in the Peloponnesian Wars. Similarly, modern social theory began during the seventeenth and eighteenth centuries when passionate religious conflict, disruptive economic change, and fierce political struggle stimulated urgent and fundamental thinking about society. Perhaps the most radical, systematic, and influential theorist of that time was Thomas Hobbes. I shall briefly indicate the significance of Hobbes' theory and shall consider its attempted refutation by John Locke before moving to the great intellectual debate that surrounded the French Revolution a century later.

The "Hobbesian Problem"

Thomas Hobbes (1588–1679) was an Englishman who lived in the period of religious and political strife that culminated in the great English Civil War and the Interregnum of 1642–1660. His book *Leviathan*, which was written from exile in Paris in 1651, presented an argument for the legitimacy of political absolutism. For their own good, Hobbes argued, men ought to respect the sovereignty of government; if they failed to do so, they risked the very sort of unhappy violence that was then plaguing his native land. To the twentieth-century liberal mind, the point of his argument seems highly conservative, and even reactionary. Yet, conceptually, his theory was radical because it self-consciously rejected older, more complacent modes of thinking. For Hobbes, social order was inherently precarious, no longer something to be taken for granted. Its understanding and reconstruction required a thoroughly systematic analysis, unfettered by wishful thinking. In common with the contemporary founders of modern scientific method, Francis Bacon (1561–1626) and René Descartes (1596–1650), Hobbes resorted to what he considered first principles, abandoning inherited preconceptions and proceeding on the basis of naturalistic reasoning.

The starting point for Hobbes' theory was man,[5] and a very secular man at that. Man, Hobbes stated, is a creature of reason and passion, or, more precisely, of reason in the service of passion. By "passion," Hobbes meant the restless desire for material well-being—"restless" because things could not be enjoyed if they were not secure and they could not be made secure without ceaseless striving after the power to make them so. Thus, he wrote, the "general inclination of all mankind" is "a perpetual and restless desire of power after power, that ceaseth only in death." By "reason," Hobbes meant the ability of man to calculate the means necessary to reach the ends sought by his passion (and not man's disposition to act in terms of justice and compromise, as a different connotation of "reason" suggests). Hobbes viewed man as a cunning, egoistic animal.

The material welfare that Hobbes' men desire is always in short supply, and, moreover, the power to protect and extend one's own supply inherently implies conflict with others who have competing passions. Thus the "state of nature" is a state of war—one in which individuals are restrained only by the limits of their intellectual and physical capacities and by other, similarly inclined individuals. Hobbes does not mean that men will always be fighting, but rather that they must always be inclined to do so. Each of them must therefore be continually fearful of the intentions of his neighbor. And such fear, Hobbes knew, was ill suited to the enjoyment of a secure and productive existence. It seemed that precisely what man's nature desired, that same nature prevented him from realizing. In the state of nature, then, man lives in a state of war, "and such a war, as is of every man, against every man." Hobbes' view of the state of nature was summarized in this famous passage:

In such condition, there is no place for industry; because the fruit thereof is uncertain: and consequently no culture of the earth; no navigation, nor use of the commodities that may be imported by sea; no commodious building; no instruments of moving, and removing such things as require much force; no knowledge of the face of the earth; no account of time; no arts; no letters; no society; and which is worst of all, continual fear and danger of violent death; and the life of man, solitary, poor, nasty, brutish, and short [1651, p. 62].

Given this dismal prognosis, how is society possible? That is the "Hobbesian problem." Hobbes' solution is "Leviathan," or the absolute political state, to which each individual cedes his right of self-protection (that is, his right to violence in the protection of his own interests). Hobbes argues that men's reason will commend to them this alienation of rights as the only way to arrange for the security they desire, and that they will and ought to respect the sovereignty of the state. Of this sovereignty, there can be no qualification, and against it, no appeal. To reserve rights of appeal or to insist that there must be some authority higher than the state is to risk falling back into that awful condition of conflict which all men desire to avoid. Hobbes poses a simple, if unattractive, choice: either a war of each against all or a respect for political absolutism.

The history of the twentieth century may suggest that Hobbes was justifying totalitarianism, but this would be a serious misreading. For one thing, the techniques of political domination in his day were simply inadequate for the purposes of totalitarian domination of an entire nation. For another, Hobbes maintained that the sovereign would permit to subjects such civil liberties as freedom of economic contract and education of children. The raison d'être of the state is its provision to its subjects of military and police protection. It was not Hobbes' intention to establish a political order that would invade and mold their very lives.

Although Hobbes' theory may lack ethical appeal for us, and although events of the two centuries after Hobbes spelled the defeat of political absolutism in most of Western Europe, his theory was profoundly influential. For Hobbes, social order is highly desirable, but it is artificial; it is a contrivance of reason for the mutual control of destructive passion. There is no natural or providential (that is, God-given) society.

The natural condition is one of isolated, fearful individuals who, on the basis of their own powers of reasoning and without divine intervention, can agree to establish a political body to guarantee order. Hobbes does not say that they did in fact so agree at some time in the past; he merely says that they can perceive what the consequences of the lack of such an agreement would be. Much of the inspiration for later social thought —especially for utilitarianism, nineteenth-century liberalism, and classical economic theory—was found in Hobbes' conceptualization of social order as an artifice intended to protect the interests of individuals.

Influential though Hobbes' theories were, they were not without certain sociological weaknesses. His starting point of fearful, cunning individuals can be recognized as a reflection of the events of his own time and milieu. There is no reason to suppose that human beings, who are, after all, formed by social experience, are "naturally" any more inclined to violence than to cooperation, nor to suppose that they will, in the absence of an awe-inspiring political overlord, break into solitary individual units rather than into families, tribes, clans, or classes. Moreover, Hobbes' limited vision of the functions of society (with Hobbes, society and Leviathan are coincident) perilously disregards the great power that social order can have over all aspects of man's existence. Nonetheless, he posed in remarkably lucid terms a fundamental problem for social theory: how is society possible?

So powerful was Hobbes' theory that one of its great, and equally influential, opponents, John Locke (1632–1704), took many of the fundamentals of his own theory from it.[6] Locke is rightly regarded as the father of modern liberalism. His *Second Treatise on Civil Government,* written thirty years after the *Leviathan,* is replete with ideas that were used by the liberal and radical ideologists of the Glorious Revolution in England (1688–1689), of the French Revolution, and of the American Revolution. The keystone of his theory was his view that social order is based on a contract among individuals, a view which was, as we have seen, formulated by Hobbes.

Locke argued that the kind of sovereignty recommended by Hobbes was injurious to the purposes for which it was presumably established. If there is no limit on the sovereign, as Hobbes insisted, then there is no restraint on the sovereign's abusing his power by confiscating the property of a subject (to cite an example much used by Locke). What Hobbes' Leviathan does, then, is to transform a war of one person against another person into a potential war of one subject against a sovereign armed with the might of a hundred thousand. In Hobbes' social order, the individual is defenseless in the face of the state. Reason could hardly recommend to us such a step from an unhappy condition to a far worse one. Locke's theory thus broached the question of limits on political power.

Locke held that "the people" (a term he preferred to Hobbes' "subjects") retain the right of revolution against an unjust government. (This right was repeatedly exercised by citizens in Europe and America during the next two centuries, in no small part under Locke's inspiration.) A government is unjust if it violates the "inalienable rights" of its people to life, liberty, and property. Locke here resorts to an old tradition of natural law, which establishes a criterion by which the performance of the government can be judged and to which the government can be held accountable.

To Hobbes' warning that the alternative to submission of subjects to political authority is a fearful anarchy, Locke presents a somewhat confused and inconsistent but ethically compelling argument that there are several acceptable gradations of order between a state of war and an intolerable tyranny. Locke begins with the idea that the "state of war" is not an immanent potentiality, but is rather a corruption of man's natural state, which is peaceful and cooperative. To be sure, without government, there is no agreed-upon arbiter of disputes, and conflicts may get out of hand. Therefore, men do contract with each other to establish a commonwealth, but not because of the dire compulsion that drove Hobbes' fear-ridden men.[7] Moreover, the contract of men in civil society is one thing, and the contract of that society with a political agency is another. If the political agency or government abuses its trust, the people can revoke its claim to rule without falling back into destructive anarchy.

The corollary to this derivation of legitimate authority from the consent of the governed and to this conception of people as maintaining inalienable rights is a view of human nature at variance with that of Hobbes. For Locke, men are naturally sociable and naturally desirous of order.[8] Thus they will not grasp at each and every opportunity to overthrow existing governments. If, under great provocation, they do rebel, they will not find it extraordinarily difficult to establish a new political regime. (It may well be that Hobbes' admonition that men should direct their energies toward economically productive activities and should leave political affairs to the sovereign, in combination with the expanding economic activity of the late seventeenth century, was sufficient to moderate the political passions expressed during the Civil War of mid-century. Locke could thus take for granted what Hobbes had labored mightily to accomplish.)

In sum, if Hobbes' men were possessed of "reason"—in the sense of cunning—Locke's men were "reasonable"—in the sense of being prudent, restrained, and moderate. If Hobbes' world requires a hard choice, Locke's world is harmonious and, within some ill-defined limits, permits the realization of the rights and values of all people. In the differences between Hobbes and Locke there is an early statement of what has become the familiar polarization in sociology between conflict theory and consensus theory.

Yet, for all their disagreements, Hobbes and Locke show a substantial area of agreement about the ingredients of social theory. Both assume that it is unproblematic to speak of autonomously formed individuals, each of whom seeks his own welfare, is endowed with powers of reason, and has to be shown a good reason to establish social institutions. Their views of society, furthermore, coincide in regarding it (whether in its entirety, as Hobbes did, or partially, as Locke did) as a contrivance to be justified on the basis of how well it serves its constituent elements, individual men. These ideas, which are theoretically, but not ethically naive from the point of view of modern sociology, had far-reaching implications for social thought and for concerted political action.

The Enlightenment: Society Is Man's Creation

During the eighteenth century, thinkers from many lands criticized and rejected the superstitions and errors of the past. They did this with the use of what they regarded as the light of reason. In the English-speaking countries, it was the Age of Reason, in France the *Siècle des lumières*, in Germany the *Zeitalter der Aufklaerung*. Great advances were made in science and philosophy, advances regarded as qualitative and thoroughly bound up with a revolution in thought. In the words of Alexander Pope:

Nature and nature's laws lay hid in night.
God said, "Let Newton be!" and all was light.

Ignorance and bigotry were to be extirpated, not only in science but also in the realm of social and political philosophy.

France was the center of this intellectual revolution, and such *Philosophes* as Montesquieu (1689–1755) and Voltaire (1694–1778) were among its most important figures. Yet France was suffering under the legacy of a crushing military debt and a decadent absolute monarchy. Montesquieu and Voltaire looked to England and John Locke as sources of critical inspiration. Parliamentary supremacy had been established in England by the success of the "Glorious Revolution" of 1688–1689, and the French thinkers saw in England an enlightened regime of political and religious tolerance and social mobility. Because of censorship in France, socially radical ideas had to be expressed indirectly through parables and metaphors, and because of the ancient system of feudal estates, men of common birth but uncommon abilities were frustrated in their attempts to gain political influence. In England, by contrast, religious toleration and freedom of social movement meant that men of dissenting views and humble origins could nevertheless contribute to the well-being of society.

These contrasts were satirically presented in such works as Montesquieu's *Persian Letters* (1721), in which two purported visitors to Paris make tongue-in-cheek observations about French institutions, and Voltaire's *Letters Concerning the English Nation* (1733), which, although officially banned, received widespread underground circulation. The flavor of the disgust Voltaire felt toward French institutions and of his admiration for England is expressed in a comment comparing the corrupt aristocracy of France to the dynamic merchant class of England:

I will not . . . take it upon me to say which is the most useful to his country . . . : whether [it is] the powdered lord, who knows to a minute when the king rises or goes to bed . . . and who gives himself airs of importance in playing the part of a slave in the ante-chamber of some minister; or the merchant, who enriches his country, and from his counting house sends his orders into Surat or Cairo, thereby contributing to the happiness and convenience of human nature [1733, pp. 18–19].

Contained in this remark, and in the many others like it to be found in the writings of the French *Philosophes*, is a vigorous criticism of existing social institutions in the light of the criterion of "reason" as it was manifested in the institutions of another nation. Reverence for the past is derided, and the view is put forward that social institutions must be judged by their usefulness and reasonableness. By using satire as an ideological weapon (a tactic forced on them by repressive intolerance), Montesquieu and Voltaire imply that the institutions being criticized derive their viability from ignorance, and that once these institutions are subjected to a clear-eyed examination, in the light of a "reason" accessible to all intelligent readers, their power will be weakened.

Therefore, despite the bitterness and disgust that are expressed in the writings of the *Philosophes*, there is in them an overarching optimism, a faith that a more just society can be established once ignorance has been banished. If it is true that less effort was expended in understanding how a just society was to be established than in exposing the corruption of existing institutions, then this is evidence of the eighteenth-century faith that the principles of social reconstruction were simple and easily accessible. Although the *Philosophes* were men of letters rather than men of action, their writings nonetheless sounded a clear call for social change. They said, in effect, that society is not sacrosanct, that its forms vary from nation to nation, and that if you are unhappy with your society, you should make a new one. These were radical ideas. As Voltaire wrote in 1757:

It is difficult to point out a single nation living under a system of good laws. . . . [L]aws have proceeded, in almost every state, from the interest of the legislator, from the urgency of the moment, from ignorance, and from superstition, and have accordingly been made at random, and irregularly, just in the same manner in which cities have been built. . . . It was only after London had been reduced to ashes [1666] that it became at all fit to be inhabited. The streets, after that catastrophe, were widened and straightened. If you are desirous of having good laws, burn those which you have at present, and make fresh ones [1757, p. 79].

Men of action heard and heeded words such as these, with effects that shattered the old regimes so reviled by the *Philosophes*.

The Age of Reason was not confined to Europe, but reached across the Atlantic to the New World. In fact, among the great and influential documents of the Enlightenment was the Declaration of Independence, drafted by a young American philosopher and politician, Thomas Jefferson (1743–1826). Those of us who are accustomed to thinking of the Declaration of Independence in the context of complacent and self-congratulatory high-school civics courses may miss its extraordinary implications. For in this document we encounter an expression of the political principles of John Locke, those principles having greater force and urgency because of their restatement in the more comprehensive critical stance of Montesquieu and Voltaire and because of the grievances and ambitions of the American colonists. Above all, the Declaration takes for granted the revolutionary principle that government, and by extension any social institution, is a voluntary creation of free men [see Arieli 1964]. The Declaration confidently enumerates certain purportedly obvious but actually controversial principles:

We hold these truths to be self evident: that all men are created equal; that they are endowed by their Creator with certain inalienable rights; that among these are life, liberty, and the pursuit of happiness; that to secure these rights, governments are instituted among men, deriving their just powers from the consent of the governed; that whenever any form of government becomes destructive of these ends, it is the right of the people to alter or abolish it, and to institute new government, laying its foundation on such principles, and organizing its powers in such form, as to them shall seem most likely to effect their safety and happiness.

These principles are presented as beyond debate or logical justification; they are announced. The appeal to a Creator is an assertion of the primordial nature of things. In that state, men are equal and there are no hereditary rulers. Men have inalienable rights, rights that no one, not even those who hold and enjoy them, can take away. These rights set limits on the legitimate purview of government. Governments, therefore, are deliberately created institutions, which are given their legitimacy not by hallowed tradition but by their utility in the service of human rights. Governments, thus, are subject to criticism, to alteration, and to overthrow by the people, who retain the ultimate sovereignty.

The process of reasoning involved here proceeds from man to government, from the individual to society. As conservatives of the time recognized, it was a process of reasoning that profoundly subverted existing social institutions—even despite the Lockean disclaimer added by the author and signatories of the Declaration that long-established governments should not and likely would not be abolished "for light and transient causes." The moderation that this passage expresses may have reflected both the caution and circumspection of its signers as well as a more accurate portrayal of human nature than that provided by Hobbes. It did not, however, compromise the contractual concept of government, which was the common coin of Hobbesian, Lockean, and Enlightenment social theory.

The example of the Americans, who used the critical social theory of the Enlightenment to shape their political destiny, influenced the French Revolution a decade later. Once again, men took it upon themselves to change their social order and to announce their reasons and premises for so doing. In effect, the French Declaration of the Rights of Man and of Citizens (1789) incorporated many of the ideas of the American Declaration of Independence and Bill of Rights. The French Declaration, as had the American, solemnly asserted that men are by nature free and equal and that government is an instrument for the preservation of human rights. It, too, expressed the faith that a just social order could be founded on the twin principles of reason and utility. And it presented a radical challenge to existing institutions. (There were, however, significant differences between the American and French declarations; these will be considered when we discuss Rousseau.)

The French Revolution, to be sure, followed a far more radical course than did the American. Not only were political ties broken and a republican form of government established, but the institutions that constituted the very fabric of French social order (the Church and the nobility) were attacked as well. So also, the American Revolution had been more radical than the earlier English Glorious Revolution of 1688: in England a Parliament took to itself the right to determine monarchical succession, whereas in America a people declared itself a political entity. Nonetheless, the critical, activist, and contractualist principles of Enlightenment social thought were important in all three movements. If it seems curious that the same principles could justify a constitutional monarchy in England, a federal republic in America, and a legislative dictatorship in France, the explanation lies in the vagueness of the "self-evident" Reason to which all appealed. In English "reason" partook of a large dose of prudence and tradition (as it did for Locke but not for Hobbes). The more radical application of "reason" in America did not have to confront the rigid and decadent social class system that was a cause and justification for the radical measures of the French revolutionaries [see Huntington 1968]. In France "reason" meant the thoroughgoing dissolution and reconstruction of society itself. (As we shall see, it was the very abstraction of the principle of reason that was to inform Edmund Burke's attack on the French Revolution.)

The differences among these outcomes do not, however, deny the fact that all three revolutions were shaped by the liberal philosophies of Locke, Montesquieu, Voltaire, and Jefferson. These philosophies established an idea of great sociological and political significance: that society can neither be understood nor justified as an unchanging order established by superhuman agency but is, rather, something enacted and reenacted by human beings.

Rousseau: Man Is a Social Product

As mentioned a short while ago, the French Declaration of the Rights of Man and of Citizens differs significantly from the American revolutionary documents. The keystone of that difference is stated in the third article of the French Declaration:

III. The nation is essentially the source of all sovereignty; nor can any *individual* or *any body of men*, be entitled to any authority which is not expressly derived from it.

The idea that the "nation" is the source of "sovereignty" is quite unlike the idea expressed in the American Declaration, and later in the Constitution, that the legitimacy of government rests in the consent of the people. The French article expresses a concept of the unity and reality of a political body—the nation—which is absent in the contractualist principles of the American document. To understand this difference, as well as to explicate another element of what was to become the sociological tradition, we must turn to the thought of Jean-Jacques Rousseau (1712–1778).

His dates and adopted French nationality place Rousseau squarely in the milieu of the French Enlightenment; he moved in Parisian society, and many of the key figures of the Enlightenment were at one time or another his friends and associates. The English statesman Edmund Burke, as we shall see, thought of Rousseau's theory as the epitome of the Enlightenment Rationalism that he so roundly condemned. The German philosopher Immanuel Kant (1724–1804) regarded Rousseau as a great moral philosopher of the Enlightenment. Yet, Denis Diderot (1713–1784), a powerful figure among the French *Philosophes* and for several years Rousseau's close friend, regarded Rousseau (after their break in 1757) as a figure at odds with the temper of the rationalist movement. He wrote that Rousseau "makes me uneasy, . . . and I feel as if a damned soul stood beside me . . . . I never want to see that man again; he could make me believe in devils and Hell" [quoted in Cassirer 1963, p. 91].[9]

Rousseau's theory espouses a desire for wholeness and authenticity and a skepticism of the intellect and of superficial conviviality; this outlook presages the attitudes of the Romantic movement of the early nineteenth century and is more characteristic of that period than of the rationalism of the eighteenth century. Rousseau's rejection of the social order of the eighteenth century was more thorough than that of Voltaire and, consequently, his vision of the means required for its reorientation was more radical.

Like Hobbes, Locke, and Jefferson, Rousseau was a theorist of the social contract, as is indicated by the treatise of that title which he published in 1762. But unlike them, Rousseau did not conceive of a legitimate social and political order proceeding from the wishes of men taken as autonomous units. He inquired further into the manner by which social experience molds and corrupts the desires men are capable of expressing. Rousseau tells us that his theoretical career was set in motion by his reading of a question posed for a prize essay competition in 1749: "Has the restoration of the sciences and arts tended to purify morals?" A sudden and overwhelming inspiration struck him, and he perceived on the spot the profound corruption of the social system and, through it, the corruption of the naturally pure human spirit. The guiding concern of his thought for the next decade and a half was thus an interrelated set of questions: "What is the nature of man?" "What has been the price paid for civilization?" "What are its benefits?" "How can these benefits be retained while regaining the purity of natural existence?"

28

Rousseau's answers are presented, not always consistently, in several works, including the *Discourse on the Sciences and Arts* or *First Discourse* (1750; his essay did win the prize); the *Discourse on the Origin and Foundations of Inequality* or *Second Discourse* (1755); *Social Contract* (1762); and *Emile*, or *Treatise on Education* (1762). I shall summarize Rousseau's theory by looking at his view of man in three stages of existence: the state of nature, social dependence, and the social contract or community.

State of Nature

To discover the original nature of man, Rousseau recognized from the outset that we must conceive of a being who is untouched by the shaping power of society. It was not enough to have recourse to statements about primitive tribes or to suppose that the debased men who populated Hobbes' world of anarchic competition were "natural." We must, Rousseau insisted, perform mental experiments that will give us a picture of a hypothetical state which may never have existed but about which we must know in order to understand the effects of social experience. Rousseau's natural man is an unsocial, but not antisocial, animal who walks erect and is able to use his hands; he is possessed of a keen native intelligence but has not yet acquired knowledge:

To strip this being . . . of all the supernatural gifts which he may have received, and of all the artificial faculties which he must have by slow degrees acquired; to consider him, in a word, such as he must have come from the hands of nature, I behold in him an animal weaker than some, and less active than others; but, taking all things together, the most advantageously organized of any. I see him satisfying his hunger at the first oak, and slaking his thirst at the first brook, in his way; finding his bed at the foot of the same tree, which afforded him a repast; and behold all his wants are supplied [1755, p. 169].

This unsocial being has no possessions and no social ties and therefore cannot be coerced: he is independent. He has no cares other than an instinct for self-preservation (*amour de soi*): he is insouciant. He has no knowledge of good or evil: he is innocent. And he satisfies his needs when he experiences them: his life has the quality of immediacy.

Rousseau thus radically rejected several earlier conceptions of the nature of man, including the Christian idea of original sin; Hobbes' picture of egoistic, antagonistic, and calculating men in a state of war; and

Locke's view of naturally sociable individuals. At the same time, he acknowledged that this primeval state was not something to which we can aspire to return. For Rousseau, "natural man" is, in a sense, a deliberate fiction (with the partial exception of infants), used to pass judgment upon the social state of man as we know him.

Social Dependence

Rousseau's judgment on the social state of man is severe, as has already been implied. He was repelled by what he considered to be the shallowness and hypocrisy of the society of his day, and he was especially repelled by the Parisian elite. Man had fallen far indeed, but social experience was responsible for the fall.

In Rousseau's imaginative recapitulation of primitive social history, the idyll of natural man is upset when—perhaps because of climatic changes and material privation—new needs emerge that require tools and the coordinated labor of two or more men. Thus are introduced possessions and the division of labor, from which flow all the evils of social life. A man with possessions is a man with something to lose, and a man who is dependent on the activities of others is also dependent upon their dispositions.

Behold, then, all the human faculties developed; the memory and imagination in full play; self-love become interested; reason rendered active; and the mind arrived almost at the highest point of its perfection. Behold all the natural qualities put in action; the rank and condition of every man assigned him; not merely as to his share of property and his power to serve or injure others, but also as to genius, beauty, strength or address, merit or talents: and these being the only qualities capable of commanding respect, it of course presently becomes necessary to possess or to affect them.

It became now the interest of men to appear what they really were not. To be and to seem, became two things totally different; and thus from this necessary distinction sprung insolent pomp and artful knavery, with all the numerous vices that compose their train [1755, pp. 229–230].

The poor man needs the help of the rich; the rich, the services of the poor. All are enmeshed in a web of circumstantial dependence and invidious comparison. From the envy and calculation so produced comes the state of war that Hobbes mistook for the state of nature. And from this emerges the necessity for government to protect the property of the rich and the meager remaining rights of the poor. Art, science, and philosophy are, then, only so many floral garlands that decorate the iron chains that now bind men and that stifle in them any desire for liberty.

Though Rousseau's indictment of society is harsh, he is not arguing for a return to primitive nature. That is impossible, for social existence is here to stay. Moreover, it is only through society that man acquires language, knowledge, reason, and a moral sense. We are endowed by nature with immense capacities, which, however, are realized only in society.

Social Contract or Community

Rousseau answers this dilemma by going beyond mere social dependence and by establishing the kind of social order in which the attributes of natural freedom can be combined with the benefits of social existence. The circumstantial dependencies and conflicts of interests that require social men to dissemble and thus to violate their own true nature must be overcome. This is Rousseau's theoretical task:

To find that form of association which shall protect and defend, with the whole force of the community, the person and property of each individual, and in which each person, by uniting himself to the rest, shall nevertheless be obedient only to himself, and remain as fully at liberty as before [1762, p. 18].

Achieving this requires both psychological and institutional reforms. Men must be made to see that their interests do not consist in striving to outdo each other but rather in the mutual efforts incumbent upon citizens. Freedom, Rousseau argued, is not the absence of restraint but rather the recognition of necessity. Like the order of nature, the social contract is impartial to individuals, and they must be individually powerless to influence it by cunning means. Those who refuse to see this, Rousseau frankly stated, may be "forced to be free." Rousseau's conception of "freedom," combined with his appreciation of the immense and profound power that society has over the individual, have led some later commentators to see Rousseau as a forerunner of modern totalitarianism.

The institutional changes Rousseau had in mind were intended to allow the "general will" of the community to manifest itself. Rousseau's community was a democratic association, not a dictatorship, and it was crucial for his process that the will of the people be heard. This could happen, however, only if the unequal privileges and partial combinations that were the bane of mere social dependence were abolished. Ideally, Rousseau conceived of a social order in which each citizen stood in a direct relationship with the community, just as original man had with nature. Thus kingship, monasticism, temporal-spiritual dualism, political partisanship, delegation of authority and responsibility—indeed, all institutions and practices that mediated the direct relationship of man to community or that divided man's loyalty—were declared illegitimate. The participation of the individual directly in the affairs of the community was to be maximized.

The better the constitution of a state, the greater influence have public affairs over private, in the minds of the citizens. They will have, also, much fewer private affairs to concern them; because the sum total of their common happiness, furnishing a more considerable portion to each individual, there remains the less for each to seek from his own private concerns [1762, p. 124].

However little this conception of direct and unmediated citizen participation in the life of an overarching political community corresponds to current pluralist political theory, and however impractical this conception may appear for the organization of a vast nation-state, it, nonetheless, greatly influenced the political theory of the French Revolution. For Rousseau and the French Revolution, the political order was not a mere utilitarian compact; it was a comprehensive association, the potential source of the realization of the true nature of man.

In Rousseau's theory we find ideas that later social theory was to elaborate: men as we know them are formed by society, they are malleable, and their social and political participation is potentially inherently rewarding. At the same time, however, Rousseau's constitutional theories, especially insofar as they influenced the course of the French Revolution, were subject to vigorous dispute by later theorists. One of these was Edmund Burke, whose reaction to the French Revolution I shall now consider.

Burke: Society Is an Objective Reality

In the decade following the American decision to declare independence, revolution broke out in France. The monarchical government of Louis XVI, saddled with an immense debt incurred largely through unsuccessful warfare, attempted to impose new taxes. These impositions were resisted by the aristocratic assemblies or *parlements*. Recognizing the crisis, the government summoned for May 1789 a meeting of the Estates General. The Estates—a body composed of the representatives of the three orders of the realm (the clergy, the nobility, and the residual category of the commoners or bourgeoisie)—had not met since 1614. If the government believed that through this extraordinary measure it could use the assembled bourgeoisie to crush the aristocrats, or if the latter believed that they could use the convocation to reassert their ancient prerogatives against the crown, a swift succession of events proved them both out of touch with social reality.

First a privileged sector of lawyers and merchants and then increasing numbers of French citizens of all stations made their will felt upon the structure of their society. In June 1789 the Third Estate of commoners declared itself to be a National Assembly, with sweeping constitutional powers. On July 14 the Bastille, a state prison symbolic of royal absolutism, was seized by the Parisian masses. In July and August a massive series of uprisings swept the countryside, as the peasants made known their grievances against the exactions and privileges of their aristocratic overlords. In August the National Assembly proclaimed the Declaration of the Rights of Man and of Citizens and, over the next year, followed it with decrees that administered a mortal blow to the tottering system of feudal authority. Status qualifications for office and privileged municipal and feudal corporations were abolished; monasticism was suppressed; church properties were expropriated; and, above all, legal equality was declared in principle and articulated in manifold statutes.

Further and more radical measures were to come. The revolution was spread by ideological and military force across the face of Europe in the years ensuing. But already at the end of 1790, Edmund Burke (1729–1797) saw the French Revolution as "the most astonishing that has hitherto happened in the world," and he proceeded to condemn not only its excesses but its very conception. He did this by means of a sustained assertion of what he regarded as appropriate principles of political action, especially those he claimed to have followed in his own parliamentary career. Burke's *Reflections on the Revolution in France* [1790] was an immensely influential and powerfully written political pamphlet, destined to become a bible of political conservatives. Moreover, it contained the germ of the nineteenth-century conservative ideology that had a profound impact on the development of sociological thought.

Yet Burke had been for years a self-conscious reformer, who had taken up a series of "great causes" on the often unpopular and often defeated liberal side. He had opposed religious repression in Ireland, colonial exploitation in India, and the burdensome taxes imposed on the American colonies by the ministers of George III, and he had defended as well the established privileges of Parliament and the Anglican church. So closely had he been identified with the cause of reform, especially because of his defense of the Americans, that Thomas Jefferson upon reading Burke's *Reflections* could say, "The Revolution of France does not astonish me so much as the revolution of Mr. Burke."

In reply to such criticisms Burke maintained that he, and not the advocates of the French Revolution, was faithful to Lockean principles and that the philosophical and ideological impulse behind the French Revolution was something very different from that of the English and American revolutions. Although he abhorred abstract social philosophy, which he saw as a cause of the fearful events in France, the controversy forced him to articulate in general terms his own social philosophy. This philosophy can be found in the *Reflections*, beneath its rhetorical excess and ungenerous temper.

Burke objected above all to the revolutionaries' belief that they could wholly remake their society on the basis of principles of universal reason. Society is not a mechanical artifact, he argued, but an organic, living entity whose complex and superficially contradictory institutions ought to be viewed with a spirit of reverence, even during the process of reform, rather than with shortsighted arrogance. He wrote,

Society is, indeed, a contract. Subordinate contracts for objects of mere occasional interest may be dissolved at pleasure; but the state ought not to be considered as nothing better than a partnership agreement in a trade of pepper and coffee, calico or tobacco, or some other such low concern, to be taken up for a little temporary interest, and to be dissolved by the fancy of the parties. It is to be looked on with other reverence; because it is not a partnership in things subservient only to the gross animal existence of a temporary and perishable nature. It is a partnership in all science, a partnership in all art, a partnership in every virtue and in all perfection. As the ends of such a partnership cannot be obtained in many generations, it becomes a partnership not only between those who are living, but between those who are living, those who are dead, and those who are to be born [1790, p. 359].

Although Burke's view of the comprehensive purposes of social life echoed a classical Greek ideal and was thereby in agreement with the vision of community contained in Rousseau's writings and in the spirit of the documents of the French Revolution, Burke believed himself wholly at odds with them. In some respects he was, for he insisted that the nature of society discloses itself only over time and that society's constituent units included corporate bodies as well as individuals. If Burke and Rousseau could agree on the all-inclusiveness of social life, Burke, nonetheless, rejected the view that social order can be conceived of as an unmediated relationship between individuals and the community and that it ought to be remade in that imagery. Burke wrote of the English, "We fear God; we look up with awe to kings; with affection to parliaments; with duty to magistrates; with reverence to priests; and with respect to nobility" [1790, p. 346]. He made this remark not only as a contrast to what he believed to be the inclinations of the French revolutionaries, but also as a statement about the way in which societies ought generally to be organized.

Burke's view of human nature corresponded with this organic view of society. He viewed men as requiring more than a minimal framework of laws to protect their rights. Men also require a sense of identity, dignity, and direction that only socially sanctioned authority can give them. Burke rejected both Hobbes' view of self-sufficient reasoning men and Rousseau's view of man as perfectible, even as he agreed with Hobbes about the necessity of restraint and with Rousseau about the social sources of realized human personality. "You see," he wrote of the English,

that in this enlightened age I am bold enough to confess that we are generally men of untaught [unsophisticated] feelings: that, instead of casting away all our old prejudices, we cherish them to a very considerable degree; and, to take more shame to ourselves, we cherish them because they are prejudices; and the longer they have lasted, and the more generally they have prevailed, the more we cherish them . . . . Many of our men of speculation [in implicit contrast to the *Philosophes*], instead of exploding general prejudices, employ their sagacity to discover the latent wisdom which prevails in them. If they find what they seek (and they seldom fail) they think it more wise to continue the prejudice, with the reason involved, than to cast away the coat of prejudice, and to leave nothing but the naked reason; because prejudice, with its reason, has a motive to give action to that reason, and an affection which will give it permanence. Prejudice is of ready application in the emergency; it previously engages the mind in a steady course of wisdom and virtue, and does not leave the man hesitating in the moment of decision, skeptical, puzzled, and unresolved. Prejudice renders a man's virtue his habit, and not a series of unconnected acts. Through just prejudice, his duty becomes a part of his nature [1790, pp. 346–347].

Reason, for Burke, is but a subordinate capacity for calculation; it cannot be the sole basis for action or for social order. Burke thus anticipates the concept of common *values* that is found in contemporary sociology, particularly in the works of Talcott Parsons.

Burke's arguments were both hortatory and analytical; he sermonizes, but he also attempts to understand. To be sure, much of the dismay he feels about the events in France stems from his evaluative conviction that the revolutionaries acted unjustly and irreverently. Yet he is also certain that they acted unwisely. That society is not a petty business enterprise and that man is not a self-sufficient and clever isolated being are not merely Burke's metaphorical expressions of moral outrage. They are theoretical conceptions carrying the implication that the natures of society and of man will reassert themselves despite the efforts of the revolutionaries to remake them. Concerted social action surely has effects, but, on a large scale, it seldom has the effects intended. If the French Revolution brought about in the years after Burke's death (1797) a political order more violent and more dictatorial than the one that it replaced, Burke would not have been surprised. Burke and the conservatives after him thus argue along two different but not wholly contradictory lines: do not attempt to introduce too much change too fast; if you do so attempt, you will be surprised and distressed by the result.

These principles oriented Burke in his official conduct as a member of Parliament. Given the complexity and organic nature of society and given the limitations of man's reason and forethought, political action ought to be taken with great caution. This does not mean that no change should be undertaken, since "a state without the means of some change is without the means of its conservation." But change must be undertaken prudently and with a view toward its consequences; purity of intentions is not justification enough. Consequences have to be foreseen in light of the context of the situation.

The science of constructing a commonwealth, or renovating it, or reforming it, is, like every other experimental science, not to be taught *a priori*. Nor is it a short experience that can instruct us in that practical science; because the real effects of moral causes are not always immediate, but that which in the first instance is prejudicial [harmful] may be excellent in its remoter operation, and its excellence may arise even from the ill effects it produces in the beginning. The reverse also happens; and very plausible schemes, with very pleasing commencements, have often shameful and lamentable conclusions [1790, p. 311].

It was the error of the "professors," as Burke scornfully calls the French *Philosophes* and revolutionaries, to ignore this principle of the necessary *contextual* application of programs derived from social philosophy. Yet, at the same time, Burke is contributing theoretical principles of his own: the reality of society as something beyond the moment, the nature of man as a being requiring social fulfillment, and the complexity of social action as involving the paradox of unintended consequences.

CHAPTER 3

Alexis de Tocqueville: Aristocratic Analyst of a Democratic Age

By the first third of the nineteenth century, Napoleon's attempt to spread his version of the French Revolution to all of Europe had been defeated. England had undergone a great surge of industrial growth, and the new nation of the United States had consolidated its independence and formed a national identity. Economic, political, and social upheavals were rapidly changing the order that men had come to know. According to the ancient economic system, production had been carried out in households, small shops, and countryside manors, and goods had been exchanged in town markets. In the early nineteenth century, this system ceded to one in which cities became vast, densely populated, swiftly changing centers of industrial production; here, the wretched, crowded conditions of the laboring poor contrasted sharply with the dynamic, productive power of the factories, run by a few men bent on economic gain. At the same time, however, the ancient prescriptions of status, occupation, and residence, which had so long held sway over the European masses, broke down to produce a social order of ever-increasing popular participation and mobilization. Surely a great transformation of the social order was taking place.

38   Alexis de Tocqueville (1805–1859) was born a nobleman, a representative of the old order, in the midst of these changing times. His lifelong struggle to understand and to influence their direction produced two masterpieces of social analysis, *Democracy in America* [1835, 1840] and *The Old Regime and the French Revolution* [1856]. In these two great works, and in other lesser ones, he employed the method of systematic *comparative analysis* to give to the understanding of society a sociological depth that was greater than that of the *Philosophes*, of Rousseau, and of Burke. At the same time, however, he carried on the moral effort of those authors to outline viable and humane social institutions. While his basic sympathies were conservative and aristocratic—he lamented what he regarded as the incapacity of a democratic social order to protect leisured, aristocratic excellence—he recognized that the new democratic and industrial order was an irrevocable fact.

Tocqueville's efforts were directed toward moderating the effects of the new social order and toward smoothing the process of its institutionalization so as to avoid both disruptive revolution and political tyranny. Viewing the United States as an image of democratic society, he sought to determine the causes for its degree of civility and to influence, so far as possible, the democratic trend in his native France in a similarly benign direction. His political efforts he judged to be unsuccessful. His theoretical efforts, however, are a lasting contribution, the most important aspect of which was his attempt to estimate the effects of two great tendencies of modern social life: social equality, on the one hand, and governmental centralization, on the other.

Like Burke, Tocqueville was both a politician and a man of letters whose sociological ideas were nurtured in a life of reflection and practical experience. Following a private tutorial education and a period of training in the law, he took a position in the government of the restored Bourbon monarch, Louis XVIII, in 1827. When the revolution of 1830 brought to the throne King Louis-Philippe, whom traditionalists regarded as of dubious legitimacy, Tocqueville (and his friend Gustave de Beaumont) obtained a leave to study the penal system of the United States. This was the occasion for his travels to America in 1831–1832. Although his and Beaumont's book on American penitentiaries was published in 1833, the greater fruit of his travels was the first part of his *Democracy in America* published to immediate acclaim in 1835. The second part, published in 1840, was less well received at the time, but it has now been recognized as a sociological classic.

Meanwhile, after resigning his government position, Tocqueville traveled to England and Ireland in 1833 and 1835, where he observed still other variations on the theme of modern society and strengthened his conviction that a complex and pluralist system of social organization was a better guarantor of liberty than the more centralized and unitary system that he saw in France. His written works brought him intellectual and political distinction, and in 1839 he was elected a representative to the French legislature, in which he served through 1851. During this period, he took an active role in foreign affairs and made several trips to Algeria to study problems of colonization there. When the revolution of 1848, which he had foreseen and warned about, toppled Louis-Philippe and ushered in the Second French Republic, Tocqueville became Minister for Foreign Affairs. He retired from politics when Louis Bonaparte declared himself emperor in 1851. For the rest of his life, Tocqueville devoted himself to his writings, embarking on what was planned as a multivolume work about the great French Revolution of 1789. He traveled in Germany and England, doing research in archives there and in France, but was able to publish only one volume of the work (1856) before his death in 1859.

Throughout his career, Tocqueville was conscious of being caught between conservative and liberal ideologies and between the pressures of political expediency and the demands of his intellectual integrity. He tried to state the truth as he saw it but complained of being misunderstood. Already in 1835, he wrote to a friend about the reception of his book on America: "I please many persons of opposite opinions, not because they penetrate my meaning, but because, looking only at one side of my work, they think they can find in it arguments in favor of their own convictions" [quoted by Bradley 1945, p. 403]. This was particularly true for Tocqueville's analysis of equality in modern society, to which I shall now turn.[10]

The Tension Between Equality and Liberty

Tocqueville saw in the United States a society in which the principle of equality had at the time been most thoroughly institutionalized. Since he regarded social equality as the dominant trend of modern societies, he thought that, from his experiences in America, he might divine a prognosis for the societies of Europe. He began with a series of presuppositions that were at odds with the Jeffersonian ideology of the United States, which tends to regard equality and liberty as wholly compatible, if not identical, principles. Coming from an aristocratic heritage in which many liberties had been traditionally enjoyed by the dominant class in a highly unequal social order, he wanted to see whether any of this heritage of liberty might be maintained under an egalitarian system. Because of his background, he was intellectually attuned to render problematic the very heart of the American experiment.

Tocqueville was not in the habit of providing precise definitions of his key concepts, but it is clear from context that "liberty" and "equality" took their meanings from Tocqueville's European background. Liberty, for Tocqueville, was individual freedom of action, of conscience, and of life style. He strongly opposed Rousseau's principle that freedom is the recognition of necessity and the realization of one's true nature. For Tocqueville, therefore, one index of liberty would be the appearance of differences among individuals. Right from the beginning, then, we can see that Tocqueville would be at least skeptical about a social order that renders men equal.

If Tocqueville had *defined* liberty and equality so that logically they were mutually exclusive, he might have won a merely rhetorical victory by demonstrating the impossibility of their combination. Such, however, was neither his intent nor his result. His implicit definition of equality was subtler than a crude notion of "alikeness." "Equality" for Tocqueville (and "democracy" as well, since he tended to use the two terms as synonyms) meant formal equality before the law, or the absence of prescriptive status differences among men. According to the older European "estate" systems, some men had been *born* to rule and others to obey, and all had taken these prescriptions to be facts. In the United States, by contrast, such prescriptive assumptions were not made, and increasingly in the Europe of his day they were being abolished.

Tocqueville could and did recognize that a complete equality of social and economic conditions did not exist in the United States, and he wrote chapters on the relations between masters and servants and between powerful industrial capitalists and factory laborers.[11] The important thing for his definition of equality was that the principle of mobility between groups of greater or lesser wealth and greater or lesser power was taken for granted in the United States. In the terminology of contemporary sociology, he saw the social system of the United States as based on "achievement," in contrast to the older European system of "ascription." As we shall see, Karl Marx, whose theory forcefully exposes the limitations of this kind of formal equality, nonetheless agreed with Tocqueville that it was a key organizing characteristic of what Marx called "bourgeois society."

To say that the United States has a democratic or egalitarian social order is not, therefore, to proffer only a *description* of the relative status of the people, although Tocqueville certainly perceived a much greater equality of condition in the United States than in England or France. Equality was for him a powerful *force* shaping the institutions and customs of modern society—from its political procedures through its intellectual habits to its interpersonal manners. Tocqueville did not focus on providing a systematic *description* or enumeration of the life conditions of the people of one nation with "equality of condition" as a finding of such a study. Rather, he viewed the issue from an analytical perspective—from the standpoint of the ways in which past and present, France and the United States, differed in a fundamental *principle* of social organization. And he proceeded to outline what he perceived as the manifold effects of those differences.

Equality or "democracy" had many consequences of which Tocqueville approved and others of which he disapproved. On the one hand, equality brings about greater mutual respect among people of different occupations and between the sexes. It renders social interaction easier; yet it reinforces morality. At the same time, however, it leads to impatience with refined and subtle works of literature and philosophy and with the effort required to produce them. It tends as well to produce in all men a restless, but mundane, ambition for material well-being. The matter that concerned Tocqueville most, however, was the effect of equality on liberty. Whether to drive home his warning or to reformulate and clarify the matter in his own mind, he returned time and again to the theme of what he variously called the "tyranny of the majority" and "democratic despotism." His analysis of this phenomenon is probably the greatest theoretical contribution of *Democracy in America*.

In typical fashion, Tocqueville has in mind a contrast between aristocratic and democratic forms of social organization. In the former, prescriptive rights held each person in his appointed place and thus set limits upon men's aspirations as well as upon government's power. In the democratic forms, however, the horizons of opportunity are opened to all, and this may lead men to hand over greater authority to government than is desirable for the maintenance of liberty. Man in democratic society, according to Tocqueville, is afflicted with a restless and envious temper:

When all the privileges of birth and fortune are abolished, when all professions are accessible to all, and a man's own energies may place him at the top of any one of them, an easy and unbounded career seems open to his ambition, and he will readily persuade himself that he is born to no vulgar destinies. But this is an erroneous notion, which is corrected by daily experience. The same equality which allows every citizen to conceive these lofty hopes renders all the citizens less able to realize them. . . . They have swept away the privileges of some of their fellow-creatures which stood in their way; but they have opened the door to universal competition: the barrier has changed its shape rather than its position.

However democratic then the social state and the political constitution of a people may be, it is certain that every member of the community will always find out several points about him which command his own position; and we may foresee that his looks will be doggedly fixed in that direction. When inequality of conditions is the common law of society, the most marked inequalities do not strike the eye; when everything is nearly on the same level, the slightest are marked enough to hurt it. Hence the desire of equality always becomes more insatiable in proportion as equality is more complete [1840, pp. 146–147].

In the United States, Tocqueville argued, the universal competitive envy that is produced by egalitarianism both increases the ambitions of the people and tends to separate them each from another. So at the same time that they have decreasing patience with remaining inequalities, they also, divided among themselves, have decreasing power to act on these inequalities.

This tendency toward the atomization of the people can be manipulated only too easily by the centralizing ambitions of governmental agents. Tocqueville's aristocratic sympathies understandably rendered him suspicious of the powers and inclinations of central governments. His own parents were narrowly saved from the guillotine during the Reign of Terror in the French Revolution. Tocqueville was convinced that "every central government worships uniformity" and therefore that those tendencies within the social order that also foster uniformity must be counteracted if liberty is to survive. For one example, the willingness with which citizens use governmental power to overcome social inequality renders them more dependent on government, as he perceived had happened in France. For another, Tocqueville worried about the possibility that citizens would become so atomized that they would be incapable of resisting governmental attempts to divide them further so as the better to rule them.

Despotism, which is of a very timorous nature, is never more secure of continuance than when it can keep men asunder; and all its influence is commonly exerted for that purpose. No vice of the human heart is so acceptable to it as egotism: a despot easily forgives his subjects for not loving him, provided they do not love each other . . . .

Thus the vices which despotism engenders are precisely those which equality fosters. The two things mutually and perniciously complete and assist each other. Equality places men side by side, unconnected by any common tie; despotism raises barriers to keep them asunder; the former predisposes them not to consider their fellow-creatures, the latter makes general indifference a sort of public virtue.

Despotism then, which is at all times dangerous, is more particularly to be feared in democratic ages [1840, p. 109].

It would be a mistake, therefore, to see in Tocqueville's concept of democratic despotism merely a snobbish disdain for public opinion or a privileged man's fear of the common masses. He is by no means above such smaller emotions, but the power and value of his message rest on his sociological distinction between the *uniformity* democracy produces and the *solidarity* it may preclude. He gives a friendly warning to the Americans (and, more especially, to his countrymen) to guard not so much against the dangers of anarchy and mob rule, as against the quiet surrender of liberty to a powerful, even if benign, government. Thus, his anxiety about the masses is not a fear of numbers or even of equality in itself but a fear of the powerlessness of an amorphous, atomized population.

The Role of Associations

We see in Tocqueville a number of the themes earlier identified as recurrent in sociological analysis: the tragic sense that not all values can be simultaneously maximized; the disposition to see intention as at variance with consequence; and the idea that man is shaped by social experience. Thus, societies cannot maximize both equality and liberty; the attempt to do so may produce democratic despotism; and desire for greater equality is fostered by the experience of equality. Yet, as I have said, Tocqueville wrote to persuade his fellow men and to influence the course of history, and he was reluctant to leave his readers with a pessimistic conclusion. "I am the last man," he noted, "to contend that these propensities are unconquerable, since my chief object in writing this book has been to combat them" [1840, p. 313]. The tendency toward democratic despotism was mitigated in the United States, and Tocqueville sought to use the American experience, insofar as possible, as a general lesson.

In aristocratic societies, the centralizing tendencies of government are combatted by the competition among centers of power (especially the powerful aristocrats themselves) supported by the services and energies of their subordinates. Democratic societies, however, tend to raise or reduce all citizens to a common level and thus to diminish such potential sources of opposition. This problem is exacerbated, Tocqueville said, in those lands, such as France, whose social equality had been obtained by forceful revolution. In France, a legacy of suspicion surrounded the centers of power which were independent of the whole nation, as we saw in the third article of the Declaration of Rights of Man and of Citizens. In the United States, social equality, in Tocqueville's sense of the term, was established from the outset, without the ill effects of revolutionary change. Moreover, the Americans enjoyed residence on an underpopulated continent, where economic ambition was more readily accommodated than in old Europe and where international warfare, with its concomitant pressures toward political centralization, was less likely. The customs of the Americans, especially their civility and respect for religion, also buttressed their resistance to political tyranny. In France, a legacy of clerical ambition and anticlerical bitterness militated against the tendency of religion to increase social solidarity. Tocqueville thus placed heavy emphasis upon a lesson of social organization that the Americans had, perhaps unconsciously, put to good use: that a *pluralist* social system is a functional alternative to the political competition provided by the aristocratic systems of the past. The terminology is the contemporary sociologist's, the insight was Tocqueville's.

In the United States the federal governmental system, prescribed constitutionally and historically, was an aspect of such a pluralist system. Writing before the Civil War, Tocqueville was undoubtedly more impressed with the independent power of the constituent states of the union than an observer would be today. But he also emphasized the role of municipal governments (especially the towns of New England) as arenas in which citizens can oversee many matters of public concern without relying on the federal or state government. He paid attention, also, to the role of lawyers as a quasi-aristocratic status group[12] whose prestige and influence serve to enhance the salutary effects of the rule of law.

Above all, however, Tocqueville focused on what he regarded as the peculiar habit of the Americans to form voluntary associations for all manner of causes. He was struck during his visit by the seemingly ludicrous news that one hundred thousand men had formed an association to bind themselves to abstaining from alcoholic beverages. He thought that in increasingly democratic France, people would have gone about this quite differently: each one of the hundred thousand would have individually abstained from alcohol and would have written a letter to ask the government to regulate taverns. He then realized that the effect of the Americans' joining together was that their combined action would command greater respect and their combined voice a greater hearing. Such an association, he reasoned, is precisely the kind of buttress against centralization and despotism that the increasingly democratic societies of Europe required.

Years later, when Tocqueville analyzed the conditions that had led to the French Revolution of 1789, he returned to this theme of the importance of association in warding off the effects of centralization or, to put it negatively, of the unholy alliance between centralization and social atomization. Long before the Revolution, monarchical policies had combined with aristocratic rigidities and bourgeois ambitions to erode the social structure of France. Tocqueville wrote that

once the bourgeois had been completely severed from the noble, and the peasant from both alike, and when a similar differentiation had taken place within each of these three classes, with the result that each was split up into a number of small groups almost completely shut off from each other, the inevitable consequence was that, though the nation came to seem a homogeneous whole, its parts no longer held together [1856, pp. 136–137].

Even in 1840, the lessons for the future were abundantly clear to Tocqueville:

In democratic countries the science of association is the mother of science; the progress of all the rest depends on the progress it has made.

Among the laws which rule human societies there is one which seems to be more precise and clear than all others. If men are to remain civilized, or to become so, the art of associating together must grow and improve, in the same ratio in which the equality of conditions is increased [1840, p. 118].

The Uses of Comparison

We can see, then, that Tocqueville would side with Burke, and against Rousseau, on the importance of maintaining or establishing decentralized organs of political power. Burke, of course, was speaking primarily about the English feudal heritage of prescriptive privileges and mediating authorities; Tocqueville was exploring what might be their functional equivalent for modern society. What Tocqueville added to Burke's analysis of the French situation was a concern for the viability of such institutions. It was not enough for him to decry the institutional destruction presumably wrought upon France by the revolutionaries of 1789 and after. He went further to ask how well the institutions of the old regime had been working. The complex, seemingly self-contradictory political system of England may have been antique, but Tocqueville could agree with Burke that it served its citizens well. He could not agree that the old regime of France had been by 1789 much more than a house of cards. In effect, he takes more seriously than Burke himself did the latter's admonition that social institutions and political policies must be evaluated in their particular context. Much of Tocqueville's book on *The Old Regime and the Revolution* carries the message that in the France during the decades preceding the Revolution, the old, decentralized, complex feudal order had already ceased to exist.

Three aspects of prerevolutionary institutional change are especially worthy of mention. Tocqueville illuminated each through the use of comparative analysis, in which he delved beneath superficial differences and similarities of institutional labels to uncover the actual structure of society. The first aspect is the administrative centralization under the old regime. It is a fiction, Tocqueville declared, that the Revolution and the reign of Napoleon had deliberately or carelessly destroyed an ancient system of government by autonomous municipal and provincial corporations and aristocratic assemblies. Burke had taken this view of the effect of the French Revolution, but Tocqueville showed that France in the prerevolutionary eighteenth century was ruled by thirty *Intendants*, or royal commissioners, each overseeing a province as the agent of the Royal Council. Except for judicial matters, nearly every detail of political and economic affairs was subject to the decrees of the Royal Council through the *Intendants*. A few feudal administrative titles remained, but they afforded little more than deference to their incumbents. Real power was centralized.

Second, the relationship between the noble lords and the peasantry had changed drastically from the medieval system. In the earlier period, the nobles provided services, such as care for the needy of their domains, in exchange for their immense privileges, such as rights to various taxes and rents on serfs' and peasants' lands and an exemption from many royal taxes. By the second half of the eighteenth century, the privileges remained while the rationale for their existence had long disappeared. The resulting disproportion was intensely resented:

When the nobles had real power as well as privileges, when they governed and administrated, their rights could be at once greater and less open to attack. In fact, the nobility was regarded in the age of feudalism much as the government is regarded by everyone today; its exactions were tolerated in view of the protection and security it provided. True, the nobles enjoyed invidious privileges and rights that weighed heavily on the commoner, but in return for this they kept order, administered justice, saw to the execution of the laws, came to the rescue of the oppressed, and watched over the interests of all. The more these functions passed out of the hands of the nobility, the more uncalled-for did their privileges appear—until at last their mere existence seemed a meaningless anachronism [1856, p. 30].

In those countries such as Germany where the functions of the nobility had not eroded to the extent they had in France, the privileges of the nobility could be as great or greater than in France without exciting popular resentment. Thus, Tocqueville did not regard (nor, as an aristocrat, was he likely to regard) inequality alone as a generator of unrest, but rather inequality without function. Twenty years earlier, he had developed similar ideas on the basis of a comparison between the aristocracies of England and Ireland, the former being an aristocracy that served, the latter an aristocracy that exploited. He concluded, "Aristocracy then can be subjected to particular conditions which modify its nature and its results, so that in judging it one must bear circumstances in mind . . . . It would not be fair to make a theoretical judgment about aristocracy on the strength of either of these examples" [1835, pp. 151–152]. Comparison enabled him to focus on the question of the viability of an aristocracy, a question Burke disregarded.

Third, in many respects the peasantry was objectively more emancipated and prosperous in France than in the nonrevolutionary areas of Europe. Far from dampening the peasants' desire for change, this state of well-being, given the moribund institutions of France, heightened it. Despite what historians of his day usually maintained, Tocqueville showed that peasant land ownership was more widespread in eighteenth-century France than in other countries, where peasants were tenants or even legally unfree serfs to feudal lords. The French peasants passionately desired title to their land, and in much of France they had obtained it. Yet, at the same time, feudal exactions remained. Forced labor, bridge tolls, marketing fees, numerous taxes, and processing monopolies were some of the burdens the peasants still had to bear, and they were the more galling for seeming anachronistic. Moreover, France had enjoyed prosperity in the decades before the revolution, and "it was precisely in those parts of France where there had been the most improvement that popular discontent ran highest." Tocqueville delights in the paradox, and formulates the general principle that "the social order overthrown by a revolution is almost always better than the one preceding it." In terms reminiscent of his analysis of the effects of equality in America (and anticipating Durkheim's analysis of *anomie*), Tocqueville says, "Patiently endured so long as it seemed beyond redress, a grievance comes to appear intolerable once the possibility of removing it crosses men's minds" [1856, pp. 176–177].

In these ways, Tocqueville's comparative method allowed him to see
that the French social order was not what Burke, using only the English
model, had presumed it to be. Tocqueville is less satisfied than Burke
with the supposition that a causal analysis of the French Revolution
could be provided by attributing the responsibility for it to capricious
"professors." In fact he argued, once again, that a structural contrast
between England and France predisposed the French thinkers toward
abstract political ideas. In England, men of letters were often men of
political influence and, hence, of political experience. In France, by
contrast, men of letters were thoroughly excluded from political affairs.
They saw before them "ramshackle institutions" but, lacking political
experience, "they completely failed to perceive the very real obstacles
in the way of even the most praiseworthy reforms, and to gauge the
perils involved in even the most salutary revolutions" [1856, p. 140].
Once again, Tocqueville uses comparative analysis to give greater
sociological depth to Burke's rhetoric.

Tocqueville's comparative method is not always wholly successful nor
are his conclusions always correct. Recent research has cast doubt
upon the idea that relative deprivation can be a cause of revolution
[see Snyder and Tilly 1972], while Tocqueville's discussion of equality
in the United States errs by overstatement. His use of polar contrasts
between aristocracy and democracy, though a powerful analytical tool,
inclined him to overestimate both the rigidity of the French social order
and the social equality within the American order. While he was aware
of the massive exception to equality represented by American slavery
and made a few prophetic remarks on what would become the issue of
"race relations" in the twentieth century, he tended to regard social
equality as an irreversible achievement at least for the American white
population. His descriptions of American society, therefore, please
those who regard our institutions as egalitarian, but they miss the mark
for those who have studied or have experienced the massive persistence
of poverty and underprivilege in America.

Tocqueville's discussion about the possibility of the emergence of an
"aristocracy of manufacturers" exhibits the limitations of his analysis.
He acknowledged that the American business orientation might rein-
troduce a persistent form of inequality. Factory laborers must spend
long hours on minute and monotonous tasks, which tend, Tocqueville
said, to circumscribe their imaginations and to brutalize their spirits.
At the same time, the wealthy manufacturer is stimulated by the initiative his position requires; his knowledge grows even as he grows
wealthier. These differences may cumulate so that there are, in the
end, two permanent classes of rich and poor. Thus Tocqueville warned

the "friends of democracy" to guard against this trend. Yet he himself did not take the warning very seriously. He saw in the universal mobility and competition of democratic society a barrier against the permanent domination of an individual workman by any particular industrial magnate and also against the solidarity of the rich themselves. "To say the truth, though there are rich men, the class of rich men does not exist; for these rich individuals have no feelings or purposes in common, no mutual traditions or mutual hopes: there are therefore members, but no body" [1840, p. 171].

As sensitive as he was to the power of political systems and to the political aspect of social structure, Tocqueville could not readily understand the power of concentrated wealth and the influence it would have on the development of democratic society. He provides a profound analysis of the effects of egalitarianism on the American mind, a social psychology of modern society, and a study of the social foundations of political constitutions. But for an understanding of modern social structure as deriving from resurgent economic inequalities, the works of Karl Marx provide a more compelling insight.

CHAPTER 4

Karl Marx:
Theorist of Revolution

Karl Marx (1818–1883) was the son of a Jewish lawyer from the Rhineland for whom career opportunities had been opened by Napoleon's progressive reforms and then closed with the restoration of conservative German rule. Marx was thus in a better position than Tocqueville to appreciate the contributions of revolution to historical progress. Friendly critic of democracy though he was, Tocqueville looked backward to an era of institutions that protected the individual liberties of the privileged, and he sought to define their functional analogues for a vastly changed society. Marx, however, used the record of the past as the prologue to a future that would permanently emancipate the underprivileged. For this purpose, Marx fashioned a theory that considered history as a series of qualitative changes, and he drew upon such diverse sources as German philosophy, French socialism, and English economics. His life was utterly devoted to this theory, both to its articulation in words and to its realization in practice. His influence has deeply shaped the modern political and intellectual world.

Marx originally aspired to a career in law, but his student days at the University of Berlin drew him to philosophy, especially to the radical heirs of G. W. F. Hegel (1770–1831). When the possibility of an academic career was foreclosed by the government's ouster of one of his mentors, he began a brilliant career as a liberal journalist in Cologne. This work brought him experience with political affairs and reinforced his sense of frustration with the conservatism and complacency of the German regimes. His increasingly outspoken ideas ran afoul of the censors, and he was exiled to Paris in 1843. There he encountered politically conscious workers, socialist theoreticians, and Friedrich Engels (1820–1895), a fellow radical and the son of a textile manufacturer. Engels quickly became his friend and collaborator; later, in Marx's years of impoverished devotion to his theoretical system, Engels acted as his benefactor. Meanwhile, Marx had begun the series of notebooks and manuscripts—largely written for purposes of self-clarification and memorandum—that were to become after his death such a major part of the Marxist canon. They included *The Economic-Philosophic Manuscripts*, the *Theses on Feuerbach*, and *The German Ideology*.

Those of Marx's writings that were published at the time got him into trouble once again. He was expelled from Paris, moving to Brussels in 1845. There he and Engels associated with a radical workers' organization, which commissioned them to write an official theoretical statement. They quickly produced *The Manifesto of the Communist Party* [1848], just in time for the outbreaks of revolution that occurred throughout Europe during that year (over which, however, the *Manifesto* exerted no influence). At the time that Tocqueville was lamenting the occurrence of yet another revolution in Paris, Marx and Engels viewed the event in another light: they took it as a signal to return to Germany expecting that, as Marx had earlier expressed it, "the day of German resurrection [would] be proclaimed by the crowing of the Gallic chanticleer." They were soon disappointed. The revolutions of 1848 were defeated all over Europe, and Marx was once again a refugee. He moved to London this time, where he lived from 1849 to his death.

Marx attempted to analyze the failure of the 1848 revolution in Paris in the lively and masterful historical study *The Eighteenth Brumaire of Louis Bonaparte* (1852). (The title refers to and deprecates the same self-proclamation as emperor by the nephew of Napoleon that caused Tocqueville to retire from public life.) Marx then turned his powerful energies and meticulous attention to an attempt "to lay bare the economic law of motion of modern society." Through the 1850s and into the

1860s, when he was not engaged in the journalism that provided much of his meager income and that kept him abreast of current events, Marx did daily research into economic theory and history. From these labors, he hoped to forge a multivolume systematic treatise, but he was able to publish during his lifetime only *A Contribution to the Critique of Political Economy* [1859] and the first volume of *Capital* [1867].[13]

After many years of watchful waiting, Marx joined and soon dominated an international workers' movement, the First International, founded in London in 1864. He thought that this association would become the vehicle for the revolutionary change that he ardently desired. Although it did bring his theories a great influence in the socialist movement and his writings an admiring readership, the International foundered when the bloody suppression of the Paris Commune of 1871 divided European socialists. Marx, growing older and pessimistic, returned to his scholarly labors. He continued to write in his notebooks and to outline his arguments, but his own health and that of his family had been undermined by years of poverty. His wife died in 1881, and his eldest daughter soon after; Marx himself died in his study in 1883. Engels interpreted Marx's message in his own books and edited Marx's manuscripts, publishing the second and third volumes of *Capital* before his own death in 1895. Many other manuscripts, notes, and letters of both men were posthumously published. The collected works of Marx and Engels in German (there is no standard or complete English edition) now run to forty-one large volumes.

Marx's life was one of passion and dedication. He was painfully conscious of having sacrificed the happiness of his family to his theoretical and political efforts. In the eyes of posterity, however, his wide experience and his voluminous reading produced an invaluable work of synthesis in the theory and practice of revolution.

Universal Emancipation Through Revolution

To say that Marx is above all a theorist of revolution is not to say that he concentrated on the strategy of violence. His friend Engels was much his superior in the understanding of military matters, and Lenin and Trotsky made greater contributions to the theory and practice of organized revolutionary struggle. Rather, Marx was convinced of the need for a radical break with the society that he knew, and he believed that radical change is always produced by struggle. Though he was understandably given to temperamental outbursts against the society that had rewarded him so meagerly, Marx saw his revolutionary commitment as part of an all-embracing historical movement of progress from narrow

provincialism through dynamic but callous egoism to universal fulfillment.

In his youth Marx imbibed the Enlightenment ideals of social activism
and human perfectibility. His vision of the ills of society and of the
changes needed to overcome them deepened until his theory crystallized
around 1848. At first repelled by German censorship and political back-
wardness, he came to see that even the more progressive institutions
of France prevented the full development of human potential. He began
to question the presuppositions of a social order based on the contradictory principles of individual self-interest and political association.

Recognizing the great steps forward taken by the French Revolution,
he criticized nonetheless the dualism implicit in a declaration on "the
rights of man and of citizens." Why, he asked, should there be two categories to provide for the rights of a unitary being whose real nature (what
Marx called "species-being") is realized only in society? Only, he answered, so that the emancipations produced by the Revolution would be
limited to the eighteenth-century ideals of political and religious liberty,
including the principles of popular sovereignty and the separation of
church and state, and would avoid the fundamental area of nongovern-
mental power relations within society. True, he said, property qualifications for voting and for political office had been abolished in the United
States, but this simply allowed private property to manifest itself as a
divisive and uncontrolled force within what he called "civil society."

Civil society, *bürgerliche Gesellschaft* in German, is sometimes also
translated as "bourgeois society." Its etymology and theoretical lineage
connote a society of townspeople formed in opposition to, and in emancipation from, the prescriptive restraints of feudal society. Bourgeois
society is a society whose primary business is business and family,
rather than war or politics. In Marx's time the term "bourgeois" had distinctly positive overtones of peaceful progress, though Marx among
others gave it a connotation of narrowness and egoism. In Marx's time,
the *middle class* of merchants and manufacturers (or "capitalists") were
bourgeois, as distinguished from the remnant of the feudal class, from
the "proletariat" of industrial laborers, and from the peasantry. In our
own time, the *upper class* of American society is the most "bourgeois"
in Marx's sense.

In modern bourgeois political life, Marx said, man is a citizen, enjoying rights of expression and the franchise; he is conscious of having
citizenship in common with other citizens. In civil society, however, he
is a private person, who "treats other men as means, degrades himself
to the role of mere means, and becomes the plaything of alien powers"
[1843, p. 13]. Man's bourgeois liberties consist in his right to do anything

that does not harm others, but this, Marx complained, defines liberty negatively and without considering the social nature of man. Specifically, the right of *property* "leads every man to see in other men- not the *realization*, but rather the *limitation* of his own liberty" [1843, p. 25]. In terms strongly reminiscent of Rousseau's critique of the contract theories of Locke and Hobbes, Marx wrote,

None of the supposed rights of man, therefore, go beyond the egoistic man, man as he is, as a member of civil society; that is, an individual separated from the community, withdrawn into himself, wholly preoccupied with his private interest and acting in accordance with his private caprice. Man is far from being considered, in the rights of man, as a species-being; on the contrary, species-life itself—society—appears as a system which is external to the individual and as a limitation of his original independence. The only bond between men is natural necessity, need and private interest, the preservation of their property and their egoistic persons [1843, p. 26].

Like Rousseau, Marx wanted to overcome the inequalities and divisions of the society of his day and to establish a true community: "In place of the old bourgeois society, with its classes and class antagonisms, we shall have an association, in which the free development of each is the condition for the free development of all" [1848, p. 31]. And like Rousseau, he located the barrier to fulfillment in the circumstantially developed divisions among men, especially the division of labor:

The division of labor offers us the first example of how, as long as a man remains in natural society,[14] that is as long as a cleavage exists between the particular and the common interest, as long therefore as activity is not voluntarily, but naturally divided, man's own deed becomes an alien power opposed to him, which enslaves him instead of being controlled by him. For as soon as labor is distributed, each man has a particular, exclusive sphere of activity, which is forced upon him and from which he cannot escape. He is a hunter, a fisherman, a shepherd, or a critical critic, and must remain so if he does not want to lose his means of livelihood; while in communist society, where nobody has one exclusive sphere of activity but each can become accomplished in any branch he wishes, society regulates the general production and thus makes it possible for me to do one thing today and another tomorrow, to hunt in the morning, fish in the afternoon, rear cattle in the evening, criticize after dinner, just as I have a mind, without ever becoming hunter, fisherman, shepherd or critic [1846, p. 22].

Unlike Rousseau, Marx outlined a program for the creation of such a community, concentrating not on the suppression of factional divisions through constitutional reforms but on using the very antagonisms of bourgeois society to bring about its downfall. For this purpose Marx turned to the proletariat.

The Proletariat as Agent of Revolution

Marx liked to say that bourgeois society—as well as the capitalist economic system upon which it is based—produces its own gravediggers. No group suffers more from the circumscribed nature of bourgeois emancipation than the class of those who work in the factories owned by capitalists. True, these workers have been drawn out of earlier modes of economic life, including agricultural and home-based craft production, and they have been released thereby from life conditions that limited their wide-scale social interaction and their political awareness. (Marx's contempt for "rural life" is one index of his own bourgeois attitudes.) But factory workers have also been emancipated in a negative sense of the word: they have been emancipated by technological obsolescence from trades in which they could earn a self-sufficient livelihood and emancipated from locational or occupational restrictions that gave them a measure of narrow security. Now they have only their labor power to sell, and to earn a living they must hire themselves out to those who own the instruments of production.

A new kind of slavery emerges and Marx is vehement in his denunciation of it:

Hence it is self-evident that the laborer is nothing else, his whole life through, than labor-power, that therefore all his disposable time is by nature and law labor-time, to be devoted to the self-expansion of capital. . . . [Capital] usurps the time for growth, development, and healthy maintenance of the body. It steals the time required for the consumption of fresh air and sunlight. It higgles over a meal-time, incorporating it where possible with the process of production itself, so that food is given to the laborer as to a mere means of production, as coal is supplied to the boiler, grease and oil to the machinery [1867, pp. 264–265].

Surely this is the depth of man's reduction to a mere means and the utmost violation of his true nature. The picture was all too true of the early factory system. It could be transformed, Marx said, only if the ability of one class of men to control, command, subdivide, and enjoy the fruits of the labor of another class of men were to be abolished. This transformation required the abolition of the system of private property in the means of production and a leap beyond the limited bourgeois rights sought by the French Revolution into the domain of the universal rights of communism.

It would be wrong, however, to dwell too long on the inhumane treatment of the proletariat by the bourgeoisie, for Marx saw in the proletarians not only the *victims* of capitalism but also the *agents* of its transformation. His argument is not only moral, but predictive as well.

57

Marx held that the proletariat would, over time, develop both the will and the capacity to create a social revolution. To see how they could do so, he employed an analogy to what he regarded as the process leading to the French Revolution. Whereas Tocqueville tended to concentrate on the weaknesses and errors of the superordinate classes as a cause of revolution, Marx looked to the dynamism of the subordinate classes. For Marx, the French Revolution was brought about by a socially subordinate bourgeoisie increasingly frustrated by the political limitations placed on it by the feudal order and increasingly capable—through its growing wealth, organization, and political sophistication—of taking action against these limits. In analogous fashion, the proletariat would become in time the numerical majority, would occupy the points of economic productivity, would realize its common interests, and would organize to take control by force.

At the time of its revolt against feudalism, the bourgeoisie was a minority, one that had only a partial grievance against society and established only partial reforms in its own time. By contrast, the proletarian revolution would be complete. The bourgeoisie would be quite ready to emancipate society "as a whole, but only on condition that the whole of society is in the same situation as this class; for example, that it possesses or can easily acquire money or culture" [1844, p. 55]. The proletariat, however, is "a sphere of society which has a universal character because its sufferings are universal, and which does not claim a *particular redress* because the wrong which is done to it is not a *particular wrong* but *wrong in general*" [1844, p. 58]. In other words, "the proletarians have nothing to lose but their chains" [1848, p. 44]. Only through the action of such a class could the humane and optimistic ideas of the Enlightenment, of Rousseau, and of the German philosophers of Marx's own day be put into practice.

The Economic Theory of History

When Marx discovered the proletariat to be the agent of change, he turned to the study of economics in order to understand the dynamics of class formation. He soon acquired an impressive mastery of the economic literature, as was shown with the publication of *Capital*, which made substantial contributions to technical economic theory. (A fine critical analysis of Marx's economic theory and of its sociological predictions is presented by Neil Smelser in the accompanying essay, *Sociological Theory: A Contemporary View.*)

Marx's "economic theory of history," goes beyond economics, in the narrow sense of that term, and presents a synthesis of historical, economic, political, and sociological ideas. Its basic presupposition is that men have to produce the means of their existence. They do so with the methods at hand (which Marx called the "forces [or means or instruments] of production") and under institutionalized conditions (called "relations of production") that amount to property rights over the forces of production. At every stage of society prior to communism, the relationship between the forces and relations of production is one of "antagonism": the forces of production (technology, science, materials, methods of factory organization) are dynamic, while the relations of production (property rights) are more or less rigidly defended by the privileged class.

The combination of forces and relations of production at any given time Marx called the "mode of production" of society. He identified four such modes prior to communism—"Asiatic," "ancient," "feudal," and "modern bourgeois"—thus informing his reader that the well-recognized periods of European history—Graeco-Roman, medieval, and modern—could be understood in Marxist terms. (The "Asiatic" mode was a late addition which poses special problems beyond the scope of this essay [see Lichtheim 1963 and Warner 1971].) Thus the foundation of Marx's theory of history includes both a "material" element (forces) and a sociolegal element (relations). His theory is not a simple technological or economic determinism.

The antagonism within a mode of production and the transformation of one mode to the next is carried out by the actions of classes, one representing the past and narrow privileges, the other representing the future and growing emancipation. A class is defined by the criterion of its relationship to the means of production. Under capitalism, a few men (capitalists) own concentrations of these material means, while others (proletarians), constantly growing in numbers, own nothing but their labor power. Under feudalism a few men (lords) own land, while others (serfs) are legally tied to the land and to the lord. In each type of society a subversive element is necessarily present (a nascent bourgeoisie under feudalism to carry out trade, a proletariat under capitalism to do industrial labor) whose interests are opposed to those of the dominant class. The subversive, future-oriented class increasingly comes to regard the dominant class and its institutions as obstacles or fetters to be overthrown. The insurgents develop an organization and an ideology that are in opposition to their oppressors, and the dominant class, increasingly on the defensive, tries by every means to maintain its hold on its privileges.

When all of the possibilities for development under the dominant order have been realized and when the rising class has acquired sufficient maturity, the revolution occurs, putting a new class in the saddle. The newly dominant class uses political power to transform rapidly the social order, and for a time social progress (coupled, however, with new forms of oppression) is swift. However, the limits of the new order sooner or later become apparent, and the process of conflict begins anew. All of this continues to happen, with each social form reaching a higher level, until finally the proletarian revolution ushers in an order that is free of antagonisms.

The bourgeois relations of production are the last antagonistic form of the social process of production—antagonistic not in the sense of individual antagonism, but of one arising from conditions surrounding the life of individuals in society; at the same time the productive forces developing in the womb of bourgeois society create the material conditions for the solution of that antagonism. This social formation constitutes, therefore, the closing chapter of the prehistoric state of human society [1859, p. 13].

Only with the abolition of "antagonisms" can human nature, or "species-being," be fulfilled. Only then will the real history of human community begin.

Structure and Dynamics of Capitalism

Marx thus treats the whole of human experience as a meaningful process that leads up to a harmonious future. He did not, however, dwell long upon the organization of future society, and as a result the picture of communist society quoted above is of more polemical than analytical value. Marx's analytical attention was focused, rather, on the process by which bourgeois society will cede to communism. His scheme of history has an air of finality and inevitability which Marx wanted to convey rhetorically. Yet when he said that the whole march of progress was "inevitable" or "inexorable," he did not mean to say that it was automatic or above human agency. He meant that it was an intricate self-contained process, one in which the internal dynamics of capitalist contradictions would be worked out.

The fundamental structure of capitalism consists of two antagonistic properties: the concentration of the means of production in private hands, on one side, and the expropriation (deprivation of property) of a mass of formally free laborers on the other side. Each of these structural properties has a long history, extending back into the Middle Ages and continuing into the present. Marx accurately predicted that masses of capital would become ever larger—that the size and market share of business firms would grow—and that a larger proportion of the labor force would lack independent ownership of the means of production and be forced to work for others. Corresponding to these structural properties are the two great classes of the bourgeoisie and the proletariat. Marx did not ignore other classes—for example, the *petite bourgeoisie* of shopkeepers and independent artisans and the land-owning peasantry, who do own their means of production—but he predicted that they would become increasingly negligible elements in society. It is the struggle between the two great camps of bourgeoisie and proletariat that produces the history and the demise of bourgeois society.

Marx insists that the bourgeoisie has a crucial role to play in this story. Though his denunciations are fierce, his scheme of history openly acknowledges that the "bourgeoisie has played a most revolutionary role in history." *The Communist Manifesto* includes several pages emphasizing this role:

The bourgeoisie, wherever it has got the upper hand, has put an end to all feudal, patriarchal, idyllic relations. . . . It has drowned the most heavenly ecstasies of religious fervor, of chivalrous enthusiasm, of philistine sentimentalism, in the icy water of egotistical calculation. . . . It has been the first to show what man's activity can bring about. It has accomplished wonders far surpassing Egyptian pyramids, Roman aqueducts, and Gothic cathedrals. . . . The bourgeoisie cannot exist without constantly revolutionizing the instruments of production, and thereby the relations of production, and with them the whole relations of society. . . . And as in material, so also in intellectual production. The intellectual creations of individual nations become common property. National one-sidedness and narrow-mindedness become more and more impossible, and from the numerous national and local literatures there arises a world literature [1848, pp. 11–13].

These statements are only partly ironic. True, Marx was not about to give moral credit to the bourgeoisie for these contributions. Nor did he morally approve of the actions of the British empire for the similarly revolutionary role it played in disrupting what he regarded as the stagnant social structure of India. The bourgeoisie and the British imperialists were impelled by the most callous of motives. Yet their actions had the effect of being historically progressive. Marx thus invokes an idea of his philosophic mentor, Hegel, who spoke of the "cunning of reason" in using men to bring about its historical ends. The bourgeoisie acted to produce the material abundance that a truly free society would require. It concentrated the means of production so that they could be employed by associated laborers. It opened men's minds to new possibilities. When Marx says that it is necessary to "abolish" the bourgeois social order, he uses a German term employed by Hegel, *aufheben*, which has three simultaneous meanings: to abolish, to incorporate, and to transcend. The course of history will not merely turn its back on the bourgeoisie; it will use what the bourgeoisie has done, go beyond it, and sweep the bourgeoisie aside. Although it is hardly their intention, the bourgeoisie contributes to the realization of communism.

Still the bourgeoisie has accomplished its miracles through the exploitation of the proletariat. Those who must labor using instruments owned by others are in a powerless position. Their labor power becomes a commodity, to be bought and sold like any other. A commodity exchanges in a free market, Marx said, for its "exchange value," which is what it costs in labor to produce it. Every commodity, therefore, can be expressed as incorporating a certain amount of "socially necessary labor time." This, the "labor theory of value," was a widespread concept in Marx's time, though it is no longer popular today.

To this concept, Marx added the perception that labor power is unique among commodities because it can produce more exchange value than the exchange value of its price. The worker's wage is what it costs to assure his regular appearance at the factory gate every morning; under bourgeois standards, his fair wage is subsistence. But, let us suppose that the worker can produce commodities equal in value to his subsistence wage within six hours (his own socially necessary labor time). The capitalist, having hired him for the day, can require him to work an additional six hours. The value produced in the hours beyond the socially necessary labor time is the capitalist's "surplus value," the source of his profit as well as the source of the immense economic growth of bourgeois society.

We see then, that, apart from extremely elastic bounds, the nature of the exchange of commodities itself imposes no limit to the working-day, no limit to surplus-labor. The capitalist maintains his rights as a purchaser when he tries to make the working-day as long as possible, and to make, whenever possible, two working days out of one. On the other hand, the peculiar nature of the commodity sold implies a limit to its consumption by the purchaser, and the laborer maintains his right as seller when he wishes to reduce the working day to one of definite normal duration. There is here, therefore, an antinomy, right against right, both equally bearing the seal of the law of exchanges. Between equal rights force decides [1867, pp. 234–235].

This contradiction produces the first great struggle of the proletarian movement: the conflict over the length of the working day. It would be a tragic conflict were it not for Marx's faith and prediction that it will be transcended by the harmonious order of communism.

The contradiction cannot be resolved within the capitalist system itself. The growing industrial concentration and technological sophistication of capitalism produce an army of unemployed laborers upon whom the capitalist can draw should any of his workers demand a better deal. The individual capitalist is also subjected to the rigors of competition and could himself raise wages only at the cost of losing out to the competition and joining the ranks of the proletariat. Any inroads upon the competitive system in the direction of national planning or regulation are denounced by the whole bourgeoisie as assaults upon "such sacred things as the rights of property, freedom and unrestricted play for the bent of the individual capitalist" [1867, p. 356]. Such are the rigidities of the bourgeois mind and of bourgeois relations of production.

Meanwhile, the workers come to a consciousness of their position. Drawn out of the fields, hamlets, and shops of precapitalist economic relations and into urban factories, they come to form a class. Their similarity of position (what Marx called "class *in* itself") as wage laborers brings them common experiences and new ideas (including Marxian ideas) and cedes to their awareness of and action upon their common interests (what Marx called "class *for* itself"). Though Marx never deduced in rigorous fashion the inevitability of the revolution, he presented it in stirring terms, which it is appropriate to quote at length:

That which is now to be expropriated is no longer the laborer working for himself, but the capitalist exploiting many laborers. This expropriation is accomplished by the action of the immanent laws of capitalistic production itself, by the centralization of capital. One capitalist always kills many. Hand in hand with this centralization, or this expropriation of many capitalists by few, develop, on an ever-extending scale, the co-operative form of the labor-process, the conscious technical application of science, the methodical cultivation of the soil, the transformation of the instruments of labor into instruments of labor only usable in common, the economizing of all means of production by their use as the means of production of combined, socialized labor, the entanglement of all people in the net of the world-market, and with this, the international character of the capitalistic regime. Along with the constantly diminishing number of the magnates of capital, who usurp and monopolize all advantages of this process of transformation, grows the mass of misery, oppression, slavery, degradation, exploitation; but with this too grows the revolt of the working-class, a class always increasing in numbers, and disciplined, united, organized by the very mechanism of the process of capitalist production itself. The monopoly of capital becomes a fetter upon the mode of production, which has sprung up and flourished along with, and under it. Centralization of the means of production and socialization of labor at last reach a point where they become incompatible with their capitalist integument. This integument is burst asunder. The knell of capitalist private property sounds. The expropriators are expropriated [1867, p. 763].

Problems with Marx's Deductions

It is now over a century since Marx issued this prognosis. We know that the proletarian revolution has not occurred in England, upon whose economic development Marx's model was largely based; that it has been repeatedly aborted in France, whose socialist and revolutionary tradition served as Marx's political model; that it was preempted in Germany, whose philosophy inspired Marx's theory, by the fearful and retrogressive Nazi revolution; and that in the quintessentially capitalist United States it has always been more of a specter haunting conservatives than an imminent probability. Much to Marx's surprise, it was in Russia, whose regime he despised as a bulwark of reaction, that his theories gained the most enthusiastic audience. It was also in Russia, a half century after *Capital*, that a revolution came to power in his name, a revolution whose totalitarian outcome under Stalin surely would have been disavowed by Marx. What went wrong?

Some maintain that Marx was right and that the proletarian revolution in the Western capitalist countries is still to come. They point out that many of Marx's predictions have actually been borne out. Capital has been massively concentrated, and huge monopolies and oligopolies have come to dominate capitalist economies—potentialities that were not at all obvious to observers in Marx's day. The capitalist system has continued to experience periodic and staggering crises in which the productive apparatus of the economy and armies of workers stand idle. Although the standard of living has increased across the board, no great redistribution of income shares has occurred; Marx's class society is still a reality. If the revolution has been forestalled, the argument goes, this is because of the irrational and wasteful but job-producing investments that the capitalist economies make in arms production and in planned obsolescence and because of the increasingly international character of capitalism (called *imperialism*) in which the working classes of the advanced capitalist countries in effect join with their masters in the lucrative exploitation of the Third World. Contemporary Marxists have invested a great deal of time in the attempt to understand the longevity of capitalist systems.

In Marx's theory itself there are points of slack in the deduction of the inexorability of revolution, some of which will be important in our subsequent discussion. First, Marx may have erred in his claim that the bourgeoisie was too rigid to countenance regulatory measures that would dampen the overt manifestations of capitalism's contradictions. Contemporary Marxist scholars have illuminated the leading role that capitalists took in the reforms of the progressive era in the United States (1900–1920). If the rigors of competition can be alleviated, much of the inherent dynamic of Marx's law of capitalist development loses force. The very monopolistic concentration that Marx predicted may have allowed such regulation to take place, but his revolutionary commitment ill-disposed him to see its implications.

Second, Marx's supposition that the proletariat was a uniform body of workers with only their labor to sell and with "nothing to lose but their chains" seriously understated the consequences of differentiation within the labor force. Marx was aware of skill differentials among laborers, but the part of his theory that he was willing to publish himself (volume I of *Capital*) assumed such differentials to be theoretically negligible. Marx knew that racial and ethnic antagonisms, as well as the kind of universal competition so stressed by Tocqueville, could stand as barriers to working class unity. Indeed, Marx struggled to overcome them in his own role as a leader of the International. He may have underestimated their persistence. Moreover, despite his own sensitivity to the complexity of "relationships to the means of production," he may not have adequately analyzed the ways in which highly trained skills, which are required by the nature of capitalism itself, and job security and job incentive guaranties serve as new forms of property for significant numbers of industrial workers and give them much to lose in the event of revolution. Those who have nothing to lose are now a minority whose structural position as a class of the permanently underemployed is a social disgrace but not a sufficient base for Marx's revolution. In Max Weber we shall see an analyst who was less committed to revolution and more willing to emphasize (even overemphasize) the complexity of stratification structures.

Finally, events may have shown that the most trying period of capitalism is the period of its introduction. Its rigors and miseries are most painful in the beginning, not at maturity. Thus, if a regime can weather the first crises of capitalism (as England did in the 1830s, but Russia in 1917 did not) its path may be smoothed for the years of capitalist advancement. In this view, held as we shall see by Emile Durkheim, periods of transition are disruptive in themselves. The reintroduction of regulatory mechanisms and institutionalized norms would render conflict unnecessary.

The Roles of Politics and of Ideas

Two further aspects of Marx's analysis of the structure of society and of the contigencies of revolution remain to be discussed: the role of politics and the role of ideas. In general, political and ideological factors play a conservative role in society. Marx adduced them in his attempt to understand why the contradictions of bourgeois society were often muted in manifest expression. Yet, politics and ideas were crucial parts of Marx's own revolutionary strategy.

In an often-cited passage, Marx presents a general formula for the relationship between the economic structure of society, or "mode of production," and the political and ideological "superstructure." The economic structure of society (which, as we have seen, is a combination of material and sociolegal relations) is, he writes,

the real foundation, on which rise legal and political superstructures and to which correspond definite forms of social consciousness. The mode of production in material life determines the general character of the social, political, and spiritual processes of life. It is not the consciousness of men that determines their existence, but, on the contrary, their social existence determines their consciousness [1859, pp. 11–12].

By this formula, Marx expressed his disagreement with the German idealist view that the political state was the highest form of community yet produced by the evolution of ideas. He insisted that politics and ideologies are weapons used in the more basic economic struggle, and he scoffed at the view that they stand neutrally above it. "Political power, properly so called, is merely the organized power of one class for oppressing another" [1848, p. 31]. "The ruling ideas of each age have ever been the ideas of its ruling class" [1848, p. 29].

This is not to say that politics and ideas are unimportant. In capitalist society, the bourgeoisie uses the state as an "executive committee" for the management of its affairs. Marx would feel his theory vindicated by the use of court injunctions to deter strikes, of national guardsmen to suppress revolts, and of the federal budget to induce unemployment-causing recessions. He knew that ideologies of opportunity and patriotism could be accepted by the "false consciousness" of the working class, directing their energies away from the conflict with the bourgeoisie and toward "opportunistic" social mobility and retrogressive xenophobia. Much of his skepticism is a healthy corrective to liberal rhetoric; he admonishes us not to take the ideology of a society at face value "just as our opinion of an individual is not based on what he thinks of himself" [1859, p. 12].

To accept as the whole story the foundation-superstructure imagery, however, would be to regard the evolution of capitalism and the revolution of the proletariat as wholly automatic processes, somehow above human agency, and thus to misread fatally Marx's message. For Marx held that politics and ideas and not only economic dynamics must play a revolutionary role.

He recognized that the bourgeoisie, in its own revolutionary consolidation of power, employed the state not merely as a stabilizer but as a propeller of capitalist development. Workers must be disciplined and the great machine put into motion.

It is not enough that the conditions of labor are concentrated in a mass, in the shape of capital, at the one pole of society, while at the other are grouped masses of men, who have nothing to sell but their labor-power. . . . The organization of the capitalist process of production, *once fully developed*, breaks down all resistance. . . . It is otherwise during the historic *genesis* of capitalist production. The bourgeoisie, at its rise, wants and uses the power of the state to "regulate" wages, i.e. to force them within the limits suitable for surplus-value making, to lengthen the working-day and to keep the laborer himself in the normal degree of dependence [1867, p. 737; italics added].

Analogously, the coming-to-be of communism after the successful proletarian revolution will require a period of forcible consolidation, in which remaining bourgeois practices are rooted out. In this period, Marx wrote, "the state can be nothing but the *revolutionary dictatorship of the proletariat*" [1875, p. 18], a remark that has been often invoked and much abused. Thus, for Marx both the rise and demise of a social order are brought about through active political intervention.

It is in regard to the role of ideas, however, that Marx has been most misunderstood, and his statement that men's "social existence determines their consciousness" has often been taken out of context. Marx was not invoking a "bucket theory of the mind" in which perception has no active role to play; he did not believe that man is what he eats.

First, note that Marx says that *social* existence determines consciousness. He is saying that each of us is dependent upon social relations that are independent of our will and that shape our thinking, surely by now an uncontroversial statement. Second, Marx was arguing against the idea that human emancipation requires only an emancipation of thought —a point of view held by some of the German philosophers with whom he had studied. This view, an extreme form of Enlightenment optimism, obscures the fact that men are enslaved by real chains, and not merely ideological ones, and that these real chains must be broken. Marx satirized the philosophers' view with a parable:

Once upon a time an honest fellow had the idea that men were drowned in water only because they were possessed with the idea of gravity. If they were to knock this idea out of their heads say by stating it to be a superstition, a religious idea, they would be sublimely proof against any danger from water. His whole life long he fought against the illusion of gravity, of whose harmful results all statistics brought him new and manifold evidence. This honest fellow was the type of the new revolutionary philosophers in Germany [1846, p. 2].

Marx argued that the power of ideas should not be misapplied. Ideas appropriate to an objective situation could most certainly have effects; those not appropriate could only mislead.

Theory and Practice

For Marx, the leading idea for the proletariat's struggle was his own theory. The working class must be convinced that capitalism is a transitory system, whose "laws" were not eternal and whose days were numbered. Thus, he worked to demonstrate both the historical specificity of the bourgeois social order and its internal contradictions. The working class must come to recognize its common interest as a class and to organize to promote that interest; it must not be discouraged by momentary setbacks. Moving back and forth from the reading room of the British Museum to the headquarters of the International, Marx sought to uncover the long-term dynamics of capitalism and to emphasize its inevitable downfall, not as an excuse for passivity but as a goad to action.

In 1845 Marx jotted down eleven short notes, known as the *Theses on Feuerbach*, in which he stated his attitude on the intimate connection between ideas and action. Those who take the simple, materialistic position that thought is shaped by external circumstance ignore the fact that men change circumstances. They cannot answer the question of how it is that new circumstances come about unless they suppose that a select few are able to exempt themselves from this materialist determination and thus to produce change. "This doctrine has therefore to divide society into two parts, one of which is superior to society" [1845, p. 198]. On the contrary, Marx said, the would-be revolutionary educator of the masses (Marx included) "himself must be educated." In a real sense, Marx regarded his own revolutionary activities as part of a practical process informing his theory.

On the other hand, those who take the purely idealist stance that thought is independent of circumstance ignore the importance of practical activity and suppose that critical debate will suffice to emancipate mankind. They have rightly developed the idea that the mind shapes experience, but their obsession with merely destroying ideological illusions condemns their efforts to sterility:

68 The question whether objective truth is an attribute of human thought—is not a theoretical but a *practical* question. Man must prove the truth, i.e., the reality and power, the "this-sidedness" of his thinking in practice. The dispute over the reality or non-reality of thinking that is isolated from practice is a purely *scholastic* question [1845, p. 197].

Marx thereby argues that society is a human product, that men's thinking and acting shape the social world. At the same time, he insists that man is a social product, enmeshed in social relations, and not an isolated individual who only needs to change his mind to change his life. Furthermore, Marx holds that to change society, it is necessary for men to grasp its objective reality of inherent contradictions. When the "prehistory" of class societies has ceded to the real, human history of communism, men will be able to transcend conflict and they will be free to shape society according to their needs. Until that time, vigorous thought and action are required. Marx ended his eleven theses with this summons: "The philosophers have only *interpreted* the world differently, the point is, to *change* it" [1845, p. 199].

CHAPTER 5

Emile Durkheim: Sociologist and Physician to Modern Society

Like Marx, Emile Durkheim (1858–1917) was a man of consummate dedication to an overriding cause. Whereas Marx's cause was the revolutionary transformation of society through a theory that would directly inspire action, Durkheim's cause was the reintegration of society based on a definitive scientific understanding of its nature. Marx argued that the structure of the society of his day was transitory; Durkheim recognized no society that would be a fundamental advance beyond his own although he held that its institutions required completion and rectification. Thus, the one was a revolutionary; the other, a reformer. And whereas Marx wished to organize the proletariat to carry out his program of political action, Durkheim organized scholars to establish the authority of the social sciences as the grounds on which reforms could eventually be based. Marx was impatient with never-ending philosophical interpretations of the world; Durkheim had a deep-seated contempt for sterile polemics and insisted on the urgency of concerted study.[15] "We believe," he wrote,

that the time has come for sociology to spurn popular success, so to speak, and to assume the exacting character befitting every science. It will then gain in dignity and authority what it will perhaps lose in popularity. For, so long as it remains involved in partisan struggles, is content to expound common ideas with more logic than the layman, and consequently, presumes no special competence, it has no right to speak loudly enough to silence passions and prejudices. Assuredly, the time when it will be able to play this role successfully is still far off. However, we must begin to work now, in order to put it in condition to fill this role some day [1895, p. 146].

Marx's theory helped to shape sociology even as it was changing the world; Durkheim's influence on sociology is unparalleled.

Durkheim, like Marx, was born into a family with a heritage of rabbinical service. His hometown was Epinal in the old region of Lorraine, about a hundred miles up the Moselle River from Marx's home of Trier. Both towns were situated in that region between the heartlands of France and Germany that has for centuries been disputed and influenced by both countries. During Durkheim's youth the balance of political leadership in Europe was passing over from a demoralized France to a Germany undergoing rapid industrialization and long-awaited political unity. When Durkheim was twelve, his town was briefly occupied by German troops, the victors in the Franco-Prussian War. Whereas Marx, in the 1840s, looked to the West as a source of progress, Durkheim, a generation later, looked to Germany for sociological inspiration. Despite this regard for German scholarship, he was very much a French patriot.

Durkheim decided early on a scholarly career in preference to becoming a rabbi. He assiduously prepared himself for the leading French academic training center, the *Ecole Normale Supérieure*, displaying both hard work and a keen mind but having difficulty with what he regarded as the questionably useful studies of the classics and traditional rhetoric (though he ultimately became a master of sociological rhetoric). At the *Ecole Normale* he earned a reputation as an exceedingly serious student with a distaste for dilletantism and for the literary and nonempirical mode of thought predominant among his peers and teachers. He graduated in 1882 and began his academic career teaching in preparatory schools. From 1885 to 1886 he took a leave to study German social science, finding there a conceptual model of society as a collective entity and a methodological model of disciplined empirical inquiry. These modes of thought impressed him as superior to the individualistic and speculative biases that he had encountered in his studies in France. Having made an intellectual impression with his published reports on German social science, Durkheim was appointed to the faculty at the University of Bordeaux in 1887, where he remained until his appointment to the Sorbonne at Paris in 1902.

His years at Bordeaux were filled with unremitting and productive effort: a heavy teaching load, with new courses every year in sociology and the theory of education; the completion of the required Latin and French doctoral dissertations in 1893 (the first on Montesquieu, the second on *The Division of Labor in Society*); the writing of two other sociological classics, *The Rules of Sociological Method* [1895] and *Suicide* [1897], and scores of articles and reviews; and the organization and editing of the journal *L'Année Sociologique*.

Durkheim was now in the position to put into motion his campaign for the institutionalization of scientific sociology in France. He initiated the university teaching of self-proclaimed sociology and held the first professorship of social science in France. He energetically propounded and defended his ideas, and his conception of society and social science earned him a circle of hard-working disciples, as well as a number of outraged critics. His efforts were rewarded at last by the Sorbonne appointment at Paris in 1902; he achieved the pinnacle of French academic life in 1906 with an advancement to full professor. His scholarly and organizational efforts continued unabated. By the end of his life he had profoundly shaped not only the field of sociology, but also the French educational system in the direction of a secular and sociologically informed curriculum. World War I mobilized Durkheim's patriotism and inspired him to write two tracts defending France's cause. Tragically, his only son, André, a disciple as well, was killed in action in 1915; Durkheim, his energy sapped, died two years later.

He left behind four great sociological classics (the three mentioned above, plus *The Elementary Forms of the Religious Life* [1912]), innumerable articles (especially his contributions to *L'Année Sociologique*), and manuscripts and lecture notes (many published posthumously by his associates and disciples). His lifelong struggle to render sociology academically respectable and systematically cumulative must be judged on its own terms a great success. His lasting influence is felt in the substance of his concepts of society and of the social nature of man and in his scientific methodology. I shall first discuss these fundamental contributions and shall then conclude the chapter by considering Durkheim's sociological ethics.

Society and the Individual and Social Reform

The Priority of Society

For Durkheim to establish sociology, it was necessary to demonstrate first that society is a reality and consequently that any explanation of social phenomena that proceeds from individuals considered as autonomous units must be fallacious. Durkheim agreed with both Rousseau and Burke that society is prior to man-as-we-know-him. He asserted this point in several ways. First, in *the life of the individual*, what is recognized as distinctively human exists only as a capacity in the infant; this capacity is realized only through social experience and education. "Considering the facts as they are and as they have always been, it becomes immediately evident that all education is a continuous effort to impose on the child ways of seeing, feeling, and acting which he could not have arrived at spontaneously" [1895, pp. 5–6]. That the force of such impositions is not consciously recognized by the adult is evidence of their success in shaping his character. Far from presenting this idea as a critical exposé of a deleterious state of affairs, Durkheim held it to be a fact of all social existence. As a dedicated reformer of the French educational system, he intended to use that fact to shape a social character appropriate to a modern democratic society.

Second, Durkheim argued that *individuality*, as we understand it, has emerged *historically*. The primitive condition of social man is one of uniformity, and systematic differences among men are a result of social evolution. Durkheim introduced for this purpose a significant terminology. The societies of the past—he had in mind the tribal societies being documented by anthropologists and the ancient societies of Israel, Germany, Egypt, and Greece rather than the feudal society that provided Tocqueville and Marx with their images of the past—were characterized by what Durkheim called "mechanical solidarity." Those societies were integrated through the alikeness of their members. Each person was, in effect, a replica of every other, able to perform the same simple tasks and believing in the same fundamental ideas. Under such conditions the "collective conscience," which Durkheim defined as "the totality of beliefs and sentiments common to average citizens of the same society," is robust, and individuality is underdeveloped. Modern societies, by contrast, are characterized by "organic solidarity," in which members specialize and develop individual uniquenesses. Society is integrated through the interdependence among men.

Durkheim was aware that this terminology and the imagery it evoked flew in the face of a romantic notion that modern society is artificial or "mechanical" whereas traditional societies were natural, authentic, and "organic." Much of the appeal of the denunciations by Rousseau and Marx of the division of labor no doubt rested upon such romantic ideas, even though neither argued that man could or should return to such an idealized past. Rousseau and Marx recognized the contributions of the division of labor to historical progress but wanted to transcend them. Durkheim took the developed division of labor as essential to "the progress of individual personality."

It is, accordingly, a real illusion which makes us believe that personality was so much more complete when the division of labor had penetrated less. No doubt, in looking from without at the diversity of occupations which the individual then embraces, it may seem that he is developing in a very free and complete manner. But, in reality, this activity which he manifests is not really his. It is society, it is the race acting in and through him; he is only the intermediary through which they realize themselves.

Thus, the progress of individual personality and that of the division of labor depend upon one and the same cause. It is thus impossible to desire one without desiring the other [1893, pp. 404–405].

Although Durkheim came to see that modern society also required a minimal solidarity of alikeness—an attenuated collective conscience— he nonetheless always maintained that individuality is a product of history. It is not, contrary to Hobbes, the natural condition of man.

Third, the *analytical understanding* of the individual must therefore begin with society. Much of Durkheim's scientific output is in effect a sociologist's inroad upon the presumably ineluctable preserve of individual self-determination. He shows that the propensity to suicide is a *social* fact, not explainable by reference to individual motives; that the sacred preserve of religion is an imposition of society upon the individual consciousness; and that even the very categories of our thinking processes are derived from society. In opposition to Immanuel Kant's theory of knowledge, that perception is possible only on the basis of certain innate or a priori categories in the mind, Durkheim held that fundamental concepts come from social experience. Only by living in society, in a group, could we come to conceive, for example, of the idea of a "totality." The "idea of *all*," Durkheim writes,

could not have come from the individual himself, who is only a part in relation to the whole and who never attains more than an infinitesimal fraction of reality. . . . The theorists of knowledge ordinarily postulate it as if it came of itself, while it really surpasses the contents of each individual consciousness taken alone to an infinite degree [1912, p. 489].

Durkheim's language is uncompromisingly assertive, and his message strikes many as uncongenial to liberal individualism. He was well aware of his rhetorical impact, but he complained when he was misunderstood. He did not reject utterly the individualistic *values* of Western society, but he insisted that the *analytical* individualism that would explain social phenomena on the premise of autonomous individuals and that would deny the reality of society was simply an inadequate basis for understanding and, therefore, for social reconstruction. Durkheim's commitments to sociology and to social reform went hand in hand.

74

Durkheim's reformism was distinctly cautious, even conservative. Like Burke, he held that the burden of proof rested with those who would change the social order. Yet, also like Burke, his image of human nature argued for social institutions to meet human needs, needs that were unfulfilled in his society. Social realist though he was, Durkheim made certain psychological assumptions that formed a premise of his reformist drive. He was reluctant to express these assumptions as first principles in the manner of Hobbes, but they nonetheless inform his theory.

The Social Nature of Man

We can approach Durkheim's psychological assumptions by looking at his theory of suicide. In modern society, he said, two forms of suicide are increasingly prevalent: egoistic suicide and anomic suicide.[16] Egoism is a state of insufficient solidarity in which the individual is too much thrown on his own devices, has too few socially structured sources of support, and lacks a sense of responsibility to others outside himself. Protestants—as opposed to Catholics—and those in small families are especially prone to egoistic suicide, because they are too little involved in society. Although social life, especially if centered around a large family and a day-to-day involvement in a religious community, involves definite burdens for the individual, these are more than offset by the benefits derived:

There is, in short, in a cohesive and animated society a constant interchange of ideas and feelings from all to each and each to all, something like a mutual moral support, which instead of throwing the individual on his own resources, leads him to share in the collective energy and supports his own when exhausted [1897, p. 210].

The same theme of the psychic support provided by social bonds is present when Durkheim, in his last major work, writes of the contribution of collective religious ritual: "The only source of life at which we can morally reanimate ourselves is that formed by the society of our fellow beings" [1912, p. 473]. One aspect of Durkheim's social reform was thus the strengthening of social bonds to increase psychological well-being.

The second type of suicide, anomic, was chronic in the rapidly changing societies of Durkheim's day. It is the suicide of those who are suddenly thrown into circumstances that unduly excite their imaginations but provide an insufficient regulation of their passions. Durkheim's central examples of anomie were divorce and the upheavals of business life. It is not the *disappointment* of marital and economic crises so much as their *disruption of expectations* that occasions suicide. Durkheim liked to say that not only sudden economic busts but also booms are "suicido-genetic." "Every disturbance of equilibrium, even though it achieves greater comfort and a heightening of general vitality, is an impulse to voluntary death" [1897, p. 246]. His own society, still in transition between the stable states of mechanical and organic solidarity, was replete with such disruptions. These are states of "anomie" or normlessness, which is an anguished state for man to be in.

In a remarkable passage in *Suicide* [1897, pp. 246–254], Durkheim argues that, unlike animals, men have no inherent point of satiation because they have imaginations that can be stimulated by their environment. Without external regulation "our capacity for feeling is in itself an insatiable and bottomless abyss." "Inextinguishable thirst is constantly renewed torture." To achieve happiness, passions must be limited. "But since the individual has no way of limiting them, this must be done by some force exterior to him . . . . The force can only be moral." Under ordinary circumstances society provides moral norms, norms that are regarded by the majority as legitimate, to restrain and discipline the individual. "But when society is disturbed by some painful crisis or by beneficent but abrupt transitions, it is momentarily incapable of exercising this influence," and that is the painful condition Durkheim called "anomie." Durkheim thus presumes that men desire order, law, and equilibrium to maintain their well-being, a presumption common to such members of the conservative tradition as Burke and Tocqueville. Thus another aspect of Durkheim's social reform was to be the strengthening of norms.

Occupational Groups

To reintegrate man into society, to counteract the egoist and anomic currents of modern social life, Durkheim proposed a concentration on occupational groups or "corporations." He insisted that social reform must work with the materials at hand and that earlier forms of social integration based on locality, family, and religion were waning in significance in modern life. The wholesale breaking down of earlier forms of social organization, which was promoted by Voltaire and Rousseau and accomplished (Durkheim thought) by the great transformation that occurred from the eighteenth to the nineteenth centuries, seemed to leave only political and economic groupings with enough vitality to serve as organs of social integration. The state as a political organ, however, is too remote from the individual for its ministrations to be adequate to his needs.

A society composed of an infinite number of unorganized individuals, that a hypertrophied state is forced to oppress and to contain, constitutes a veritable sociological monstrosity. For collective activity is always too complex to be able to be expressed through the single and unique organ of the State [1902, p. 28].[17]

Durkheim, like Tocqueville, worried over the evidence of atomization in his society, though his concern was more for individual welfare than for constitutional stability. Durkheim, too, urged the strengthening of secondary or intermediate institutions. Accordingly, at the end of his book on *Suicide* [1897] and in a preface to the second edition of his *Division of Labor* [1902], he prescribed the occupational group as a remedy. "The only decentralization which would make possible the multiplication of the centers of communal life without weakening national unity is what might be called *occupational decentralization*" [1897, p. 390]. Occupational groups would be "formed by all the agents of the same industry, united and organized into a single body" [1902, p. 5]. In recognition of the metropolitan scale of the modern economy and of the provincialism that had doomed the medieval guilds to oblivion, these groups could only be national in scope. "Society, instead of remaining what it is today, an aggregate of juxtaposed territorial districts, would become a vast system of national corporations" [1902, p. 27].

Durkheim never provided a detailed plan for such groups, but he had in mind that those earning their livelihood in a single industry would be part of the "corporation." He recognized that differences in interest between labor and management would require that at the lowest levels employers and employees should be separately organized. But the corporations themselves were intended to represent all levels of workers in an industry. They were not, therefore, to be the same as American industrial or craft unions. The function of the corporation would be to mediate, not just articulate and advocate, conflicts of interest. Most of Durkheim's discussion of corporations was devoted to demonstrating that other forms of decentralization would be inadequate to the task (a form of argument by elimination, a favorite device of Durkheim's) and to analyzing the functions that such corporations would perform rather than to analyzing their proposed structure. He held that they would reduce egoism by providing the individual with social bonds at the site of his most consequential activity, his job. Corporations would oversee retirement benefits, industrial legislation, and labor-management mediation (thus guaranteeing their utilitarian viability), but they would also be a locus for social involvement per se. Durkheim foresaw corporations sponsoring cultural and social events. The corporation is for Durkheim "a source of life *sui generis*. From it comes a warmth which animates its members, making them intensely human, destroying their egotisms" [1902, p. 26].

On the other hand, corporations would serve to reduce anomie by establishing just rules and giving them moral authority. These rules would meet the needs of the individual and yet remind him of his place:

By forcing the strongest to use their strength with moderation, by preventing the weakest from endlessly multiplying their protests, by recalling both to the sense of their reciprocal duties and the general interest, and by regulating production in certain cases so that it does not degenerate into a morbid fever, it would moderate one set of passions by another, and permit their appeasement by assigning them limits. Thus, a new sort of moral discipline would be established, without which all the scientific discoveries and economic progress in the world could produce only malcontents [1897, p. 383].

The social order to be reinvigorated by the establishment of occupational groups would simultaneously serve to mitigate *egoism* and *anomie* by means of social *bonds* and limiting *rules*.

This illustrates how Durkheim's twin commitments as sociological advocate and social reformer are intimately related through his image of man. Disequilibrium in modern society is injurious to individual well-being. To promote equilibrium, certifiable knowledge about the workings of society is required. Then, by an only apparent paradox, individualistic forms of explanation must cede to sociological ones. So, without contradiction, Durkheim in his role as a social reformer devoted to promoting individual psychic well-being could doggedly fix his eye on the establishment and progress of the new science of sociology. If his presentation of the methods and tenets of this science frequently invoked a troublesome series of expressions and images that seem to endow "society" with a mystical reality, such rhetorical devices should be understood in the context of Durkheim's solemn devotion to his causes.

Sociology as a Science

In his student days and early academic career Durkheim expressed himself as an embattled pioneer of an emerging discipline. From the very beginning he rejected philosophical speculation and methodological individualism as modes of thought. He insisted that a discipline with any value to serve the needs of modern society must be scientific and must treat society as a realm in its own right.

For Durkheim, science was a mode of inquiry founded on reason and empirical knowledge. His method has often been called that of "positivism," and he argued that sociology deserved a place among the positive sciences. In the dictionary sense of "positivism" as a viewpoint holding that firm knowledge can be based only on the study of natural phenomena through empirical methods and not on metaphysics or religion, this is a true, if partial, characterization of Durkheim's method. By maintaining that the methods appropriate to natural science are also appropriate to social science, Durkheim placed himself at odds with the dominant tendency in Marx, for whom theory should shape as well as reflect the world. In our terms, Durkheim was a positive, rather than critical, thinker. He believed that empirical and naturalistic study was required for a science of society, and he criticized those who took no account of factual evidence or who arranged "evidence" according to a preconceived philosophical theory. He accused the English sociologist Herbert Spencer of this fault among others.

Yet Durkheim's own method was as much dominated by a process of thought as by empirical investigation. He was an uncompromising rationalist who, in the tradition of Descartes, believed that knowledge could be deduced through logic from axiomatic principles. His writings, accordingly, are replete with syllogisms, arguments by elimination, and analogies that purport to scientific status, often to the dismay of the reader. A few examples will suffice. He argues that all natural phenomena are governed by necessary laws (scientific laws, not juridical ones) and that society, which is a part of nature, must therefore also be so governed. He argues that social phenomena, which are by definition external to the individual, cannot be explained by psychology: "If social life were merely an extension of the individual being, it would not thus ascend toward its source, namely, the individual, and impetuously invade it. . . . When the individual has been eliminated society alone remains" [1895, pp. 101–102]. Sociology is therefore necessary. He argues that the exteriority of social forces cannot be denied on the ground that such forces are often unperceived, just as air pressure cannot be denied simply because we do not feel it. Persuasive to some, such rhetorical devices are only irritating to others. They clearly indicate that Durkheim's science of society was by no means confined to a method of induction from observed facts.

Durkheim's science had an object as well as a method. Its object was society, studied through its manifestations in what Durkheim called "social facts." Durkheim's polemical stance led him to use immoderate expressions that long obstructed the reception of the valuable part of his message. He said that social facts are "things," that there is a "group mind," and that when anyone attempts to explain social phenomena psychologically, "we may be sure that the explanation is false." But Durkheim was quite correct in pointing to the facts that the moral obligations observed by individuals are social in origin and in persistence, that such institutions as governments exist independently of any individual, that the currents of emotion that sweep a crowd "can carry us away in spite of ourselves," and that a given society has specific characteristics that distinguish it from other societies.

Much effort has been expended in debates over the ontological (thing-like) status of "society" in Durkheim's theory, but to see the importance of his ideas, it is only necessary to observe, for example, that a church is not simply a sum of the beliefs of its member-individuals taken as units. Rather, the member-individuals orient their behavior toward what are conceived to be common practices and beliefs, whether or not such beliefs are to be found in any one person. In this sense, society is indeed greater than the sum of its parts.

Durkheim's most sustained demonstration of the utility of his concept of social facts is found in his treatise on *Suicide*. Using data available from official sources, he demonstrated that the rate of suicide per million of population varied remarkably among European societies of the late nineteenth century, that each society (Italy, England, Sweden, France, Prussia—"Germany" being still a federation—and Denmark) had a characteristically high or low rate of suicide, and that the suicide rate of a society changed over time in regular patterns rather than randomly. Durkheim took on the toughest problem imaginable—what is ultimately the most personal act—and showed how it could be understood as a social phenomenon. The rate of suicide is a fact, he said, "peculiar to each social group," and it could be explained by those other "social facts" that he grouped under the categories of egoism, anomie, and altruism.

In practice, Durkheim vacillated between the attempt to account for these *variations in rates* and the claim that his theory was sufficient for the explanation of *any given suicide*. However, given that only a tiny proportion of those identifiable by his method as especially prone to suicide—Protestants, the unmarried, military officers, businessmen— do take their own lives, this latter claim is obviously unsupportable. Durkheim, nonetheless, succeeded in demonstrating the power of a distinctively sociological mode of analysis, which seeks to transcend (or at least to supplement) explanations based upon individual motives and personal pathologies. At a minimum, his method requires that the investigator adopt a special attitude toward the perhaps intangible but nonetheless real level of experience that we call the social. Society, he endlessly repeated, is a reality *sui generis* ("of its own kind") and must be approached scientifically as such. (For a fuller analysis of Durkheim's *Suicide*, see the accompanying essay.)

The basic methodological principle for which Durkheim argued is that sociology is a *science* that deals with a special level of reality called *social facts*. He did, however, outline more specific sociological procedures, both in his book on *The Rules of Sociological Method* and in his works of empirical research. Rather than summarizing *The Rules* (which Durkheim himself did not always follow), I shall examine several of the steps that he took in his attempt to arrive at sociological knowledge, and I shall draw upon his studies of the division of labor, suicide, and religion. Three distinctively Durkheimian methodological strategies will be attended to: his concern for definitions, his attempt to refute alternative explanations, and his effort to produce sociological explanations, both causal and functional.

Definitions

As prophet of a new science, Durkheim insisted on the independence of sociology from psychology and other sciences and also from common sense. This required a break with accepted modes of thought: "[If] there is to be social science, we shall expect it not merely to paraphrase the traditional prejudices of the common man but to give us a new and different view of them; for the aim of all science is to make discoveries, and every discovery more or less disturbs accepted ideas" [1895, p. xxxvii]. Like Bacon and Descartes, Durkheim urged that scientific study begin with a purge of received opinion.

Durkheim thus approaches very self-consciously the problem of defining a given phenomenon. To define religion, for example, he rejects the notion that religion is bound up with a sense of the "supernatural," because the category of the supernatural presupposes the category of the natural, which is a historical development of thought that postdates primitive religion. He rejects as well the notion that religion is a matter of worshipping "gods," because there are such nondeistic religions as Buddhism. Durkheim then focuses on what he holds to be the essential traits of religion: its division of the world into things "sacred" and "profane" and its collective, social embodiment. At the end of a chapter he gives his own formal definition: "A religion is a unified system of beliefs and practices relative to sacred things, that is to say, things set apart and forbidden—beliefs and practices which unite into one single moral community called a church, all those who adhere to them" [1912, p. 62].

In parallel fashion, Durkheim held that "crime" is not to be defined by reference to the content of certain acts which can be presumed to be in themselves inherently criminal. Rather, he says that, in effect, crime is what society says it is: "In other words, we must not say that an action shocks the common conscience because it is criminal, but rather that it is criminal because it shocks the common conscience" [1893, p. 81]. Using such definitions and working within the realms of experience circumscribed by them, Durkheim goes on to consider explanations of the phenomena of religion and crime.

These efforts of Durkheim's contain great insight and have influenced later sociological and anthropological work. Only by transcending such common-sense definitions, as Durkheim does, is it possible, for example, to entertain the potentially fruitful idea that extremist political movements partake of the qualities of religions and can be compared to them. Durkheim's definition of crime expressed the truth that moral standards are social variables, and it thus contained the germ of the cultural relativism that was later developed in such works as Ruth Benedict's *Patterns of Culture*. His definition of crime also pointed the way for a new understanding of the problems of deviance and social control, for an approach that questions not so much why certain people commit deviant acts, but rather how some acts come to be perceived or "labelled" as deviant. With respect to sumptuary legislation, for example, the latter question often appears to have greater practical and theoretical significance.

Yet at another level Durkheim's definitions profoundly affirm common sense. He assumes that the layman is correct in taking for granted that Buddhism is a religion and that it is therefore fundamentally the same phenomenon as Christianity. He assumes that the category of "the criminal," if not its common-sense definition and explanation, isolates a phenomenon (one might almost say a "thing") that is worthy of sociological treatment. Thus Durkheim affirms that the lay categories of religion and crime are legitimate topics for sociological analysis, and he also affirms the common-sense notion that each of these topics partakes of a sufficient number of internal common properties to be treated as an entity. There can be sociologies of religion and crime. Epistemologically as well as politically, Durkheim is a reformer rather than a revolutionary.

Refutation of Alternative Explanations

Durkheim's considerable polemic vigor was most thoroughly invested in his attempts to dismiss current, and in his view wrong-headed, explanations of the subjects that he selected for study, whether the division of labor, suicide, or religion. These refutations regularly asserted the inadequacy of explanations based on nonsociological reasoning, especially of those based on individualistic psychology, biology, or the natural environment. Durkheim spent whole chapters explaining that religion could not be understood as merely an intellectual reflection of natural phenomena and that the division of labor cannot be the result of innate human propensities to exchange goods.

In *Suicide*, an entire section of nearly one hundred pages is devoted to the task of refutation. Although some of the theories that Durkheim dismissed seem exotic and even silly today—for example, that variations in suicide are caused by seasonal or daily variations in sunlight—his methods were serious and astute. To counter the hoary argument that suicide, as well as other sorts of social behavior, resulted from hereditary "racial" predispositions, Durkheim used a kind of statistical logic that has become fundamental to contemporary empirical sociology. He began with a correlation between nationality and suicide rate to the effect that Germans were more prone to suicide than Frenchmen. On the basis of such a correlation, some made the argument that suicide varied by "race" with "Germanics" being more self-destructive than "Celto-Romans." On the contrary, Durkheim argued, the national differences are the result of religious differences, Germany being much more heavily Protestant than France. He then tested his assertion in the multi-ethnic confederation of Switzerland, where Germans and Frenchmen of both the Protestant and Catholic religion reside in relatively homogeneous cantons (territorial units of Switzerland). Looking simultaneously at religion and at "nationality" as variables, Durkheim showed that the presumed German tendency toward suicide is in fact a Protestant tendency: the Catholic cantons, whether German or French, have a comparatively low rate of suicide; the French Protestant cantons have a suicide rate five times as high. "Facts thus concur," he wrote, "in showing that Germans commit suicide more than other people not because of their blood but because of the civilization within which they were reared" [1897, p. 89].

These and some of Durkheim's other methods are not above reproach. Official statistics on suicide rates, on which Durkheim relied, are notoriously subject to error and bias. His use of ecological correlations is problematic, and his refutations bypass the possibility of multiple causation.[18] Attempting to prove a thesis by refuting alternatives is in principle close to impossible: *all* alternatives would have to be shown incorrect in order to establish Durkheim's thesis as the only one valid. In effect, Durkheim's refutations are an aspect of his rhetorical strategy of establishing sociology by reducing its rivals. Of course, he did not stop with negative arguments. The real power of his work is to be found in the substance of his own sociological explanations.

Durkheim's Sociological Explanations

We have already encountered some of Durkheim's attempts to make sense of social phenomena, and we have seen the basic sociological and social-psychological domain assumptions on which they were based. Here, somewhat more formally, I shall explicate two kinds of explanations that he offered, the causal and the functional. Suicide, for example, is *caused* by social malintegration. Occupational groups would *function* to promote reintegration. Durkheim was well aware of the two different kinds of thinking represented by these two terms, but he upheld the legitimacy of each. "When, then, the explanation of a social phenomenon is undertaken, we must seek separately the efficient cause which produces it and the function it fulfills" [1895, p. 95]. He proceeded to offer what has become a very famous example:

. . . the social reaction that we call punishment is due to the intensity of the collective sentiments which the crime offends; but, from another angle, it has the useful function of maintaining these sentiments at the same degree of intensity, for they would soon diminish if offenses against them were not punished [1895, p. 96].

Both kinds of explanation—those that focus on how social facts come to be and those that look at their contributions to society—are worthwhile.

Each type of explanation is represented in Durkheim's study of *The Division of Labor in Society*. Given the observation that in the advanced societies of his day, and of our own, there is greater variation among individuals' occupational roles than is to be found in simpler societies, Durkheim wanted to explain how this change to "organic" from "mechanical" solidarity had come about. His *causal* explanation centered on demographic factors, that is, on the size and distribution of population. He was aware that as a population increases in size, a greater specialization of tasks becomes possible. (For example, the greatest variety of types of restaurants is found in large cities because there also is found a sufficiently large population to support the unusual tastes of small population proportions.) But the specific factor Durkheim stressed was the "dynamic density" of the population, by which he meant the rate of social interaction. Dynamic density is increased as the concentration of the population and the means of communication increase; more people come into more contact. But if everyone pursues essentially the same occupation (that is, if the society is still characterized by mechanical solidarity), an increase in dynamic density produces an increase in competition. This competition produces specialization.

Durkheim called upon Darwin for an understanding of the logic of such competition. Just as different species of organisms can coexist in the same territory because their physical needs are complementary instead of conflicting, so the division of labor in society moderates competition:

> In the same city, different occupations can co-exist without being obliged mutually to destroy one another, for they pursue different objects. The soldier seeks military glory, the priest moral authority, the statesman power, the business man riches, the scholar scientific renown. Each of them can attain his end without preventing the others from attaining theirs [1893, p. 267].

Thus Durkheim claimed to have uncovered a general causal law of social development: "The division of labor varies in direct ratio with the volume and density of societies, and, if it progresses in a continuous manner in the course of social development, it is because societies become regularly denser and generally more voluminous" [1893, p. 262]. Incorporated in an altered terminology—that structural differentiation is the result of technological advances and population density—Durkheim's law still has currency in sociology. Those whose scientific goal is the derivation of a set of laws about properties of societies taken as units can claim Durkheim as their intellectual ancestor.

Durkheim, however, was not satisfied with causal explanations of the genesis of social phenomena; he also wanted to understand the functioning of these phenomena. Taking seriously the idea of society as a reality *sui generis*, he believed that societies have a kind of internal economy in which most social facts have a role to play:

> Indeed, if the usefulness of a fact is not the cause of its existence, it is generally necessary that it be useful in order that it may maintain itself. For the fact that it is not useful suffices to make it harmful, since in that case it costs effort without bringing in any returns. If, then, the majority of social phenomena had this parasitic character, the budget of the organism would have a deficit and social life would be impossible. Consequently, to have a satisfactory understanding of the latter, it is necessary to show how the phenomena comprising

it combine in such a way as to put society in harmony with itself and with the environment external to it [1895, p. 97].

Durkheim insisted that this presupposition that social phenomena be analyzed in terms of their usefulness was distinctively sociological. It was not to be confused with a concentration on what might be the purposes of individuals in society. Individuals may not be aware of or concerned about the social effects (or functions) of their practices; these effects are often unanticipated. Instead, "the function of a social fact ought always to be sought in its relation to some social end" [1895, p. 111].

The *Division of Labor* provides additional examples of functional explanations. Durkheim held that the proportion of two different types of law changes as societies move from mechanical to organic solidarity. Societies with *mechanical solidarity*—with the solidarity of alikeness—have higher proportions of penal laws, which specify rules of correct behavior and are backed up by "repressive sanctions." Such sanctions threaten the wrongdoer with loss: "They make demands on his fortune, or on his honor, or on his life, or on his liberty, and deprive him of something he enjoys" [1893, p. 69]. As the division of labor increases, however, and as society becomes integrated by *organic solidarity*, other types of law become prevalent—civil, commercial, procedural, and administrative—for which the enforcement mechanisms are "restitutive sanctions." Restitutive sanctions do not so much inflict a loss upon the law-breaking agent as function to return things to the way they were. An example of a restitutive sanction is the awarding of damages in a civil suit. Looking over a large range of historical and anthropological findings, Durkheim claims to have confirmed this macroscopic correlation between the type of solidarity and the type of law.

To make sense of this correlation, he invokes the imagery of society as a functioning entity. We can expect, Durkheim might have said, that society will be so organized as to reproduce the conditions of its existence. Where mechanical solidarity prevails, the cohesion of society depends upon the strength of the common conscience. The social function of penal law and repressive sanctions—in short, of punishment—is not so much to rehabilitate the criminal or to deter the repetition of his act as to reenforce in each member of society a sense of union with the collectivity. Penal law strengthens the common conscience, "both in demanding from each of us a minimum of resemblances without which the individual would be a menace to the unity of the social body, and in imposing upon us the respect for the symbol which expresses and summarizes these resemblances at the same time that it guarantees them" [1893, p. 106]. Durkheim thus explains not only the cause of punishment—the outrage occasioned by criminal behavior—but also its effects or social functions.

With the advent of the division of labor, the problem for society is no longer to maximize the similarity among member individuals but rather to integrate complementary forms of behavior. Individuals now pursue very different lines of work, although Durkheim insisted that his analysis was not confined to the narrowly economic area of goods-production. Individuals are not self-sufficient; they must engage in multiple exchanges with one another. Thus it is not enough for each of them to pursue some identical, fully charted course of action. Rather, there must be some mechanism to facilitate their interaction:

> For at each instant, and often at the most inopportune, we find ourselves contracting, either for something we have bought, or sold, somewhere we are traveling, our hiring of one's services, some acceptance of hostelry, etc. The greater part of our relations with others is of a contractual nature. If, then, it were necessary each time to begin the struggles anew, to again go through the conferences necessary to establish firmly all the conditions of agreement for the present and the future, we would be put to rout [1893, pp. 213–214].

Contract law with its merely restrictive sanctions functions as a mechanism for reducing the costs of constant negotiation; it thus promotes organic solidarity. Contract law "expresses the normal conditions of equilibrium. . . . A résumé of numerous, varied experiences, what we cannot foresee individually is there provided for, what we cannot regulate is there regulated, and this regulation imposes itself upon us, although it may not be our handiwork, but that of society and tradition" [1893, p. 214]. The society with an advanced division of labor, therefore, is not an ever fluctuating jumble of juxtaposed atoms. Its organic solidarity is guaranteed by newly developed types of law. Once again, Durkheim has approached the understanding of social institutions with the inclination to illuminate their positive contributions to social order. In this respect, he is the fount of the school of functionalism in modern sociology.

Sociology and Ethics

More than any other man, Durkheim deserves to be called the founder of scientific sociology. The naturalistic attitude that he adopted toward social phenomena, his astute use of statistical data, his treatment of societies as units, and his functionalist orientation have been incorporated in a cumulative effort by many present-day sociologists. Yet the basic substantive ingredients of his sociological perspective are familiar to us from earlier thinkers. He believed, with Rousseau and Burke, in the priority of society to man-as-we-know-him and in the comprehensiveness of social life; with Burke, in the reality of society and in the inadequacy of radical politics; with Burke and Tocqueville, in man's psychic need for limits. In common with all of the thinkers whom we have encountered, he was powerfully motivated by ethical concerns. It may seem paradoxical to reassert the centrality of social ethics to Durkheim's life and work. He was, after all, a prophet of science, who insisted on the necessary autonomy of sociology from common-sense assumptions and political pressures, and he argued, along with Max Weber, that facts must be distinguished from the scientist's values lest wishful thinking distort knowledge. He is therefore sco.ned by some politically activist sociologists as a precursor of the aseptic and apolitical stance of contemporary sociology. Nonetheless, Durkheim did attempt to combine his scientific and ethical commitments, and in a way that sheds an important light on his theory. The third chapter of *The Rules of Sociological Method* was devoted to his answer.

Durkheim's Proposal

Durkheim was aware of a viewpoint (represented, as we shall see, by Max Weber) according to which science, dealing with facts, can tell us nothing about what we ought to do. Ethical values can be *studied* scientifically as phenomena, according to this view, but cannot be *derived from* science: science "can indeed illuminate the world, but it leaves darkness in our hearts" [1895, pp. 47–48]. The trouble with this attitude, Durkheim said, is that it leaves science without practical utility and hence without justification. Those who would bridge this gap by subordinating science to some ideological imperative (Durkheim may have had Marx in mind) are untrue both to science and to the nature of society. Durkheim wanted to be true to both. Here is his starting point:

Briefly, for societies as for individuals, health is good and desirable; disease, on the contrary, is bad and to be avoided. If, then, we can find an objective criterion, inherent in the facts themselves, which enables us to distinguish scientifically between health and morbidity in the various orders of social phenomena, science will be in a position to throw light on practical problems and still remain faithful to its own method [1895, p. 49].

Just as a physician can be an applied scientist who prescribes courses of action to restore health, so also might the sociologist *as sociologist* pronounce upon the desirability of social facts.

Durkheim then considers what might be an "objective criterion" for the determination of social morbidity. After refuting several alternative criteria, he outlines his own criterion: what is normal or healthy is what is *essential* to a given type of society; what is unhealthy or abnormal is what is escapable. Within any given type of society or social species, an index to the essential is supplied by the *average*. Durkheim arrives at the following formula: "We shall call 'normal' these social conditions that are most generally distributed, and the others 'morbid' or 'pathological.' . . . Once we know how to distinguish the various social species from each other . . . it is always possible to find the most general form of a phenomenon in a given species" [1895, p. 56].

Two ingredients of Durkheim's theory that have already been discussed are contained in this formula. The first is functionalism, the disposition to believe that social conditions, particularly those recurrent and widespread, have a contributing role in the social order. In effect, societies as kinds of organisms select those conditions that are conducive to their well-being. Thus, the average conditions are likely to be healthy. The second ingredient is Durkheim's sociological relativism, the conviction that morality cannot be imposed by some absolute standard irrespective of time and place but is derived from society itself. Thus Durkheim defines normality, and thereby what is morally desirable, in relation to social species. (He did not go further than outlining the problem of defining social species—that is, of developing a taxonomy of societies—but it is clear that he would have used the basic criterion of evolutionary levels of social differentiation as developed in *The Division of Labor*.) Like Burke, he argued for a contextual approach to social reform; unlike Burke, he phrased his argument in the language of science and not in the language of politics.

Durkheim was thus able to make prescriptive pronouncements on social problems with the authority of science behind him. A certain level of crime, for example, is normal and healthy for a society. Crime is inevitable and essential; it is not pathological unless it rises beyond a certain unspecified level. In modern societies crime is a concomitant of their inherent increasing individuation. For all societies, the risk of crime is part of the price paid for the possibility of social change. More than that, however, crime and the punishment that it occasions function to reaffirm the common conscience and, thus, to promote solidarity. With these matters in mind, Durkheim argues that it would be an ethical error to attempt to eradicate crime.[19]

The problem of anomie in contemporary society—a condition that

Durkheim clearly wanted to remedy—mobilized his relativistic and evolutionary criterion of normality. Anomie was widespread in his day, as was evidenced by the increasing rates of suicide and by the prevalence of industrial strife. Yet its clearly widespread nature was not an index of its normality. Durkheim argued that anomie was a pathology of transition between fully developed states of mechanical and organic solidarity. It occurred in the process of evolution between two social species, and Durkheim showed that it was harmful, rather than functional, for individual and social well-being. Thus he was not embarrassed to call it abnormal and to prescribe for its eradication such means as occupational corporations.

The Social Physician and Harmony

One could take exception to several steps in Durkheim's argument; of these, his use of the analogy of the social physician is the most interesting. The medical physician can be, and is legally authorized to be, both a scientist and a moral authority in matters of health because we recognize not only the authority of medicine but also the overarching value of human life. Durkheim invokes this analogy in his drive to establish the ethical authority of social science. But the medical doctor must frequently sacrifice microorganisms (by prescribing antibiotics) and even bodily parts (through surgery) to restore his patient's health. By analogy, however, the social physician might have to sacrifice individuals—their values, dignity, even their lives—to establish social "normality." In such cases, ethical choices become more ambiguous, and the ethical autonomy of social science less compelling, than Durkheim admits. Even the authority of the medical doctor is circumscribed in those cases where fundamental human values come into conflict: abortion, euthanasia, transplantation, and hemodialysis are current and controversial examples. Durkheim's analogy of the social physician ignores such problems of value conflict, problems that are the more severe when we are considering the immensely complex topic of social ethics. But he ignores them not because of self-consciously illiberal values. Given his own values—his commitments to human dignity, to reason, and to free expression—it is unlikely that he would have consciously decided to subordinate conflicting human values to the overall value of social health. On the contrary, he believed that ethical choices were unambiguous in principle (if, indeed, arduous to work through) only because he believed in the immanent harmony of social life, because at the deepest level he did not believe in the necessity of tragic choices.

For Marx alienation was inherent in capitalist society, to be tran-

90

scended only with the abolition of that society, but for Durkheim anomie could be overcome by the reform of occupational groups within the framework of organic solidarity. Durkheim saw no ineradicable or tragic conflicts in society. Because he did not, because societies were potentially in harmony, science alone could answer ethical questions. As we shall see, it is on this point that Weber is radically at odds with Durkheim. Just as Tocqueville argued that we might have to choose between freedom and equality, so Weber saw choice between fundamental values as inherent in social life. Thus, Weber fiercely reserved for the individual the ethical autonomy that Durkheim sought to delegate to the sociologist. Durkheim could embark on that course only because conflict as an inevitability had no place in his theory.

CHAPTER 6

Max Weber:
Analyst of Rationalization

Max Weber (1864–1920) and Emile Durkheim are commonly regarded as the two most important forerunners of contemporary American sociology. Each was an apostle of scientific method and an advocate of the separation in principle of statements of fact from judgments of value. Each contributed to our understanding of religion and law, although Durkheim's special attention to deviant behavior contrasts with Weber's focus on political organization. To a degree, then, Weber and Durkheim agreed with and complemented each other. Yet the very project to which Durkheim devoted his life—the establishment of a scientific sociology with sufficient authority to "silence passions" and answer questions of ethics—was one that Weber resolutely opposed. " 'Scientific' pleading," Weber said, "is meaningless in principle because the various value spheres of the world stand in irreconcilable conflict with each other" [1919b, p. 147]. For each *individual*, not for a sociological physician speaking for the whole, "it is necessary to make a decisive choice" [1919b, p. 152].

Durkheim's presumption of immanent harmony was the implicit axiom that made his sociological ethics a possibility. By contrast, Weber was a theorist of tragedy, for whom no amount of scientific knowledge could relieve the individual of ethical responsibility. Although Weber did not explicitly express his attitude toward Durkheim's brand of sociology since neither author took account of the other's work, it is not difficult to surmise what this attitude would have been. For Weber, Durkheim's approach violated both the nature of science and the nature of ethics:

It is simply naive to believe, although there are many specialists who even now occasionally do, that it is possible to establish and to demonstrate as scientifically valid "a principle" for practical social science from which the norms for the solution of practical problems can be unambiguously derived [1904, p. 56].

Marx, who might have said that Durkheim's reformism was premature and wholly insensitive to the deep-seated contradictions of bourgeois society, could, nonetheless, advocate a fusion of scholarly and activist roles. Weber struggled to keep those roles distinct. Despite his political passion, he insisted on the separation and the autonomy of the scholarly and political callings.[20]

Weber was born in 1864 to a prosperous Protestant family. His father's successful political career brought the family to Berlin in 1869, where Weber senior served in the Prussian parliament and, after the unification of Germany in 1871, in the Reichstag (comparable to the U.S. House of Representatives). In the years of Weber's youth, Berlin was a rapidly growing city, increasingly enjoying cultural and political dominance, first in Germany and then in continental Europe, under the astute guidance of the Iron Chancellor, Otto von Bismarck. Weber's father was one of a number of erstwhile liberals who made peace with the nationalistic, alternately repressive and co-optive policies of Bismarck. The household was saturated with Weber senior's accommodationist, self-satisfied, and "realistic" attitudes. The pious social conscience and respect for Christian duty of Weber's mother combined with the heady and powerful circle of his father's acquaintances to produce in young Max a lifelong orientation to work and worldly influence. However, Frau Weber otherwise submitted to her husband's domination, a fact that was to assume great importance in Max Weber's life.

In 1882, Weber began university studies at Heidelberg, and during the following year he did a term of military service. These years brought him for the first time out of his father's house. He came under the influence of his mother's sister and brother-in-law, Ida and Hermann

Baumgarten, in the Rhineland city of Strassburg, then part of Germany. The Baumgartens refused to make the compromises that Weber's parents had. Between them they forcefully represented the older liberal ideas that Weber's father had abandoned and the Christian humanitarian ideals that his mother quietly espoused. The Strassburg sojourn heightened Weber's awareness of the value conflicts within his own family and his respect for a political stance less intimidated by Bismarck's *Realpolitik* than that of his father.

In 1884, however, his parents urged him to resume his studies at the University of Berlin, and for most of the next nine years (during Weber's twenties) he lived again in his father's house. Although he was uncomfortable with this dependent position, he worked prodigiously. He studied law, history, and economics, earning a Ph.D. by 1889; he wrote monographs on medieval trading companies, on Roman agrarian history, on eastern German agricultural workers, and on the stock market. He also practiced law and participated in the Christian Socialist reform movement. Only when Weber was nearly thirty was he able to earn his own living. He then married Marianne Schnitger and accepted the first of several university positions that German academe was quick to offer him. By 1897 Weber was established in Heidelberg as a full professor and as successor to Karl Knies, one of his former teachers. It was a meteoric rise by the standards of the day in the stodgy German academic system. Weber feared only that his new position would require him to abandon the reformist scholarly work that he had done while in Berlin.

Then, disaster struck in the form of a paralyzing psychic illness that brought Weber's research to a halt for nearly five years and that precluded formal teaching for almost two decades. Our understanding of Weber's illness and its relation to his ideas has been furthered by a recent work of Arthur Mitzman, *The Iron Cage* [1970]. Weber's breakdown was precipitated by his intervention in a quarrel between his parents on the occasion of their visit with him in Heidelberg. Years of suppressed resentment burst forth as Weber ordered his father from his house. While his mother stayed on with him and Marianne, the father returned to Berlin and died a few weeks later (August 1897). Within a few months, Weber's own mental illness became apparent: at first, irritability and diffuse pains; then, insomnia and inability to concentrate; and, finally, nearly total psychic collapse. He was excused from his teaching duties. In search of recovery he spent periods in sanatoria and in restless travels to Italy, Switzerland, Holland, and Belgium. Slowly, with relapses, he began working again in 1902. He became an editor and the guiding spirit of the major journal *Archiv fuer Sozialwissenschaft* in 1903 and was back to great productivity by 1904. Only at the end of World War I, however, was he able to return to teaching.

From 1904 until his death in 1920 from pneumonia, Weber produced those masterpieces of sociological analysis on which his modern fame rests. His psychic ordeal had deepened his self-awareness and his sensitivity to value conflict. The two major works that followed his recovery bore the marks of this self-scrutiny. The first, " 'Objectivity' in Social Science and Social Policy" [1904], was a methodological treatise insisting on the nonscientific status of judgments of ethical value and on the necessity of *isolating* phenomena for social scientific analysis rather than attempting to treat them in their fullness. The second was the famous study of the contribution of ascetic Protestantism to the work ethic of Western societies, *The Protestant Ethic and the Spirit of Capitalism* [1905].

Weber went on to defend himself against charges of ethical obtuseness, which stemmed from misinterpretations of his defense of scientific objectivity, and against claims that his studies of religion unduly neglected the influence of "material" factors. He planned a series of essays on the general relationship of religion and society in the major world culture areas and a comprehensive treatise on economy, politics, and society. Neither of these massive projects was completed, but by the time of his death Weber had written *The Religion of China* (1915), *The Religion of India* (1917), *Ancient Judaism* (1919), *Economy and Society* (first edition published posthumously in 1922), several more methodological essays, and many other works.

Weber's home in Heidelberg became a center of German intellectual life; Karl Jaspers, Georg Lukács, Robert Michels, and Georg Simmel were among the regular visitors. Meanwhile, Weber collaborated in empirical research on the experiences and attitudes of industrial workers, helped to found a German sociological association, directed military hospitals during the first year of World War I, and carried on a vigorous journalistic critique of the foreign and military policies of the German emperor William II. During the years before his death in 1920, he resumed regular academic duties, now at the University of Munich. He took an active role in the Versailles peace conference, attempting in vain to moderate the severe terms dictated by France and later vowing to work to make of the resultant treaty only a "scrap of paper." He also worked with a commission studying the structure of a proposed constitutional German republic and was himself considered for high office. However, he did not live to see the results of Germany's experiment with democracy during the Weimar Republic of 1919–1933.

Weber's biography is important because it helps to account for the fact that although his work has profound depths and brilliant facets, he never achieved closure on a single theory of society. True, he died relatively young, but the deep-seated internal conflicts so dramatically manifested in his breakdown contributed equally to this lack of closure. He was a nationalist, who approached constitutional questions holding in mind as a criterion of adequate constitutional structures their potential for the development of effective leadership of Germany. At the same time, however, he was an individualist, who refused to concede the legitimacy of allowing organizational or political imperatives to dictate his, or any person's, ethical decisions. He had the passion and rhetorical gifts of a political leader, but his respect for intellectual integrity prevented him from making politically necessary compromises. In workaday discipline Weber was the equal of Durkheim, and yet he had also a rebellious, even quixotic, streak which was seen not only in his relationship with his father, but also in his frequent involvement in lawsuits, in his defense of the rights of political underdogs in German universities (whether or not he agreed with their ideas), and in his political journalism. Weber was intellectually convinced of the durable and stultifying power of modern organizational society, which he dubbed an "iron cage," but he held fast to individualistic values even more poignantly than did Tocqueville. As he wrote in 1906, "We are 'individualists' and partisans of 'democratic' institutions 'against the stream' of material constellations. He who wishes to be the weathercock of an evolutionary trend should give up these old-fashioned ideals as soon as possible" [quoted by Gerth and Mills 1946, p. 71].[21] Much of his work centers upon the analysis of what he called "rationalization"—the long-term historical process in which Western society has been stripped of magical culture and has become dominated by technical calculation. Yet Weber was also tantalized by the possibility of a rise of "charismatic" leaders—extraordinary, routine-breaking prophets.

What unites these paradoxical displays of hope and pessimism, however, is the single overarching commitment to intellectual integrity. Weber had the utmost contempt for demagoguery and hypocrisy and a patronizing disdain for those who engage in wishful thinking. He held it to be the "primary task" of the teacher and scholar, and a "moral achievement" as well, to compel students and citizens to recognize "inconvenient facts," those facts that people find it comforting to ignore because of their own political and ethical commitments. His sociology was employed in the service of such intellectual self-confrontation and clarification rather than, as with Marx and Durkheim, in the service of revolution or reform. His work, therefore, offers no consistent guide for action, and its legacy is ambiguous. Aspects of it have been put to use by contemporary sociologists of the most diverse intellectual and political persuasions. In the sections that follow, I shall discuss three of his major concerns: the methodology of social science, the study of religion, and the analysis of social structure.

Social Science

Both Weber and Durkheim invested considerable energy in writing "methodological" treatises on the nature of knowledge in social science and on the procedures for arriving at it. These methodological writings gave rise to much controversy and debate. In other respects, however, Weber and Durkheim as methodologists differ dramatically. Weber was a methodological individualist and employed the analytical method of "ideal types"; Durkheim enunciated the reality of social facts *sui generis*.

It must be stated here, however, that Weber and Durkheim will be misinterpreted, and the differences between them exaggerated, unless one recognizes a crucial disparity between the contexts within which each wrote his methodology. Durkheim was an embattled pioneer, a would-be founder of a new approach to the understanding of society, an approach that would thoroughly supersede previous dilettantist or reductionist efforts. He was ultimately successful, in both his professional career and his intellectual influence, but the dogmatism and overstatement of his methodological writings reflect his upward struggle. By contrast, Weber was from the beginning a respectful, and respected, scion of the disciplines of law and economic history, whose orientation he brought to his sociological work. Weber could take for granted what Durkheim had had to struggle to establish: an authoritative and institutionalized social science. Unlike Durkheim, Weber did not have to defend the legitimacy of social science as a discipline; rather, he could take this as a given and proceed beyond it. Thus, Weber attempted a twofold task: first, to analyze, qualify, and rationalize the scholarly practices in which he had been trained; and, second, to mitigate by his call for objectivity what he saw as political abuses of scholarly privilege. Without false modesty, he could thus preface his last and most influential methodological essay with the remark, "The method employed here makes no claim to any kind of novelty" [1922, p. 3]. At the same time, he had axes to grind, three of which will concern us: *Verstehen*, the ideal-typical method, and objectivity.

Verstehen

There is a great contrast at face value between Durkheim's orientation toward sociological knowledge and that of Weber. Durkheim advocated a sociology that would be the science of social facts, which should be considered as "things" and be explained by other social facts:

The determining cause of a social fact should be sought among the social facts preceding it and not among the states of the individual consciousness [1895, p. 110].

Weber, by contrast, spoke of sociology as a science concerned primarily with

the interpretive understanding (*Verstehen*) of social action and thereby with a causal explanation of its course and consequences. We shall speak of "action" insofar as the acting individual attaches a subjective meaning to his behavior— be it overt or covert, omission or acquiescence [1922, p. 4].

Where Durkheim explicitly insists on the extirpation of psychological considerations, Weber claims to found sociology on the category of *Verstehen*, on "subjective" and "interpretive" analysis. Durkheim took as his model for the establishment of sociology the "positivist" method of natural science. However, the disciplines in which Weber was trained, and in whose traditions he continued to work, were oriented toward *Verstehen*. In a court of law, attorneys, judges, and juries are interested in ascertaining a *motive* and in attributing *responsibility* to a defendant or a party to a lawsuit. In economics, theorems and laws are constructed by taking as a premise that individual actors will each be motivated to maximize their economic advantage and by then assessing what actions are likely to ensue from that basis. Similarly, for the disciplines of history and for sociology to explain, for example, the contribution of religion to economic action, we must *interpret* the *meaning* of religious doctrine for the believer in order to determine the effect that it might have on his economic activity.

For Weber, only individuals act, and action is intelligible to the scholar as well as to his lay audience only when the individual's point of view is understood:

In general, for sociology, such concepts as "state," "association," "feudalism," and the like, designate certain categories of human interaction. Hence, it is the task of sociology to reduce these concepts to "understandable" action, that is, without exception, to the actions of participating individual men [quoted by Gerth and Mills 1946, p. 55].

For Weber, a mere statistical uniformity, such as the correlation between rates of suicide and of divorce, is sociologically meaningless until we can "understand" the connection. Such statistical uniformities and their subsumption under general laws may be the goal of the natural sciences, but for the human sciences the goal is something else:

> We can accomplish something which is never attainable in the natural sciences, namely the subjective understanding of the action of the component individuals . . . . This additional achievement of explanation by interpretive understanding, as distinguished from external observation, is of course attained only at a price—the more hypothetical and fragmentary character of its results. Nevertheless, subjective understanding is the specific characteristic of sociological knowledge [1922, p. 15].

A contrast between Durkheim's *Suicide* and Weber's *Protestant Ethic* illustrates this difference in purpose. Weber's book begins with an almost casual reference to the existence of a correlation between religious affiliation and social position, specifically that "business leaders and owners of capital . . . are overwhelmingly Protestant" [1905, p. 35]. In a brief chapter, he gives examples, argues that the correlation is not spurious, and surveys a few possible explanations. The rest of the book is given over to an extended attempt to *interpret* the correlation. First Weber defines the "spirit of capitalism" (using as examples Benjamin Franklin's homilies to the effect that time is money and a penny saved is a penny earned). Then he investigates the doctrines of various Protestant sects to see what contribution they might have made to this spirit. Finally he argues that Calvinism especially gave the believer a conception of his relationship to God and to other men that served to direct his activity into capitalistic endeavors. In the English translation of Weber's last revision (in 1920), this "interpretive" exercise occupies over two hundred and thirty pages of text and footnotes.

In Durkheim's *Suicide*, the emphases are reversed. The bulk of his book is devoted to astute statistical demonstrations of sociological correlations between suicide rates and such factors as religion, family size, marital status, occupation, and so forth and to arguments for the spuriousness of correlations with "race" and psychopathology. Durkheim's argument is crowned by the subsumption of the sociological correlations under the general categories of egoism, anomie, and altruism. Ultimately, it would appear, he wanted to validate a series of lawlike propositions such as "anomie generates social disorder." The formally analogous though characteristically qualified proposition—that "religious affiliation in part determines occupational position"—was for Weber merely a starting point. What was a goal for Durkheim was only a beginning for Weber.

At the same time, however, what was a goal for Weber was at least a means for Durkheim. That is, Durkheim found it necessary to *interpret* the correlations that he had discovered. Durkheim explicates the meaning of anomie, for example, through a statement of man's special need for regulation. It can be argued that not the general proposition relating anomie and social disorder but the internal understanding of the relationship between man and society is the true goal of his research. As Durkheim wrote toward the end of the book, "We start from the exterior because it alone is immediately given, but only to reach the interior. Doubtless the procedure is complicated; but there is no other unless one would risk having his research apply to his personal feeling concerning the order of facts under investigation, instead of to this factual order itself" [1897, p. 315]. In Weber's writings the concern for such a risk was subordinated to the focus on *Verstehen*.

Ideal-Typical Method

If *Verstehen* was Weber's means of codifying procedures already in use, his discussion of "ideal types" was a means of resolving a long-standing controversy, known as the "battle of methods," within the discipline of economics in Germany. That field was divided into two camps, into what are now called economic history and economic theory. The first group concentrated on the recapitulation of *particular configurations* of economic systems; the second, on the development of *general models* of economic activity. The debate centered on the role of abstraction in economics. The economic theorists argued that abstraction was necessary to the pursuit of scientific knowledge. The economic historians responded by accusing the theorists of one-sided analysis and argued that adequate understanding of a concrete economic situation requires the consideration of the full range of human motivation, not just the narrow economic self-interest emphasized by the theorists.

It was in reference to this controversy that Weber wrote of "ideal types." He insisted that *both* the historically situated concepts of the historians (for example, "the medieval city economy") *and* the self-consciously abstract concepts of the theorists (for example, "free competition") were "ideal types," concepts based on abstractions from particular historical configurations. He agreed with the historians that the theorists' models were time-bound and with the theorists that the historians' configurations were abstractions. In each case the scholar himself selects the phenomena to be highlighted and unifies the concept according to a specific point of view. Weber expressed this similarity of procedure in a tone that was for him polemical:

An ideal type is formed by the one-sided *accentuation* of one or more points of view and by the synthesis of a great many diffuse, discrete, more or less present and occasionally absent *concrete individual* phenomena, which are arranged according to those one-sidedly emphasized viewpoints into a unified *analytical* construct. In its conceptual purity, this mental construct cannot be found empirically anywhere in reality. It is a *utopia* [1904, p. 90].

In this passage Weber was performing his wonted service of clarification by articulating inconvenient propositions. The historians did not like to recognize that their concepts were analytical abstractions, nor the theorists that theirs were based on a synthesis of evanescent concrete phenomena. In effect Weber was stating what has since become a methodological commonplace; Durkheim, by necessity, also used an abstracting and isolating method. Nonetheless, Weber's emphases on the inevitable one-sidedness and unreality of concepts (his "conceptual nominalism") was distinctive in the sociological tradition. Let us examine, by way of illustration, Weber's widely discussed concept of "bureaucracy."

Modern governmental administration—and Weber was thinking particularly of the case he knew best, that of Germany—is carried out by officials who are *employees* of the state, rather than princes in their own right or personal servants of the head of state. These officials (1) have fixed *areas of jurisdiction* (within the foreign service, for example, there is a "French desk," a "Russian desk," and so forth); (2) are recruited on the basis of *specialized* training; and (3) are full-time *salaried* workers rather than laborers paid by the piece or by the hour. The functioning of the office is characterized by (4) an established *hierarchy* or chain of command (according to which it is against the rules to go "over the boss's head"); (5) reliance on *written* documents (which involves keeping everything "in the files"); and (6) orientation to *general* rules of procedure (going "by the book"). These are the defining characteristics of "bureaucracy" as an ideal type.

Weber was clearly aware that in some offices certain aspects of this model do not hold true. Officials may be granted or may usurp functions outside a narrow area of jurisdiction (for example, the "troubleshooter"). Secret arrangements may be made and kept in "unofficial" files. Officers may be remunerated by means of legitimate incentives such as bonuses or illegitimate incentives such as kickbacks.[22] And yet these six "discrete . . . concrete individual phenomena" of bureaucracy are usually "more or less present" although also "occasionally absent." What is more, the concept is "arranged . . . into a unified analytical construct" on the basis of a "one-sided accentuation." In the case of "bureaucracy," this "accentuation" is that the analytical model, and the concrete phenomenon on which it is based, is organized according to the criterion of the maximization of control from the top and minimization of possible usurpation by officials lower down in the hierarchy. The stipulations that officials are *salaried* and that processes are to be recorded in *written documents*, for example, have the "logic" of preventing an official from arrogating to himself his office as a personal property. Ideally, a bureaucracy is a strictly neutral but powerful political tool of the governmental head.

While such a picture of modern officialdom may have numerous exceptions in actual experience, many of its aspects have become legendary in contemporary social criticism ("just routine," "I'm only following orders," "that's not my business, you'll have to see Mr. So-and-So in Room such-and-such"). It is by no means an absurd concept. Weber, however, emphasized the "one-sidedness" and "unreality" of such concepts because he was worried about the tendency of some contemporaries to attribute causal force to the phenomena synthesized under such concepts or to suppose that a synthetic concept captured an exhaustive representation of relevant phenomena. He might have had the Marxists of his day in mind, who could be accused of both of these faults in their use of the concept of "capitalism." Weber's methodological polemic stresses the role of the scientist in constructing concepts and reflects his own profound conviction that no single concept can exhaust a manifold, disorderly reality. He did not recommend, however, that sociological concepts be remote from experience.

Objectivity

The "ideal" in ideal types refers to conceptual purity, not to ethical desirability. There are, after all, "negative" utopias, such as Huxley's *Brave New World*, as well as positive ones. It was an inherent part of Weber's methodological perspective to deny that scientists *in their role as scientists* have the right to make ethical or political pronouncements. Yet Weber was an outspoken man of passionate convictions, and the question of the way in which these two parts of his character and his philosophy could be reconciled arises immediately. Weber gave his answers often, but he did so most forcefully and movingly in two speeches, "Politics as a Vocation" and "Science as a Vocation," which were delivered at the University of Munich in 1918, when Germany was in the midst of a social revolution. Since I have space for only a few points here, I urge the reader to read the lucid and easily accessible translations [1919a, 1919b].

In these speeches, Weber acknowledged that the very activity of scholarship rests on normative or ethical assumptions that are themselves incapable of scientific proof. There is no science "without presuppositions," he argued. Science supposes not only that the rules of logic are valid, but also that its findings are "worth being known." Furthermore, self-clarification and intellectual integrity were for Weber fundamental values inherent in scholarship. Beyond these concessions, however, he was unwilling to go.

Social science is neutral about social policy, he insisted. It can give us knowledge of facts and causal processes (or empirical data and sociological laws) with which we can attempt to control our fate, although even here, as American economists have recently found, its power is limited. It can provide us not only with knowledge but also with the techniques of investigation and the honing of intelligence. Most of all, in the hands of the true scholar, social science promotes clarity of judgment; it provides an opportunity for ethical self-examination. Weber put it this way:

No ethics in the world can dodge the fact that in numerous instances the attainment of "good" ends is bound to the fact that one must be willing to pay the price of using morally dubious means or at least dangerous ones [1919a, p. 121].

If you take such and such a stand, then, according to scientific experience, you have to use such and such a *means* in order to carry out your achievement practically. Now these means are perhaps such that you believe you must reject them. Then you simply must choose between the end and the inevitable means. Does the end "justify" the means? Or does it not? The teacher can confront you with the necessity of this choice. He cannot do more, as long as he wishes to remain a teacher and not to become a demagogue [1919b, p. 151].

There is a head-on confrontation between Durkheim, who insisted that without the goal of sociological ethics in mind social science has no meaning, and Weber, for whom it was "indisputable" that science can give no answer to the question, "What shall we do and how shall we live?"

Weber's insistence on the objectivity of science was for him, nonetheless, an emphatically moral achievement. The conception of an abyss between science and politics was intended to preserve the integrity of each, lest the scholar's values color his findings or the scientific establishment usurp political authority. Weber had in mind especially those academics who abused the privilege of the lectern, which inspired far more awe in his Germany than in the contemporary United States, to deliver jingoistic tirades to students. Weber wanted to protect the students' rights of choice. One suspects also that he did not want his typically pessimistic scholarly analyses to be taken as recommendations toward political quietism. He knew that "man would not have achieved the possible unless time and again he had reached out for the impossible" [1919a, p. 128].

The dominant tendency in contemporary American sociology has been to abide by Weber's idea of objectivity, or to invoke it in self-defense, while abandoning his sense of tragedy and his consequent conviction of the necessity for ethical self-clarification. As we have seen with Durkheim, it is but a short step from social science to political prescription if one holds to a harmonic conception of social order. Moral choices are then simple and scientific findings readily take on an obligatory force. Such was not Weber's intention: for him, the boundaries placed on science were meant to facilitate the separate activity of political action.

Let us now examine his substantive scholarly work.

Man and the Cosmos: Sociology of Religion

Weber is probably best known for his study of *The Protestant Ethic and the Spirit of Capitalism*. Although this book does not adequately represent Weber's whole approach, it was the starting point for his extended project on the sociology of religion, and I shall treat it here as such. In the process, a number of Weber's methodological and theoretical principles will be illustrated and his conception of human nature will be outlined.

The Protestant Ethic and the Spirit of Capitalism

Weber's purpose was to understand (*verstehen*) what he took to be the commonplace observation that there was a connection between Protestantism and the rise of capitalism. The meat of his argument begins with a puzzle: Where could the peculiar capitalist mentality have come from? It is not at all obvious, Weber points out, that large numbers of individuals should want to amass great wealth through unremitting work. More typical of the world's history, he says, are the attitudes of "economic traditionalism," the desire to earn only enough to get by, on the one hand, or the impulse of mere greed without the discipline of systematic work, on the other.

In Benjamin Franklin's writings, Weber finds the ideal type of the spirit of capitalism:

Remember, that *time* is money. He that can earn ten shillings a day by his labor, and goes abroad, or sits idle, one half of that day, though he spends but sixpence during his diversion or idleness, ought not to reckon *that* the only expense; he has really spent, or rather thrown away, five shillings besides [quoted by Weber 1905, p. 48].

Accumulate, but do not spend, and remember the opportunities lost through idleness. These are Franklin's messages and they are especially conducive to entrepreneurial activity. Once capitalism as a system is triumphant, it may no longer require such intense motivational support. But its *rise* was a qualitative breakthrough, which was given impetus, according to Weber, by such an extraordinary mentality. (Marx, too, recognized the revolutionary nature of the rise of capitalism, though his explanation of it was different.)

Weber next examines the doctrines of the Protestant churches, and this examination comprises the longest part of his book. He found that both Luther and Calvin contributed to different aspects of this mentality, although it was not the intention of either man to promote capitalism. Luther rejected the medieval Catholic notion that monasticism was the highest form of the religious life, and he argued that one's mundane occupation should be regarded as a "calling." Worldly work came to have religious significance. It was *legitimated*, and Weber insisted that such legitimation must have had great significance in a pious age.

Yet Luther's conception of the calling was traditionalistic and there was in the doctrine of his church, and its Pietist variant, no incentive toward innovative activity. Weber found that in Calvinism. Calvin's theology was austere, ruthlessly logical, and completely God-centered. Calvin took to its logical extreme the idea of God as omniscient and omnipotent. If these be His attributes, then to suppose that we can influence Him by chants, rosaries, or other pious exercises is blasphemy. Calvin's answer was the concept of predestination, a concept of man's relationship to God that put the Calvinist believer into a state of excruciating anxiety. From eternity all human beings are predestined to eternal life or to eternal damnation. No amount of intercession by priests or fellow believers can change that elemental fact.

According to Weber, the people of the Reformation believed in this concept in a way that we find difficult to appreciate today. However, they also wanted some assurance of their salvation. Their hope lay in the idea that "a tree without fruit is dead." That is, although good works cannot earn salvation, a life systematically and successfully organized toward the production of good works could be seen as an external sign of inward grace. In effect, the successful man is seen as the instrument of God's will to His greater glory. "In practice," Weber says, distinguishing this from Calvin's intention, "this means that God helps those who help themselves" [1905, p. 115]. The "extreme inhumanity" of this doctrine produced in the believer a "tremendous tension," which was relieved only by a thorough devotion to a "life of good works organized into a unified system." In the mind of the believer, this doctrine acted powerfully against the spontaneous enjoyment of possessions. . . . On the other hand, it had the psychological effect of freeing the acquisition of goods from the inhibitions of traditionalistic ethics. It broke the bonds of the impulse of acquisition in that it not only legalized it, but (in the sense discussed) looked upon it as directly willed by God [1905, p. 171].

With this conclusion, Weber's analysis comes full circle. He has shown how the psychological effect of Calvin's theology had an "elective affinity" (a favorite metaphor of his) with the acquisitive and innovative capitalist spirit, which was oriented toward work and savings. The asceticism of the religious believer contributes to the asceticism of the economic actor. Furthermore, Weber has carried one step further his analysis of "rationalization." For the Calvinist believer, all magical means to salvation—and, more broadly, all traditionalistic practices and institutions—lose their causal efficacy and moral significance. The world of the Calvinist is "disenchanted," bereft of magic, and the believer is alone before God.

A number of Weber's themes can be extracted from this summary. First, the book was self-consciously a "one-sided" abstraction. Weber held that analysis, or breaking into parts, was a necessary means to knowledge. *The Protestant Ethic* focuses on an isolable part of a fuller history, on how religious ideas affect economic action. Weber knew that an investigation of how such ideas became prevalent in the first place, which would view these ideas more as "effects" than as "causes," was equally necessary. Although he never finished his study of ideas as "effects," the work that he did complete shows that ideas are promoted by "status groups," a concept that will be discussed later.

Second, it was a *verstehende*, an interpretative exercise, that sustained a high level of interest in the *content* of doctrine itself. The contrast with Durkheim is striking. In explaining the different rates of suicide of Protestants, Catholics, and Jews, Durkheim tried to show that the *moral attitudes* of these groups toward suicide were less important than the question of whether their *social structure* was atomized or integrated. In this respect, Durkheim's approach was more self-consciously sociological. Weber also studied the social organization of religion in an essay on "The Protestant *Sects* and the Spirit of Capitalism," which directly followed *The Protestant Ethic*. However, his distinctive emphasis, when looking at the "one side" of religion as a cause of action, was to take doctrine seriously.

Third, this does not mean that he looked solely or primarily at explicit theologies or at moral commandments. On the contrary, it was important for him to point out that Martin Luther and Richard Baxter (a

Calvinist minister whom he cites) had attitudes that were hostile to capitalist acquisitiveness. Moreover, specific behavioral religious proscriptions (against usury, for instance) were not his main concern. Rather, he wanted to understand the *psychological effect* of belief in religious concepts, regardless of the intentions of the founders. (There is, in fact, much similarity in form between Weber's Calvin and Marx's bourgeoisie, both of whom unintentionally advanced revolutions of worldwide historical significance.)

Two other implications of *The Protestant Ethic* require more extended treatment.

The Role of Religious Ideas

In *The Protestant Ethic*, Weber presented his most sustained treatment of ideas as determinants of action. The topic was one to which he returned time and again—so often, as a matter of fact, that Weber's theories have been stereotyped as an "ideal determinism" which stands as an alternative to the equally stereotyped "economic determinism" of Marx. What Weber contributes, however, is an analysis of the *ways in which* ideas have an effect. The result is a theory that is not as opposed to Marx's as the stereotypes suggest.

From *The Protestant Ethic* can be extracted the two conceptions of the function of ideas that were most important to Weber. The first concept extends what he saw to be the particular contribution of Lutheranism: the *legitimation* of worldly activity. Weber's analysis of the effect of Lutheranism is part of a more general conception of the role of ideas. In Weber's view, people like to have a good conscience and a sense of the meaningfulness of their activity. Most often, this means that they want to believe those things that will justify their present lives. Depending on the social position of the individual, he is in need either of an ideological justification for his privilege or of an ideological compensation for his suffering.

The fortunate is seldom satisfied with the fact of being fortunate. Beyond this, he needs to know that he has a *right* to this good fortune. He wants to be convinced that he "deserves" it, and above all, that he deserves it in comparison with others. . . . Good fortune thus wants to be "legitimate" fortune [1915, p. 271].

The problem for the underprivileged is more complex, but for them as well, according to Weber, religious ideas can provide a needed message of justification by holding out a promise of salvation at some future time, in this world or in a world beyond. For the underprivileged, their "sense of dignity" is nourished most easily on the belief that a special "mission" is entrusted to them; their worth is guaranteed or constituted by an *ethical imperative*, or by their own functional *achievement*. Their value is thus moved into something beyond themselves, into a "task" placed before them by God [1915, pp. 276–277].

In both cases, religious legitimation serves to release the energies of whole groups by relieving them of the burden of experiencing the world as senseless.

What Weber saw as the contribution of Calvinism points to the second function of ideas—their directive or *refractive*[23] effect. Weber wrote:

Not ideas, but material and ideal interests, directly govern men's conduct. Yet very frequently the "world images" that have been created by "ideas" have, like switchmen, determined the tracks along which action has been pushed by the dynamic of interest. "From what" and "for what" one wished to be redeemed and, let us not forget, could be "redeemed," depended upon one's image of the world [1915, p. 280].

Accordingly, when Weber analyzed religious doctrines, he was interested primarily in the concepts or pictures of reality that they provide rather than in their behavioral commandments. The *image* of man as predestined by an omniscient God is the "switchman" that refracted the self-interest of Calvinists into capitalistic activity. Worldly success seemed to them to be proof of salvation, and that, in turn, gave them a powerful psychological incentive to continuous, systematic work.

Weber's uncompleted series of studies on the "Economic Ethics of the World Religions" was designed to emphasize "those features in the total picture of a religion which have been decisive for the fashioning of the *practical* way of life" of people in China, in India, in the Judaeo-Christian West, and in the Islamic world. True to his switchman metaphor, he found that ideas have refracted interests in vastly different directions.

His analysis of Hinduism provides a good example. A belief in certain metaphysical principles of Hinduism was extensive and intensive among the population of India. These principles included *samsara*, the idea of "transmigration of souls" or reincarnation; *karma*, or "ethical compensation," the idea that worldly deeds are consequential for the standing of one's soul; and the interrelated ideas of *varna* (caste position) and *dharma* (caste duty), which stipulated that one's life chances in a reincarnated existence were determined by one's adherence to the prescriptions of one's caste in this life. The contradictory idea that birth was an accident was not to be found in India. *Believing* in these presuppositions and being keenly *interested* in a better life, the Hindu was powerfully impelled to remain faithful to his traditionally appointed social role. "Hinduism did not join occupational stability to teachings of the moral nature of the person's vocational stability and humble modesty . . . but to the individual's very personal interest in salvation" [1917, p. 122]. In the economic sphere, the practical effect of Hinduism was thus powerfully conservative; for Weber this went a long way toward explaining why capitalism did not develop in India. The example underscores his point that ideas can direct courses of history even if, like Marx, he was skeptical of the motive power of merely moral exhortations.

With respect to the role of ideas, the perspectives of Marx, Durkheim, and Weber can be contrasted as follows. For Durkheim, the content of ideas is less important than the form of their institutionalization: what is important for him is whether or not ideas are shared among a population. By contrast, both Marx and Weber were interested in the content of ideas, and both highlighted the role that ideologies can play in conserving society through legitimation and in changing society through concentrating and directing the energies of social groups. Marx's theory of ideology, however, was wedded to a theory of history that determined the kinds of ideas that would be able to play a revolutionary role. Weber's switchman metaphor, by contrast, emphasized contingency rather than progress in social change. What separates Weber from Marx is, first, the greater attention that he paid to the analysis of ideas and, second, his conviction that ideas can radically *alter* (not only hinder or quicken) the course of history.

Weber's Image of Man

This is an appropriate point to sketch out the philosophic anthropology that stands behind Weber's writings and that underlies many of his differences with others in the sociological tradition. For Marx, man is at the least a self-regarding and socially conditioned reproducer of the means of his existence and at the best a searcher after and creator of the conditions for a universal fulfillment. For Durkheim, man is inherently a creature of society and is beset with anxiety when he is insufficiently surrounded by the company of his fellows and when he lacks a stable set of normative guidelines. For Weber, as seen in the ideal-typical Calvinist and Hinduist, man is motivated by worldly and spiritual self-interest, the import of which can be powerfully directed by images of the world that map out the course to personal security.

108

Weber saw man as variously motivated by the desire for material advantage, social honor, and political power, but also as sufficiently reflective to be anxious about his place in the cosmos. For Durkheim, man's anxiety centers around his social role and around the expectations others have of him. For Weber, man is anxious in the face of a social and "spiritual" world that increasingly threatens to become devoid of meaning:

Abraham, or some peasant of the past, died "old and satiated with life" because he stood in the organic cycle of life; because his life, in terms of its meaning and on the eve of his days, had given him what life had to offer; because for him there remained no puzzles he might wish to solve; and therefore he could have had "enough" of life. Whereas civilized man . . . catches only the most minute part of what the life of the spirit brings forth ever anew, and what he seizes is always something provisional and not definitive, and therefore death for him is a meaningless occurrence. And because death is meaningless, civilized life as such is meaningless . . . [1919b, p. 140].

Intellectuals and religious virtuosos, who devote their lives to a search for cosmic meaning, are a minority. However, their quest and the answers that they have provided respond to profound needs of all men and consequently have far-reaching effects, if not always the effects intended. "Calvin's theology must be distinguished from Calvinism, the theological system from the needs of religious practice. All the religious movements which have affected large masses have started from the question, 'How can I become certain of my salvation?' " [1905, p. 229]. The cosmic certainty that man desires is as concrete as his mundane attachment to worldly rewards: he wants the feeling *here and now* that he is "saved."

Thus religion, as well as worldly activity, has its wellspring in the interests and needs of the individual. "Understanding" how individuals, alone and in groups, go about meeting these needs and securing their interests is the stuff of Weber's interpretative sociology. Thus, there is a profound philosophical conviction behind Weber's methodological individualism. The analysis of religion, Durkheim's social fact *par excellence*, or even the analysis of socialism has to be stated "in terms of the actions of individuals," with all the complexity and contingency thereby implied. Methodological precepts and theoretical axioms are linked in both Weber and Durkheim, though neither was inclined to acknowledge it. And, finally, each was undoubtedly informed by secular versions of his own forsaken religious heritage: Weber, who grew up as a Protestant, was a methodological individualist, and a theorist of self-seeking, existentially searching man; Durkheim, who was born Jewish, was a methodological collectivist and a theorist of socially oriented, rule-regarding man.

Social Structure: The Organization of Interests and Domination

To speak of "social structure" is to have in mind the major constitutive divisions of society: institutions such as the state, the church, the school, and the family; and groups such as classes, parties, pressure groups, and occupational associations. Analyses of such phenomena have occupied us throughout the discussions of Tocqueville, Marx, and Durkheim. For Weber, the topic comes last for two reasons. First, Weber's structural analyses build on the elements that I have been explicating: on tragedy, *Verstehen*, ideal types, ideas, and interests. Second, Weber's methodological individualism and his conceptual nominalism have frequently been interpreted either as denying the reality of society or as contradicting his empirical work on social structure. Neither of these interpretations is correct. Weber *did* continue to employ *Verstehen*, and he *did* recognize the very real divisions within society. We shall turn first to his concepts of socioeconomic groups and then to his concepts of political domination.

Classes and Status Groups

In *Economy and Society* [1922], Weber presented a host of concepts with the intentions of clarifying usage and of orienting the reader to his distinctive point of view. One of the most famous but least understood of these conceptual discussions is contained in the essay on "Class, Status, and Party." Here Weber discussed three phenomena of the distribution of power in society: "classes," "status groups," and "parties." In one respect, Weber was acknowledging three dimensions or hierarchies on which individuals and groups can be placed and along which they usually try to move upward: economic advantage, social prestige, and political power. In his discussions, he concentrated on the first two concepts.

On the subject of "classes," Weber had two points to make. First, he provided a definition that was a variant of the one used by Marx. A class, for Weber, is a group of people in a similar market position with respect to their opportunities for income. They may be owners of marketable commodities or services, whether these involve esoteric skills or common labor, or they may be owners of land, livestock, capital equipment, money, or other aspects of what Marx called "the means of production."

Already, in his definition, Weber draws attention to class constructions that are more complex than those of Marx. For Weber, workers of different skill levels can be members of different classes, as can creditors and debtors. Yet, in Marx's more concrete analyses we find a subtle appreciation of complexities of class formation. In his analyses of mid-nineteenth-century France, for example, he distinguishes commercial, financial, and industrial sectors of the bourgeoisie. Moreover, for Weber, as for Marx, " 'Property' and 'lack of property' are . . . the basic categories of all class situations" [1922, p. 927]. About the *definition* of class (Marx's "class *in* itself"), the two are not at loggerheads.

Weber's second point, however, was a decisive disagreement with Marx. Weber argued that the "emergence of an association or even of mere social action [Marx's "class *for* itself"] from a common class situation is by no means a universal phenomenon" [1922, p. 929]. A similar economic situation, in other words, is seldom an adequate basis for group unity. Weber recognized that people in the same economic situation do act similarly under certain circumstances, but he added that they often do so only as a mass—for example, when large numbers of migrant workers move with the harvest or when scores of pedestrians open umbrellas at the onset of a shower. Indeed, they may compete with each other as much as join in common action. Class action—that is, mutually oriented, organized action directed toward a common class interest—has occurred throughout history, as seen in bread riots or, more recently, in strikes for higher wages. However, Weber hardly saw class action as the primary force of social life.

At this point, Weber turned to the concept of the "status group," which, despite its unfamiliarity to most Americans, is a translation of an ordinary German word, *Stand*, meaning social rank or position. The plural form (*Staende*) means estates of the realm such as the "nobility" or the "clergy." To make his point, Weber immediately remarked that, "in contrast to classes, *Staende* (status groups) are normally groups" [1922, p. 932], which in translation appears as a rather flat way of saying that status groups usually do have consensual unity. Furthermore, although Weber rarely asserted general and unqualified sociological propositions, his remark that "status groups are the specific bearers of all conventions" is formally parallel to Marx's statement that "history is the history of class struggles" even though it attributes action to a different agency. To overstate the matter slightly (in a way that Weber's caution would not normally allow him), it might be said that *society is an arena of status group struggles.*

What does this mean? Just as individuals are stratified by economic situation, so also are they stratified by "status situation," or social honor. An estimation of this honor is usually based on the style of life that the individual maintains, including his standard of living, occupation, choice of social equals, place of residence, and so on. Status can be a merely individual striving, but more commonly it is linked to the expectations of a specific social circle, the "status group"; within this circle, certain kinds of status-relevant social interaction, such as intermarriage and dinner parties, occur. Because the estimation of "honor" is inherently social and because of the high visibility of the style of life on which it is based, a common status situation (in contrast to class situation) *is* normally manifested in group formation. Furthermore, such groups do not simply express a common style of life; they also act to *protect* their interests by social exclusiveness and by monopolization of privileges.

Weber thus agrees with Marx that interest groups of a sort are the historically important actors. He disagrees about the typical basis of formation of such groups. However, Weber was *not* saying that snobbery is a more important motivation than material gain or, for example, that people more often vote their social resentments and anxieties than their pocketbooks. For one thing, his disagreement with Marx centers on the contention that *"honor" facilitates group formation in a way that "property" does not.* What is more, the privileges that status groups act consensually to protect are very often "material" ones, such as property values, professional prerogatives, and even educational qualifications.

For example, Weber interprets the rise of formal educational requirements for many occupations as a result of neither the technical requirements of the job nor "a suddenly awakened 'thirst for education,' but [of] the desire to limit the supply of candidates for these positions and to monopolize them for the holders of educational certificates" [1922, p. 1000]. Such demands for educational certification are typically put forth by such occupational status groups as physicians, lawyers, architects, professors and business administrators. Whatever the intent, their effect is to prevent many talented individuals from entering the group.

However, a status group may also act to propagate its religion or, more broadly, its "ideal interest," as the Brahmins successfully spread Hinduism to the native Indian population and to successive waves of foreign conquerors. Weber tends to view in a similar way regulations, laws, understandings, norms, and all sorts of "conventions" that have shaped social development; he tends to see all of these as the effects of status group action.

In contrast to Marx, Weber sees no group with a "universal character" and no end to the forms of property that may be monopolized or to the forms of ideas that may be propagated. There is motion aplenty in the Weberian scheme, with a typical alternation between periods of status group consolidation (the extreme form of which is the caste system) and periods of economic upheaval (when the would-be closure of status groups is successfully overcome by hordes of *parvenus* and *déclassés*). However, for Weber there is no ultimate revolution stemming from these actions, as there is for Marx, and no inherent direction to the process.

Politics and *Herrschaft*

In the arena of power, Weber did see a directional development. That development involves the consolidation of the "state" as an organization and the increasing prevalence of "legal" as opposed to "traditional" or "charismatic" forms of "domination" in both political and economic realms of life.

Social structure, for Weber, is built up not only on the basis of the ideal and material interests of individuals taken as units but also by their positions in structures of command and obedience. To describe such structures, Weber used the term *Herrschaft*, the translation of which has sparked many controversies.[24] Here I shall use the translation "domination." In some instances, domination may be merely de facto, as in the case of "the domination of gasoline dealers by the Standard Oil Company" [1922, p. 944]. But Weber concentrated on those relationships of domination in which there is a shared expectation that "rulers" have a *right* to issue commands and the "ruled" a *duty* to obey. Such expectations may be based on a variety of motivations—on expediency, personal loyalty, respect for law, persuasion, or fear. Relationships of domination have historically taken many forms: parent-child, master-servant, king-subject, boss-employee. What is important is that a claim to the obedience of specific persons is successfully made by the ruling party. (In Durkheim's language, we might say that domination is a "social fact.")

As we have seen, privileged persons want to justify their good fortune, and those privileged by *Herrschaft* are no different. Their claims to legitimacy may be based on one of three grounds: (1) *legal*, or *rational*, legitimation, which invokes the legality of certain rules and establishes the right of those governing by virtue of those rules; (2) *traditional* legitimation, which claims sanctification by hallowed customs; and (3) *charismatic* legitimation, which appeals to a presumed popular belief in the extraordinary character of a particular person (prophet, hero, and so forth) and in the normative order promulgated by him.

Legal legitimation is especially prevalent in the modern world and is symbolized by the slogan, "a government of laws and not of men." Traditional legitimation was typical of the medieval world; its spirit of continuity is seen in the old French exclamation, "The King is dead; long live the King!" Charismatic legitimation has sprung up in many times and places; the biblical prophets, Jesus and his disciples, Hitler, and Mao Tse-tung are all charismatic figures. The extraordinary character of this type of legitimation is exemplified by Jesus's refrain, "It is written . . . , but I say unto you . . . ," in which Jesus expressed his charismatic superiority to traditional prescriptions.

What is of special interest in this typology is Weber's proposition that the ground on which legitimation is claimed "constitutes the basis of very real differences in the empirical structure of domination" [1922, p. 953]. Thus, when he presents his "three pure types of legitimate domination" or "authority," he is not simply proposing a classification scheme; he is also advancing a series of claims about actual social structure. The legitimating principle is consequential to the extent of determining in large measure how rulership is carried on and even in establishing boundaries on the discretion of the ruler.

Legal authority is administered by a "bureaucratic" staff, which (as we saw above) is a hierarchical organization of full-time, salaried officials with specialized training and fixed areas of jurisdiction, operating according to general rules and written records. Although bureaucracy is a potent instrument of domination, the arbitrary will of the ruler is circumscribed in many ways by the institutionalized codes of the bureaucracy, as is seen in contemporary "civil service" regulations. *Traditional authority* has had many complex varieties. Its typical administrative structure has relied heavily on personal servants of the ruler, in effect his extended patriarchal "household," or on semi-autonomous, traditionally recognized persons of notability. There are, as well, many gradations in between. *Charismatic authority* is in principle hostile both to bureaucratic routine and to traditional prescriptions. Its decrees are carried out by a circle of personal devotees of the ruler who are presumed to partake of his exceptional qualities. The "Cultural Revolution" of Chairman Mao is a recent example of charismatic authority in operation.

Weber analyzed the linkages between legitimating principles and administrative structures in great historical detail. True to his insistence on the ideal-typical nature of the typology of domination, he invested much of his effort in analyzing deviations from the pure type.

Nonetheless, his overall analysis of domination was a treatise on "rationalization": the "disenchantment" of intellectual life has been paralleled by the "bureaucratization" of *Herrschaft*, both in politics and in the economy. There are three instructive comparisons with Marx. First, Weber saw the political order going through a development that was analogous to Marx's conception of the rise of capitalism. That process involves the expropriation of independent producers (in the economy) and of autonomous centers of power (in politics). Bureaucratization is one aspect of this process; the ruler seeks to assure a separation between the "powers of office" and the official who exercises them, just as the capitalist expropriates the worker from the means of production.

Everywhere the development of the modern state is initiated through the action of the prince. He paves the way for the expropriation of the autonomous and "private" bearers of executive power who stand beside him, of those who in their own right possess the means of administration, warfare, and financial organization, as well as politically usable goods of all sorts. The whole process is a complete parallel to the development of the capitalist enterprise through gradual expropriation of the independent producers. In the end, the modern state controls the total means of political organization, which actually come together under a single head. No single official personally owns the money he pays out, or the buildings, stores, tools, and war machines he controls. In the contemporary "state"—and this is essential for the concept of the state—the "separation" of the administrative staff, of the administrative officials, and of the workers from the material means of administrative organization is completed [1919a, p. 82].

The state is treated as an *enterprise*, a compulsory, territorial power monopoly, the specific means of which (though not the only business of which) is the use of force. The state, Weber said, is "a human community that (successfully) claims the *monopoly of the legitimate use of physical force* within a given territory" [1919a, p. 78]. Weber's political sociology is thus a study in the dynamics of expropriation.

Second, Weber placed greater emphasis than did Marx on bureaucratization within the economy. Marx confined his analysis for the most part to the division between bourgeois and proletarian, without paying sustained attention to the organization of the capitalist enterprise itself. (He does, however, have some prescient remarks on the rise of the modern corporation in the third volume of *Capital*, published by Engels in 1894.) Weber's stress on the bureaucratization of both political and economic enterprises was one of the bases for his lack of socialist convictions. Not only ownership but also the apparatus of control was for him decisive for the shaping of society.

Third, the "means of domination" are as crucial for social order as the "means of production." Weber would not agree with Marx that the former are in any sense subordinate to the latter. Thus Weber resists such a concept as "ruling class" because it suggests that economic dominance is ipso facto political dominance. Probably because of the immense *political* power of Bismarck, Weber had a well-developed sense of the analytic independence of the state from the economy. Reflecting upon the example of the German bureaucracy, he was convinced of the longevity of that form of organization. He saw no alternative to bureaucracy as a means of necessary administration. At the same time, he self-consciously faced up to its immense power over our lives.

Prophecy and Pessimism

In the preceding discussions, we have seen how Weber developed a battery of concepts—disenchantment, rationalization, legitimation, refraction, ideal and material interests, status groups, domination, bureaucracy, the state. Each of these involves empirical claims about the nature of social reality, and all are stated in a precise and logical fashion. These concepts are the brilliant and profound facets that I mentioned in the introduction to my discussion of Weber. I have had time only for brief consideration of them and have left out others entirely.

However, Weber self-consciously avoided conceptualizing *the whole* of social reality, because he was convinced of its manifold, tragic complexity and because he was wary of the kind of conceptual reification that he would have seen in Marx and Durkheim. Weber's overall approach has been aptly called a sociological mosaic: the parts are nicely articulated, but there are breaks between them. At the same time, the pattern of the mosaic does suggest an image of the whole, an image that is deeply pessimistic. The trend of modern development leads away from liberal values. "Everywhere the house is ready-made for a new servitude," he said in 1906. Optimistic hopes are misguided: "Not summer's bloom lies ahead of us, but rather a polar night of icy darkness and hardness," he said to his German audience in 1918. The events of the next thirty years bore out his prophecy.

Weber was, then, a prophet, a Jeremiah who lifted the torch of intellectual integrity against the false prophets of unwarranted optimism and irrational action. His prophecies were as magnificent in their rhetoric as those of Marx and rather less rigorous in their deduction from analytic premises. Here are some of the concluding sentences from *The Protestant Ethic:*

The Puritan wanted to work in a calling; we are forced to do so. For when asceticism was carried out of monastic cells into everyday life, and began to domi-

116

nate worldly morality, it did its part in building the tremendous cosmos of the modern economic order. This order is now bound to the technical and economic conditions of machine production which today determine the lives of all the individuals who are born into this mechanism, not only those directly concerned with economic acquisition, with irresistible force. Perhaps it will so determine them until the last ton of fossilized coal is burnt. In [Richard] Baxter's view the care for external goods should only lie on the shoulders of the "saint like a light cloak, which can be thrown aside at any moment." But fate decreed that the cloak should become an iron cage. . . .

No one knows who will live in this cage in the future, or whether at the end of this tremendous development entirely new prophets will arise, or there will be a great rebirth of old ideas and ideals, or if neither, mechanized petrification, embellished with a sort of convulsive self-importance. For of the last stage of this cultural development, it might well be truly said: "Specialists without spirit, sensualists without heart; this nullity imagines that it has attained a level of civilization never before achieved."

But this brings us to the world of judgments of value and of faith, with which this purely historical discussion need not be burdened [1905, pp. 181–182].

In this quotation are to be found Weber's vivid images of an uninspiring existence—"this machine," "this nullity," "iron cage," "mechanized petrification"—as well as fragments of a vague sense of an alternative—"great rebirth," "new prophets." All are presented in a manner that provokes but does not exhort. The rhetorical burst is brought short by a reminder of the incapacity of scholarly investigation to entertain judgments of value and faith. How are we to regard this mixture?

The guiding thread of Weber's life was his commitment to the value of intellectual integrity—his refusal to hide from unpleasant truth and his insistence on intellectual self-confrontation. Despite his value-relativism, he demanded the same value of others, his students and the readers of his political tracts. He spoke with respect of a value conflict even in this sphere, between those who believed in an "ethic of responsibility"—who accepted that they must be willing to provide an account of the probable consequences of their actions in view of the knowledge at hand—and those who were oriented toward an "ethic of intentions"— who believed that they must strive to represent purity in their actions whatever the consequences. However, Weber's own option *and his option for others* was the former, no matter how noble the latter could sometimes appear. From his mother and his aunt he had learned a respect for the Sermon on the Mount, but he could not take it seriously as a guide for worldly conduct, whether scholarly or political. For him, the responsible involvement in the complex interplay of multiple causes and often obscure consequences was something of an absolute ethical value for all men.

118

Thus Weber had not only to recognize the process of "rationalization," but also to find it valuable. For rationalization includes disenchantment, which overcomes illusions about the makeup of reality, and technical calculation, which increases the possibility of control and of causal accounting. He partly agreed with the German idealist view that man is most free when he can predict the results of his action because then he has most control. Weber embraced this rationalized world, even as he recognized that the control it makes possible increasingly devolves to impersonal agencies.

At the same time, he stood within another German tradition, that of Faust, Nietzsche, and the prophetic Marx, in which the exertion of will is bound up with the conditions for freedom. Thus Weber stated that "man would not have attained the possible unless time and again he had reached out for the impossible" and that "freedom and democracy are only possible where the resolute will of a nation not to allow itself to be ruled like sheep is permanently alive." His fascination with charisma is part of this, though his analyses of charisma centered on its instability and inherent tendency toward routinization.

Weber was a man of intense values, but his values were at war with each other and with his analyses. His insistence on objectivity was an answer to these conflicts. He was a man of values, but not a man of faith. Those who urgently longed for faith (or those who, like Marx and Durkheim, had it) he regarded with condescension:

To the person who cannot bear the fate of the times like a man, one must say: may he rather return silently, without the usual publicity built up of renegades, but simply and plainly. The arms of the old churches are opened widely and compassionately for him [1919b, p. 155].

His respect—and it was genuine and committed—he reserved for those like himself who had "trained relentlessness in viewing the realities of life, and the ability to face such realities and to measure up to them inwardly." In effect, although not by intention, Weber's message and the "image of the world" that it conveys discourages not only an easy faith in harmony but also an arduous search for transcendence. His stance of objectivity is not sufficient to prevent this "refractive" effect of his own analytic ideas.

CHAPTER 7

Conclusion: Unity and Diversity in the Sociological Tradition

Space and energy are limited quantities, and the time has come for me to draw this essay to a close. The book itself has another half, and insofar as this part is an interpretation of a process in time, the subject itself has no conclusion other than the present. Yet both a historical and an analytic story have been told; here I shall present these stories in a different summary form.

The Sociological View of the World

The historical part of my story has been the rise and consolidation of a distinctive, though by now well-diffused, world view, that of sociology. Beginning with the early, speculative efforts to deduce society from a fixed human nature (represented by Hobbes), I presented three aspects of the "discovery of society"; these centered on the process of change from eighteenth- to nineteenth-century Europe. That discovery was incorporated into the theories that were articulated in the late nineteenth century.

That *society is man's creation* was stated forcefully by Hobbes and by the thinkers of the Enlightenment and has been reaffirmed by the activists who have attempted to remake society ever since. Of the three major thinkers we have encountered, Marx and Weber make this concept central to their perspectives (though in different ways) while Durkheim employs it as a crucial, though muted axiom. Marx's activism, his revolutionary commitment, insists that the social world is not to be taken as a sacred given. His theoretical efforts were directed toward the identification of the possible levers of social change, and his rhetoric about the inexorability of revolution was intended to channel activism, not to counsel fatalism. For Weber, the enacted nature of society was a methodological as well as political starting point. He intended to demystify "society" by arguing that its institutions could only be the results of the actions of participating individuals. In this, he agreed with the Marx who has become clearer to us with the publication of his full corpus of writings, but disagreed with the Marx represented by Weber's Marxist contemporaries. Durkheim's scientific project militated against his saying aloud and often that society is man's creation, and in an individualistic reading of that statement he could not concur. Yet his scholarly efforts intended to show that the earlier modes of social interpretation—which held that society was determined by biology, geography, or divinity—had to cede to those centering on human agency. Most current sociology, from policy-oriented macroscopic works to microscopic studies of face-to-face interaction, also agrees, though the danger of returning to a mystified, reified concept of society is ever-present in a discipline that is devoted to the study of social life.

In our story, Rousseau was the fount of the idea that *man*, as we know him, *is a social product*, and his legacy includes the radical tradition of Marx as well as the conservative tradition of Burke, Tocqueville, and Durkheim. The priority of society to realized humanity was Durkheim's special scholarly emphasis, as we have seen, but it was also a crucial part of Marx's message. First, like Rousseau, Marx conceived of human beings as creatures whose true potential ("species-being") is realized only in social life. This was, in fact, the meaning of the famous dictum of Aristotle, upon whom both Rousseau and Marx drew, that man is a "political animal." Second, the manifestations of humanity that we see in daily life (especially greed and venality) ought not be taken as the inevitable essence of humanity (as Hobbes tended to take them) but as the effects of changeable social institutions. The social nature of man is thus a key assumption of a radical and critical social theory. If Weber spent less time than Marx and Durkheim stating explicitly its assumption, this is due both to his working in a context where a social-scientific point of view was more strongly established and to his own rhetorical inclination to emphasize the ethical priority of the individual over society. Yet Weber spent much of his time demonstrating that the fundamental ideas that we humans have of the cosmos result from centuries of social processes. Like Marx and Durkheim, Weber knew that the rugged individualist of nineteenth-century economic theory was (insofar as not wholly fictitious) a product of historical social forces.

Along with the demystification of society and of human personality, the sociological viewpoint nonetheless insists on the *objective reality of society*. Once again, this is a special emphasis of the conservative tradition, used for analytical as well as "political" purposes. In Durkheim, the insistence that society is a reality of its own kind served both his conservative reformism and his battle for sociology as a science. If in Durkheim's own rendering of the axiom, society became a monolithic thing, we have seen that it is not necessary to accept his most extreme statements in order to appreciate his most valuable message. On the other side of the political spectrum, Marx also had political and scientific reasons to present the social as real. For all of his activism and for all of his optimism about human possibilities, Marx argued that for his party's hopes to bear fruit, social activism would have to proceed in a manner consistent with the actual structure and contradictions of bourgeois society. And Weber, despite his own "unfashionable" ethical individualism and despite his conceptual nominalism, spoke of the social order of his day and later as an "iron cage," as a new apparatus of enslavement. For all three thinkers, and for the sociological point of view in general, it is crucial that social phenomena be regarded as more than aggregations of individual atoms.

It is in line with the idea of society as a reality that each of the thinkers whom we have encountered dwells on unintended consequences of action. Marx's bourgeoisie produces its own grave-diggers as it mobilizes and brings into contact a new class of factory laborers. Every "antagonistic" (that is, presocialist) mode of production contains internal contradictions produced necessarily but without conscious intent by its ruling class. Only with the advent of the classless society will the succession of such unintended contradictions cease, because only then will there be a society in which one group of men no longer lives off the labor of another. Marx, however, outlined only vaguely the form that this classless society would take. For Durkheim, the distinction between individual purpose and social function was a key methodological principle, and his sociology is replete with interpretations of social facts

122

that transcend the points of view and the anticipations of the individual participants. Individuals worshipping their god are, sociologically, reaffirming the collective conscience, and those specializing in a new line of work are moderating competition and promoting organic solidarity, whatever may be their orientations. Both Marx and Durkheim thus see individual plans of action as meshing into something new at the level of the society; for Marx that something new is subversive, and the subversive process will end with the overthrow of capitalism, whereas for Durkheim social functions are integrative and inevitable. In other words, Marx concentrates on consequences unintended and unwanted from the ruling class's perspective, and Durkheim focuses on consequences unsought but often welcomed from the point of view of society as a whole. Weber's approach less often highlights the emergent properties of the social order itself, but concentrates on the ambiguities of intention. But for Weber also "fate decreed" that the asceticism of Protestant morality should take its part in building the structure of modern economic life. Whether a sociologist claims a heritage from the Weberian principle of methodological individualism or from the Durkheimian idea of sociological emergence, the resultant world pictures will contradict the easy and naive notion that a society is merely a reflection of the desires and values of its member individuals.

Competing Sociological Paradigms

Notwithstanding this sociological consensus, Marx, Durkheim, and Weber illustrate for us three distinct answers to a set of problems confronted by any comprehensive social theory. Although these answers are not the only ones possible, I have chosen these three thinkers for detailed scrutiny partly because they represent such dissensus. My choice, however, is not idiosyncratic; I believe that sociologists as a group have kept alive these particular theories not only because of their intrinsic power but also because of the differences among them. Whichever theory, or whichever combination of theories, that you follow, it is worth being aware of the others as a reminder of the analytical paths foregone [see Sherman 1974]. The paradigmatic differences among Marx, Durkheim, and Weber are partly matters of value choices, and hence properly a topic for political debate. (These value choices involve, for instance, whether one holds social justice, social peace, or individual integrity to be one's guiding ethical norm.) Partly also, they are empirical issues, subject in principle to settlement on the basis of facts at hand or facts still to be ascertained. (Research can tell us, for instance, whether rebellion is likely to be the product of absolute or relative deprivation, and under what circumstances.) Still, however, paradigm disputes will persist as *theoretical* controversies (which can be dismissed neither as merely evaluative wranglings nor as ignorant squabbles) because they flow from divergent views of human *possibilities* and from divergent views of the *uses of knowledge.* Here, then, I shall run the risk of oversimplification and outline the views of Marx, Durkheim, and Weber on the three issues presented in the early section that discussed the main themes of this essay.

Human Nature and Social Order

All of these three authors avoid the most extreme positions on the subject of human nature and social order; they view the individual as neither a wholly autonomous entity nor a mere leaf before social winds. Yet they do represent great differences. Marx views the individual as a being with a need for society, but not for *any* society. Man has a nature that will eventually assert and fulfill itself and will do so at the expense of a decadent social order. Man's nature, that is to say, is *elastic,* susceptible of bending but maintaining an essential spring of integrity. And the social order (for Marx, the "mode of production") is immensely powerful but not so powerful as to forestall its downfall.

Durkheim's men also have a need for society, but a need that is met less by substantive principles of justice and more by social ties and normative limits. For Durkheim, social restraint works not because of the actors' short-run calculations of prudence, but because of a long-term internalization of the restraints themselves. Durkheim's view, therefore, is not identical to that of Hobbes; Durkheim sees men's passions as subject not only to control and redirection but also to diminishing or enhancement, depending on the strength and clarity of the society's norms. For Durkheim, men are *malleable,* and where the limits of this malleability may lie is not clearly indicated. (In this respect, present-day Marxists who pessimistically explain the longevity of capitalism by adducing a fundamental corruption of humanity [Marcuse 1964, for example] are closer philosophically to Durkheim than to their acknowledged mentor.) Correspondingly, Durkheim's image of social order is robust, and even the threat of anomie is less a statement of the inherent possibility of civil war or of rebellion than a forewarning of mass demoralization and of an incapacity for effective collective action.

Weber's philosophical anthropology is closer to that of Hobbes, for Weber's man needs society in a less profound way than does Durkheim's. For Weber, men need the respect, more than the company, of their fellows, and their anxieties are concerned more with cosmic forces than with social ones. Weber's man comes closest to the bourgeois ideal of individual self-sufficiency; although Weber still sees man as a creature of reason in the service of passion, the Weberian contribution is to **124** see passions (or "interests") as a socially defined variable. Society shapes man by vectoring, so to speak, his drives. Social order at any given time, correspondingly, is a temporary resultant of such vectors, and there is no principle underlying a social equilibrium. For Weber, as for Hobbes, society is theoretically precarious.

To review these divergent philosophic anthropologies is to be reminded how oversimplified is the "man versus society" dualism, either as an analytical or an ethical problem. Especially since Rousseau, we have known that it is nonsense to speak of nonsocial human beings. The foregoing review demonstrates a few variations on that theme.

Attitude toward Conflict

In their attitudes toward conflict, Durkheim and Weber present a polar opposition, with Marx falling in between. Durkheim is a theorist of *harmony*, in whose theory there is no principle or structured source of conflict. There is an image of social disorganization bound up in the concept of anomie, but it is not one seen as inherent or as involving irreducible and legitimate differences of interest. The "anomic division of labor" is a state of transition between institutionalized states of mechanical and organic solidarity. "Anomic suicide," on the other hand, is a matter of greater or fewer numbers of individuals opting out of life. Neither idea involves intrinsic mechanisms of group conflict, and both ideas are images of something lacking in society, rather than images of something active in it. The effect of this harmonic stance is that Durkheim, as we have seen, is able to make an unambiguous argument for a sociologically informed ethical system.

Weber is Durkheim's opposite, a theorist of *tragedy*, who sees multiple sources of socially generated conflict and who sociologically endows the respective points of view with the legitimacy that they claim. The struggles of groups (especially of status groups and of structures of domination) for power, honor, wealth, and a style of life, in combination with the scarcity of the means provided by society and with the variability of the ends suggested by ideas, produce an ever-varying and never-ending series of social conflicts. Weber, unwilling as sociologist to assume the absolute superiority of any one point of view (with the exception of intellectual integrity), could in his professional role only observe and analyze these struggles; he could not decide between them.

Because of Marx's theory of history, his approach is not one of harmony or of tragedy, but one of *transcendence*. Conflicts in the present are (as in Weber's scheme) intractable, but (as in Durkheim's scheme) Marx is willing to take sides and to predict a harmonic future. Social conflict prior to the advent of socialism is both necessary and inherent. After that, such conflict is literally inconceivable, since classes, the source of Marxian conflict, will have been abolished by the historical process itself.

This dimension of harmony and tragedy thus differs from the opposition of "consensus" and "conflict" views. In Weber's theory, long periods of evident order do not gainsay the potentiality of conflict, and consensus on values that imply scarcity (such as social honor) may itself generate struggle. And Durkheim's readiness to prescribe against social disorganization does not proceed from a concept of structured divisions but, on the contrary, implies their absence. Marx's theory, most often thought of as the quintessential conflict theory, combines both elements.

Knowledge and Action

From Hobbes through Weber, all of our theorists have had strong ethical inclinations, and all affirm, in one way or another, the power that knowledge can bestow. Marx is the preeminent *critical* theorist; for whom his ideas could be powerful not only because they were true to the nature of human existence but also because they could be believed and acted upon by the masses. Most theorists no doubt hope that they will have some such impact, but Marx in particular made this concept of the public nature of social theory into a guiding principle of *praxis*, the integration of theory and action. Since his day, this integration has been perhaps the most difficult of his ideas to sustain, with Marxists often tilting heavily to one side or the other. Either they ignore the imperative of educating and thus implicitly assume that the historical process is automatic, or they forget that they too have to be educated and thus implicitly minimize experience in favor of preachments. Marx's faith in the power of profoundly valid ideas combined with his faith in historical progress to produce a theory that uniquely incorporates the theorist's activity as part of the social process.

Durkheim's ethical commitment and faith in knowledge were as strong as those of Marx, but his abjuration of a public role for theoretical activity means that his is a *technical* orientation to science. The sociologist as subject must temporarily retire from the world of action and must regard that world as only an object of investigation. Only when the social world has some day yielded up the secrets of its operation to concentrated empirical investigation and to clear thought will the social scientist as actor be able to reenter the scene. Then he will convince those who have the power to enact reform that certain marginal changes are desirable. Durkheim was himself a master of both deduction and induction, formulating and testing theories on the basis of empirical evidence. This is an achievement that is itself difficult to sustain as sociology remains split between "theoretical" and "empirical" camps. But Durkheim's style of empirical work goes on against a world taken as given, with the intent of testing, not enacting, a theory. And the best test, for the technical orientation, is that which is unobtrusive. Marx was determined to be obtrusive, and though Durkheim himself had a major impact on the French educational system, his theory of knowledge makes no room for his own worldly activity.

In these two divergent ways, Marx and Durkheim are interested in knowledge for the sake of social intervention. Weber's orientation is something else, something more purely intellectual, even though his political activities were as vigorous (if not as consistent) as those of Marx and Durkheim. Weber's *interpretative (verstehende)* knowledge can be applied to the technical determination of means to nonscientifically determined ends, but for Weber it is just as crucial for the illumination of our situation that it provides. His value commitments were expressed through a role other than that of social scientist, in a principled division of self that has been characterized as comparable to the mythical half-man, half-bull Minotaur [Gouldner 1964]. Because of his fact-value distinction (shared with Durkheim) and more critically his tragic orientation (in opposition to Durkheim), Weber insisted that the social scientist has no right to prescribe social norms and has every obligation to acknowledge that any social intervention undertaken by him proceeds only from individually held, existentially arbitrary values. Yet Weber knew the power that ideas could have, and he himself emphasized that the effects of an idea were often not the ones desired or anticipated by its creator. Thus, he implicitly agreed with Marx on the public nature of theory, but unlike Marx, he did not conceptualize his own worldly activity as a theorist within his theory of knowledge. In this regard, to be a pure, philosophical disciple of Weber is to be inconsistent as well as to invite virtually unbearable tensions. Present-day sociologists have mostly side-stepped the inconsistencies and eliminated the tensions by holding fast only to the ideal of nonevaluative science and by jettisoning the tragic sense that made the ideal necessary and the understanding of the refractive role of ideas that made it inconsistent. Without either Durkheim's faith in harmony or Marx's faith in history, Weber employed his immense learning both in the critical service of self-clarification and in the technical service of exogenous values.

The relation of knowledge to action is thus a far more complex matter than is suggested by the opposition of "value-free" versus "committed" social science. Conceptions of the nature of empirical "facts" as opposed to political "values" operate only within the context of a theorist's options on other philosophic presuppositions. Moreover, there is no clearly superior position to be found even among these very different theoretic giants. Marx's comprehensiveness and consistency are bought at the price of optimistic affirmations that few today (even those who claim to be followers) can easily regard as warranted. Durkheim's scientific orientation brings with it a provisional conservatism and a principled elitism of the sociologist over the public. Not only is Weber's role differentiation an ideal that ordinarily falls far short of realization, but it is also a position that verges closely on what Durkheim would call a sociologist's anomie, devoid of realistic aspirations. If we are to judge only by the volume of continuing controversy, a viable position is far beyond immediate resolution, and certainly beyond the scope of this conclusion.

Before closing this essay, I want to underscore that these concepts—elastic and malleable, harmonic and tragic, and critical and technical—are employed here by way of summarizing the fuller analyses that have gone before. I hope that they will prove useful but will not be substituted for the contextual understanding that they are intended to facilitate. First, none of the three major thinkers can be restricted to only one of these categories. Durkheim was aware that a wider public could read his sociological writings (and thus verged on the "critical" approach), and Marx wanted data unbiased by the philosophical leanings of the observers (a "technical" orientation). Second, the approach toward understanding theories that I have taken in this essay is similar to Weber's approach to social analysis; it is interpretation with the aid of ideal types. Such types—including types of domain assumptions—cannot be found in their purity in the real world, and more to the point, they are a means to understanding rather than the end of analysis. I do not intend to present another approach to the sociology of knowledge with these concepts as its variables. They will serve a real function if they help you to understand the work of these and other theorists; they will have failed if they are reified into a scheme for pigeonholing theorists. Third, to focus on what I claim to be deep-seated philosophic differences should not obscure the fact that Marx, Durkheim, and Weber were all attempting to construct powerful schemes to illuminate the social world. In principle they are thus engaged in a cumulative enterprise, in which it is possible for people of very different inclinations to learn and to borrow selectively from each other.

Domain Asssumptions as Theoretical Axioms

For sociology as a science, the most compelling reason to focus on domain assumptions is that they often provide the implicit link of continuity within a theory. In particular, they link concepts and the derivation of hypotheses. Durkheim and Weber especially, being methodologically astute and attempting to avoid philosophic disputation (Durkheim) and philosophic reification (Weber), did not fully explicate the philosophic underpinnings of their works. Each of them devoted more attention to the articulation of concepts and of epistemologies than to substantive axioms. In science, however, a concept is first of all a claim that the aspect of existence circumscribed by it makes a causal difference in the world [Stinchcombe 1968, pp. 38–40]. Marx's concept of exploitation is elaborated in his several definitions of the rate of surplus value, but he brings it up not simply to describe and damn the capitalist system but also to further his analysis of revolutionary process. The proletarians are not only the victims of capitalism, they are the agents of its transformation. Exploitation is one of the wellsprings of their insurgency.

Durkheim's concept of anomie has been defined and measured in myriad ways, but it is sociologically important only because of the image of man that gives it force. Tests of anomie theory are one means of grounding that philosophic anthropology, but the theory as a whole is pointless without the underlying axiom. The same can be said of Weber's concept of legitimacy, which he saw as important first of all because people want to feel it and second because the type of legitimacy that they claim has consequences for the organization of their action.

In this manner, domain assumptions quite literally give meaning to sociological concepts and hypotheses, and to be aware of them is to be reminded of the purpose of definitional and logical operations. Part of the function of the present essay is, therefore, to supplement the more formal analysis of theory that is undertaken by Neil Smelser in the following study.

Notes

1. This point should not be overstressed. Although some techniques have developed to the point where classical efforts are relatively obsolete, the classics still provide models of how quantitative reasoning and operational translation can be applied to bear closely on theoretical ideas. Paul Lazarsfeld and Hanan Selvin, two major figures in contemporary empirical research, have awarded high marks, respectively, to Weber and Durkheim on this score.

2. A number of recent texts in contemporary sociological theory bear witness to this lack of paradigm consensus within the discipline [Mullins 1973; Turner 1974; Zeitlin 1973].

3. No one would deny that Marx's influence has been far greater than that of Durkheim or Weber on the shaping of the modern world. What is at issue is his contribution to an ongoing sociological dialogue. Some writers (myself excluded) maintain that Marx is too much the prophet and that his thinking too crude or antiempirical for him to be directly relevant for contemporary sociologists. Others would exclude Marx because his thought is presumably too materialistic and deterministic for the modern mind. And still others would do so because it is presumably too soft and philosophical, even religious. Such divergence may indicate that the grounds for exclusion are unsound. In any event, I side with those who view Marx's contributions as essential parts of the sociological tradition.

4. In this essay this will be shown to hold only for the four major thinkers treated. The necessity of incorporating some concept of human nature into a social theory is not psychological reductionism because it is *not* claimed either that psychological assumptions are *variables* or that they are the *only* sociologically relevant variables.

5. Throughout this essay I have followed the practice of the theorists I discuss in using the term "man" and the pronoun "he" occasionally to indicate human beings of both sexes. First, it is convenient and it avoids awkward expressions. Second, most of our theorists wrote at a time when men were conceived to be the active members of society and women were conceived to be subsumed within the family unit or not taken into account at all. For some theorists, then, "man" and "the individual" actually refer to the family unit, as is the case for much of "bourgeois" social theory. Others (Durkheim, for example) thought of men and women as constitutionally different in sociologically relevant respects. Thus, Durkheim's analysis of "anomie" is especially concerned with the male of the species. Some contributions to the analysis of the position of women in society were made by those in, or closely connected to, the tradition under study here: Alexis de Tocqueville, John Stuart Mill, Friedrich Engels, and Marianne Weber. Analysis of those contributions, however, would be a separate topic.

6. In fact, the primary target of Locke's political philosophy was the theory of Robert Filmer, whose *Patriarcha* (1680) presented an argument for absolutism on traditionalistic grounds (on the basis of the inherited and divinely ordained rights of monarchy). Filmer's theory thus differed essentially from Hobbes' secular and modern theory, which was popular with neither liberals nor, understandably, those who wanted to uphold the mystique of kingship. Nonetheless, Locke was both influenced by and responsive to Hobbes' statement, and his theory is conventionally and usefully taken as an alternative to that of Hobbes.

7. The logic of Locke's rationale for the establishment of government leaves much to be desired, even if the effect of that logic is to defend a cherished liberal principle. Some authorities maintain that, in fact, Locke had in mind a society divided between property owners and those without property and that the establishment of government was a measure for the protection of the interests of the former against the latter (see MacPherson 1962). This might explain an otherwise puzzling step. As it is presented, however, Locke's theory pictures a relatively undifferentiated society of equals.

8. Another of Locke's philosophical contributions, his *Essay Concerning Human Understanding*, presents a critique of innate or natural human qualities. Yet his political theory is based on a theory of innate qualities. This is one of several problems in Locke.

9. Rousseau, who is among the most controversial of all of the writers we will consider, has been variously characterized as a rationalist or irrationalist, an individualist or collectivist, a moralist or an apostle of irresponsibility. His influence extends to thinkers as divergent as Kant, Hegel, Marx, and Durkheim. The brief treatment presented here follows only one of several possible lines of interpretation. For a judicious assessment, see Cassirer 1963.

10. Tocqueville wrote concisely and perceptively about a vast range of topics. My effort has been to extract a few guiding themes, but much of value and charm is sacrificed in the process. Fortunately, his own writings are the most accessible of all the authors considered.

11. Tocqueville wrote also about the black population in the United States, giving an early warning of what became known as the "American dilemma." Moreover, he was aware that women and children did not fully enjoy the rights of "democracy." At the same time, however, he emphasized that relations between the sexes and between parents and children were affected by the march of equality in the United States.

12. For an explanation of the term *status group*, see the later section on Max Weber's theory.

13. Recent discussions of Marx's theory have highlighted the importance of a series of notebooks Marx wrote in 1857 and 1858 but which were published in the original German only a half-century after his death and in English translation only in 1973. These notes, known as the *Grundrisse (Foundations of the Critique of Political Economy)*, were drawn upon by Marx in the writing of the *Critique of Political Economy* of 1859 and *Capital* and have been taken into account in preparing this essay. The Moscow edition of *Capital* has been used in this essay.

14. We recognize in this instance a distinct ideological difference between Rousseau, for whom the "natural" was preferred, and Marx, for whom "nature" was giving way to the conscious control of socialized humanity, a process Marx hoped to further.

15. This contrast between Durkheim and Marx is not absolute. At the end of his preface to *A Contribution to the Critique of Political Economy*, Marx, too, invoked the authority of science and conscientious research. He wanted at one time to dedicate *Capital* to that other misunderstood scientific pioneer, Charles Darwin. Engels' speech at Marx's funeral drew parallels between the work of the two thinkers. In my view, Marx's dominant tendency is to view knowledge of society and knowledge of nature as involving two different methodologies (see Lichtheim 1961; for a different view, see Barzun 1941).

16. A third form of suicide, "altruistic," is of lesser importance for modern society and probably also for Durkheim. See the accompanying essay, *Sociological Theory: A Contemporary View.*

17. This quotation expresses a conviction (similar to that of Burke) that Rousseau's project of abolishing all mediating bodies between man and community had regrettably been accomplished. Despite his concept of social facts, Durkheim was less ready than Marx or Weber to analyze such partial social bodies as estates and classes and more likely to concentrate on the direct relationship of man to society, as represented in the concept of the collective conscience. Evidently, he overestimated the extent to which modern society had become atomized.

18. An "ecological correlation" relates two or more population characteristics to each other within a given unit (for example, the percentage of Democrats and the percentage of blacks by voting precincts). If such correlations are intended to explain the behavior of *individuals*, the possibility of an "ecological fallacy" arises. Under some circumstances statistical methods may mitigate the severity of the problem. In other cases, not behavior of individuals, but behavior of groups is at issue and the "fallacy" is not encountered. For two different views of Durkheim's ecological methods, see Blau 1960 and Selvin 1965.

In regard to multiple causation, most contemporary sociologists would acknowledge that suicide and similar phenomena should be explained *both* "psychologically" and "sociologically." In concentrating his attention on refuting single-factor explanations, Durkheim obscures the possibility that the social fact of "anomie" may exacerbate the suicidal tendencies of psychically unstable individuals. The two forms of explanation are *not* mutually exclusive.

19. Just as Marx's analysis of the historically progressive role played by the bourgeoisie was not a moral apology for their exploitations, so also Durkheim's demonstration of the positive functions of crime was not a plea in defense of the criminal. Both arguments were intended to orient conscious social action (revolutionary or reformist) in appropriate directions and to discourage futile attempts to return to a phantom idyll of precapitalist existence or to establish a crime-free world.

20. In this discussion I use the terms "scholarly" and "scientific" as appropriate in the context. Weber's word was *"Wissenschaft,"* which, although often translated as "science," is more accurately (if awkwardly) translated as "scholarly discipline." Jurisprudence, history, literary criticism are all *Wissenschaften.*

21. "Weber uses a profusion of quotation marks as an alienating device to indicate that he employs familiar terms with reservations, with a new meaning, or in an ironic sense. This habit was the counterpoint to his concern with terminological precision and at times is a drawback" [Roth 1968, p. ci].

22. Ideal types, therefore, *are* subject to modification and criticism by empirical research. For a useful example, see Udy 1959.

23. Weber did not apply labels to his theoretical conceptions about the causal role of ideas. The term "refraction" appears in *The Religion of India* [1917] and is used here in preference to the term "canalize" as used by Parsons [1937]. Refraction suggests the contingent or switching function of ideas that was of great importance to Weber. See Warner 1970a.

24. Most literally, *Herrschaft* is "rulership." "Leadership" or "authority" are other possible translations. "Power" is too diffuse, being one's ability to get one's way. *Herrschaft* is a capacity to get others to carry out one's will. It refers, therefore, to a *relationship* between superordinate and subordinate. "Authority," however, carries the suggestion that the acquiescence of the subordinate is wholehearted and ethically motivated, which may not be the case for many of the phenomena analyzed by Weber under the rubric. See Weber 1922, pp. 53–54 and 61–62.

PART TWO

Sociological Theory
A Contemporary View

Neil J. Smelser
University of California, Berkeley

CHAPTER 8

A Simple Model of
Political Behavior

Introduction

The study of sociological theory is commonly divided into two types of academic courses: the "History of Sociological Thought" and "Systematic Sociological Theory." In the former we examine critically the ideas of the great historical schools—utilitarianism, Marxism, idealism, sociological positivism, and so on—as espoused by their most articulate representatives. We ask how these schools of thought influenced one another and thereby produced a complicated mosaic of intellectual history, and we often ask how these intellectual positions affect the ways we think and work in sociology today. In courses in systematic theory, we concern ourselves more with modern writers. We explore the logic of theory construction and address questions from the philosophy of science; we try to understand what is meant by formal terms such as "models," "hypotheses," and "derivation"; and we study various verbal and mathematical modes of theorizing.

From an educational standpoint there may be a sound rationale for this kind of division within sociological theory. From other standpoints, however, the division into the history of theory and systematic theory creates difficulties. First, it is difficult to draw any meaningful empirical line between the two aspects. Contemporary theory must be considered as a part of this history of theory, since history obviously extends right up to the present. Furthermore, I know of no point in time when the "history of theory" turns into "systematic theory." From Antiquity to the present, many thinkers have been systematic; and many modern writers who are called theorists can scarcely be considered systematic in their approach. And some theorists—Marx, Weber, Durkheim, to name the most prominent ones—are at once influential figures in the history of social thought and very systematic in their theoretical conceptualization and empirical scholarship.

I am going to try to cut through this troublesome distinction by adopting the following strategy. I shall assume that there is such an activity as *sociological theorizing* and that in pursuing this activity a thinker has to face, a definite number of *issues* or *problems*. For example, in creating a theory, a thinker must be as explicit as possible in identifying what he is trying to explain; he must avoid logical contradictions and absurdities; and he must try to ascertain whether his theoretical ideas square with empirical reality. I assume that these issues are, in some respects, timeless; that it is possible to ask whether and how Adam Smith faced them, just as it is possible to ask whether and how any modern theorist faces them. By asking the same set of questions of all thinkers, we can thereby *compare* various theories with one another, even though they differ greatly. Furthermore, by asking how well thinkers face the issues that arise in theorizing, we are in a position to *evaluate* their theories as intellectual and scientific products.

My objective in this essay is to develop a series of questions that pinpoint the issues that arise in sociological theorizing. These questions constitute a set of tools that can be used to describe, criticize, and evaluate any sociological work. I shall then apply these questions more or less systematically to the works of several very different sociological theorists—Emile Durkheim, Talcott Parsons, Karl Marx, and Robert Michels—in an effort to assess the strengths and weaknesses of the work of each. By this exercise I hope to sharpen the student's ability to evaluate critically not only the work of these and other theorists but also his own theoretical thinking.

To evaluate this theoretical aspect is to consider but one facet of any scholar's thought. There are other aspects as well—literary elegance, ideological potency, social utility, and so on—which can be assessed by applying canons other than those of theoretical adequacy. Furthermore, if and when we discover theoretical omissions or flaws in a body of thought, we are not necessarily scolding the scholar for not measuring up to his objectives. It may be that he did not intend to create a socio-logical theory in the full sense we now conceive it. Nevertheless, it is still possible and profitable to inquire in what ways his work does and does not qualify as sociological theory.

I shall begin by inventing a little theory of my own—a theory that attempts to explain the behavior of political parties during political cam-paigns. This theory has three virtues. First, it is simple, thereby permit-ting us to perceive the theoretical issues clearly. Second, it is hypo-thetical, thereby permitting us simply to posit—rather than establish empirically—the facts that it attempts to explain. Third, since the theory is simple and hypothetical, it will be possible to build into it a weakness that can be readily identified. After presenting the theory, I shall outline the general issues that arise in constructing even such a simple theory.

The largest part of this essay will be devoted to analyzing some of the work of four major theorists in the European and American socio-logical tradition. I have chosen the following theoretical topics:

Emile Durkheim's theory of suicide. It would be difficult to exclude *Suicide* from our sample, since it has been so long and so widely re-garded as a model of sociological research. In this book, Durkheim (1858–1917) took a fairly limited range of information—the suicide statis-tics available to him at the end of the nineteenth century—and erected a coherent and comprehensive theory of society to explain why some social groups are more prone to suicide than others. Written early in his career (1897), the book takes as its principal thesis the idea that the social cohesion (and lack of cohesion) of different groups is the main cause of variations in suicide rates among these groups. Durkheim's theory is remarkably complete in that it faces directly, if not always satisfactorily, all the issues that arise in sociological theorizing.

Talcott Parsons' theory of deviant behavior. Parsons (born in 1902), one of the most widely known contemporary sociological theorists, has devoted his intellectual career principally to creating a general theory of social action, with particular attention to social systems. While Durk-heim was one of the most important intellectual influences on Parsons, the latter's theory is more comprehensive than Durkheim's. Parsons has extended his theory to include the analysis of social stratification, the family, economic development and social evolution, behavior in small groups, development of personality, and he has focused on topics as specialized as psychosomatic disorders. From this wide range of investi-

gation (and especially from Parsons's writings in *The Social System*) I
shall extract some of the foundations of Parsons' social system theory
and consider the application of this theory to the explanation of the genesis and control of various kinds of deviant behavior (for example,
criminal activity).

Karl Marx's theory of capitalism. Marx (1818–1883) is best known, of
course, for having created the foundations of an ideology that has
spawned revolutionary movements and governments throughout the
world in the past century. In his own lifetime, Marx himself was certainly active as a revolutionary, but he devoted most of his energy to
creating a comprehensive philosophy of history and theory of economic
and social evolution. I shall focus on the first volume of *Das Kapital*—
the most mature statement of Marx's theory of capitalism. Here, too, I
shall cover only selected aspects of Marx's work, concentrating mainly
on the laws of development of capitalist society, exploitation, class conflict, and revolution.

Robert Michels' theory of political organization. Michels, a German-
Italian sociologist (1876–1936), was exposed to and much influenced by
Marxian thought early in his career. In his most important book, *Political Parties,* he undertook to analyze the internal structure of certain
left-wing political groups in Western European countries around the
turn of the century. His principal thesis was that these groups, despite
their commitment to ideals of equality, fail to maintain these ideals in
their own structures and instead develop rigid and permanent oligarchies. His formula of the "iron law of oligarchy" is an important sociological contribution. Since this formula strikes at the heart of both
democratic and socialist theory, it has attracted widespread attention.

These four authors differ from one another in a number of respects.
The publication dates of their books span almost a century—Marx's
Capital appeared first in 1867, Durkheim's *Suicide* in 1897, Michels'
Political Parties in 1911, and Parsons' *The Social System* in 1951. Their
works cover a large number of subfields of sociology—deviance, social
movements, economic sociology, political sociology, social stratification,
and social change. And, furthermore, the authors represent a diversity
of "schools of thought": Durkheim wrote *Suicide* at a time when he was
committed to the school of "sociological positivism"; Parsons' work is
most commonly assigned to the "structural-functionalist" tradition;
Marx, it can be safely argued, falls in the "Marxist" tradition; and while
Michels' work obviously shows the influence of Marx, he is often
grouped with Vilfredo Pareto, Gaetano Mosca, and others in the "Italian
irrationalist" school of thought.

Despite this diversity, we are going to ask identical questions of each of these authors. This approach is justified, I feel, because each theorist selected certain features of social life and attempted to develop an intellectual apparatus to explain them. Because they were engaged in the same general enterprise—however differently they went about it—a number of common intellectual issues arose for them. Let us now try to formulate these issues as simply as possible.

The Model

The notion of a model is based on a distinction commonly made in science: that between empirical phenomena (the "real" world) and the concepts that we use when we think about empirical phenomena (the "world of ideas").[1] A *model*, defined simply, is a construction of concepts, on the basis of which we make conditional predictions about what we expect to happen in the real world. A model may take the form of mathematical formulas, of words, or even of pictures. An example of a model is the economist's theory of a business cycle. He arranges the economic concepts of savings, investment, consumption, and so forth, into a set of relations with one another in such a way that they permit predictions about the fluctuations of the economy. A model, then, consists of a network of statements organized so that we expect certain phenomena to occur empirically under specified conditions.

Two general criteria permit us to decide whether a model is a good one. (1) Its logical consistency, which concerns the conceptual structure of the model itself. Are the concepts defined clearly? Are their relations to one another spelled out explicitly? Are these relations logically consistent? (2) Its empirical validity, which concerns whether the facts of the real world conform to the hypothetical outcome predicted by the model. If they do not, a further question arises: can the model be made workable by modification, or must it be rejected?

Keeping these two different types of criteria in mind, I shall now construct a simple, illustrative model of political behavior and then indicate a possible test for the model.

Let us suppose that we have noticed on an impressionistic basis that the strategies and tactics of political leaders and party officials seem to vary at different times in the electoral cycle. Big "scandals"—such as bribery in high government circles—seem to be "uncovered" as elections grow nearer but seldom immediately after the elections have occurred. Personal attacks on political leaders also seem to vary in their timing and intensity. In constructing the following model we shall attempt to explain this kind of variability in behavior.

To simplify matters we shall limit our concern to American politics and to presidential elections in particular. Furthermore, we shall assume a two-party system, ignoring the possibilities of third parties and coalitions. We shall assume further that what determines the content and timing of different political tactics is *not* the ideological character of the party—that is, whether it is Democrat or Republican—but whether the party is in or out of office. We shall consider that a party is "in" when it controls the Presidency and "out" when it does not. We shall also assume that political tactics are initiated by the "out" party in the following sequence:

Phase 1. In the period immediately after the unsuccessful election, the outs will quietly patch their wounds and *search* for new modes of attack. This is a period of political quiescence.

Phase 2. The outs will attack the *policies* of the ins and claim that they are not governing the way the outs would if they were in power. For example, the outs accuse the ins of using the wrong monetary and fiscal policies to curb inflation.

Phase 3. The outs charge the ins with *administrative incompetence.* They claim the policies of the ins as their own and maintain they could implement them better. During the Eisenhower years, for example, Democrats claimed that the Republicans were merely following out the lines of New Deal policy, and doing a poor job of it.

Phase 4. The outs accuse the ins of *breaking the rules* of the political game. Scandals are uncovered, corruption is charged, cries of "foul play" are heard.

Phase 5. In the final phase before the next election, the outs *personally attack* the leaders of the party in power.

Again for the purposes of simplicity, we shall not list a corresponding set of phases for the in party but shall assume that their behavior is directed toward defending themselves against the attacks of the outs.

This, then, is the model, or set of expectations that we have generated about the political behavior of parties between elections. Our hypotheses describe the expected sequence of tactics to be pursued by the opposition party. This sequence is the dependent variable, or what we want to explain. The independent or causal variable is the fact that the party is out of office, seeking to win the coming election.

Testing the Model

To determine how well the model works in the empirical world, we have to decide on a number of indicators for the major variables in the model. The indicator for "political tactics" will be all official statements made by the headquarters of each party and by all members of Congress over a four-year period, as reported in *The New York Times.*

Once we have chosen these indicators for the major concepts, we must devise an empirical test that will either validate or reject the hypotheses generated by the model. First, we have to decide on the time duration of the five phases. For purposes of testing we shall assume that the sequence begins immediately after a presidential election, that each of the five phases is approximately equal in length, and that each phase lasts for about nine months. This may be an arbitrary assumption, but it locates the phases in time; it provides an empirical specification for the otherwise indeterminate concept of "phase." Second, we have to choose specific electoral campaigns for a test. In this connection we shall choose two periods—from 1936 to 1940 (Roosevelt's second term) and from 1952 to 1956 (Eisenhower's first term). This is a small sample, but it does give us one "in" period for each of the two major parties.

The next step is to decide how to measure political tactics. For this we devise a set of code categories to classify the content of all political articles appearing in *The New York Times* in the relevant years (for example, "personal attacks," "attacks on policy"). Then we might have a panel of coders read and analyze the contents of the *Times;* if the coders agree among themselves, we shall assume that we have a reliable index for political tactics.

Finally, we must compare the hypotheses with results obtained from actual data. For our model, we see that in hypothetical figure 1 the total incidence of all tactics initiated by the outs rises during the first two phases, then levels off. In figure 2, policy attacks predominate in the second phase, and in figures 3, 4, and 5 the other kinds of tactics cluster in time as predicted. Assume also that we apply a statistical test to these distributions and that these tests reveal that the clusterings are greater than could be expected by chance alone. We would, therefore, conclude that this model is adequate to account for the tactics of political parties in the United States in national elections, at least for the two periods tested.

Generalizing the Model

Having developed this degree of confidence in our hypothetical model, let us now see what might be involved in generalizing it beyond the two electoral campaigns used in the test. Two strategies of generalization come to mind:

1. Simple empirical extension. The model could simply be extended to other national elections, state and municipal elections, elections in other countries, or elections in voluntary associations, such as labor unions, to see whether the same regularities would hold for the behavior

Figures 1–5. Clustering of political tactics over time, electoral periods 1936–1940 and 1952–1956.

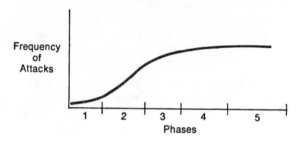

Figure 1. Total incidence of all types of tactics.

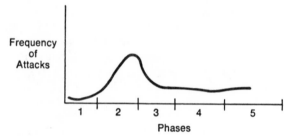

Figure 2. Incidence of attacks on policy.

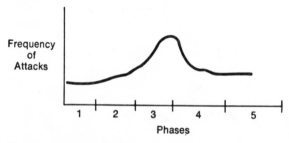

Figure 3. Incidence of attacks on administrative incompetence.

of aspirants to political office. We would, of course, have to modify some of the assumptions and some of the measures according to the different empirical settings.

2. Generalizing the major concepts and reapplying them to nonelectoral situations. Suppose we suspect that in generating this model we have uncovered a much more general and fundamental behavior pattern, one that applies to many situations other than electoral campaigns.

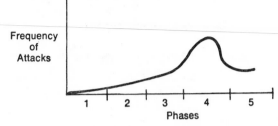

Figure 4. Incidence of attacks for breaking political rules.

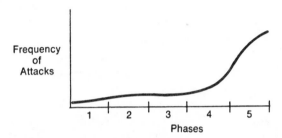

Figure 5. Incidence of personal attacks.

And suppose we suspect that, in general, people's purposive behavior will unfold in the following sequence:

Phase 1. Resources are assembled for action (this is a general category, of which the period of quiescence and the searching for new modes of attack in an electoral campaign is a special case).

Phase 2. There is a formulation of the *goals* of action (criticism of policies is a special case).

Phase 3. There is a preparation of the *means* to attain goals (attacks on administrative competence is a special case).

Phase 4. There is an assessment of the *norms* that regulate the attainment of goals (attacks for breaking the rules of the political game is a special case).

Having generalized the categories of our model in this way, we are now prepared to examine many new kinds of social settings—churches, business firms, families, and so on—and to *respecify* these general categories in terms appropriate for these new settings and to see whether people's purposive, problem-solving behavior unfolds accordingly.

Both methods of generalization—empirical extension and reformulation of concepts—involve the identification of new empirical settings; the first extends the existing variables to directly comparable situations, and the second generalizes the categories so that they can be applied to situations that would not otherwise be thought comparable with electoral campaigns.

What Is Wrong with the Model?

One possible defect in this model is that the data of electoral campaigns simply do not bear out the expectations generated by the model. But for the moment we shall disregard this possible flaw, because we have decided, for purposes of illustration, to use only fake data.

The main inadequacy of the model is that it does not *explain* anything. On the basis of the model we have no reason to know *why* the types of political tactics should have unfolded in the posited sequence. We appear simply to have announced this sequence out of the blue. Thus, the status of the "model" is only that of an empirical generalization about political behavior, and not an explanatory theory about it. True, we said that the fact that a party is out of power is an independent (causal) variable, but there is nothing about the quality of "outness" that would explain why the sequence of phases should unfold in a particular order. In short, the most that our model can be is accurately descriptive; it cannot explain.

How can the model be made genuinely explanatory? It must be supplemented by a more general set of postulates and assumptions that would reveal why one set of tactics should precede another in an electoral campaign. Or, to put it more formally, we should have a body of theoretical concepts and propositions from which the sequence could be *derived*. Suppose, for example, we develop the following body of assumptions. Assume that the several tactics can be ranked in terms of possible costs and gains to the out party. On these grounds it is relatively cheap for them to criticize the policies of the party in power, because such attacks, being mild, will not provoke counterattacks from the party in power and will not arouse much internal criticism of tactics within the out party. When, however, political leaders of the out party begin to attack the administrative competence, or even more, the political honesty and personal integrity of the party in power, they provoke retaliatory attacks from the party in power and they provoke criticisms within their own ranks that they are "hitting below the belt." So we have ranked the several tactics both by political potency (their power to discredit the party in power) and by their potential for generating political backlash and disunity within the opposition party.

Assume further that when prospective political gains are remote, opposition parties will balance gains and costs, but minimize risk. However, when the prospective gains are imminent—that is, when the elections get nearer—the opposition will continue to seek a balance between political gains and costs, but they will be prepared to risk greater losses because the prospects for their gains are nearer at hand. Thus they will be willing to engage in progressively riskier and more extreme tactics as the election approaches.

By thus setting several new variables—gains, costs, and risk—into relationship with one another and by postulating a few psychological principles about how political leaders will maximize their behavior with respect to these variables, we have created some *reasons to expect* that their tactics will unfold in the posited sequence. We have created some theoretical underpinnings for the model, and now we are able to explain why the political facts should be so, rather than merely that they are so. We have not made these underpinnings rigorous enough to say that we have derived the sequence, but we have approached the level of formal derivation. If we had formalized the principles of minimization of cost and maximization of gain into a series of postulates, had made risk-taking a function of time, and had expressed all these relations in mathematical formulas, we could have derived a sequence whereby low-cost, low-risk tactics give way to high-risk, high-gain tactics over time. This sequence could then have been tested empirically in the ways suggested in the original formulation of the model.

CHAPTER 9

Issues That Arise in Theorizing in the Social Sciences: A General Statement

From this simple model of political behavior we may now move to a more general statement of the kinds of issues that must be faced by the investigator who proposes to generate a sociological theory. In listing these issues in the order that I do, I do not mean to suggest that any one is more important than another, or that the investigator must face the issues in any particular order. Sooner or later he must face all of these issues if his theory is to be scientifically complete, and he must face them well if his theory is to be scientifically adequate.

Specifying a Problem Within a Range of Data

The first problem that arises in the construction of theoretical explanations is to identify what it is that we wish to explain. This problem has two aspects: identifying the range of data and specifying the kind of variation that is problematical.

1. In our political model we specified the tactics of political parties in electoral campaigns as that range of data toward which we wished to direct our attention. To identify this range of data is to say in general what our theory is about. In this case, we are concerned with a "theory of political tactics."

Sociological models and theories vary greatly in the ranges of data that they address. For example, the range of data may be *broad* or *narrow*. An example of a narrow range of data would be found in the theory of a trade cycle, which is designed to explain the temporal movement of several simple, aggregated economic indices—employment, income, and so on. An example of an extremely broad range of data is Talcott Parsons' "general theory of action," which is explicitly meant to apply to many different kinds of phenomena on many different analytic levels (see the section on "Parsons: A General Perspective" in the material that follows). Or again, the range of data may be *macroscopic* or *microscopic* in its focus. A model designed to predict the sequence of problem-solving activities in a small experimental group is relatively microscopic, whereas a theory designed to explain the nature and workings of industrial society—as in the case of Karl Marx—is macroscopic. Finally, the boundaries of the range of data may be *loosely* or *tightly* defined, depending on the care with which the investigator explicitly and systematically excludes phenomena that he is not interested in explaining. In our hypothetical model of political tactics, the range of data is relatively narrow because it deals with only a few of the many possible aspects of the political process; it is macroscopic because it deals with aggregated aspects of a political system rather than, for example, individual political decision making; and, finally, the boundaries of the data are rather tightly defined because we specified the precise empirical referents of the term "tactics."

A very common shortcoming of theories in the social sciences is that they do not define the relevant range of data with sufficient precision. If we are to think theoretically, it is not permissible to be vaguely interested in "political behavior" or in the "political process" in general. It is necessary to specify clearly what aspect or aspects of these general areas are to be addressed. Otherwise we are not prepared to say what phenomena interest us, and as a consequence we are not in a position to say precisely what our theory is about.

2. To specify a scientific problem, we select some observed or hypothetical line of variability within the range of data, and we pose the question, "Why does it vary in the way that it does?" In the case of our political model we failed to ask this question in a precise way; instead we asked only how political tactics seem to vary regularly over a period of

time. For this reason our theory was bound to be incomplete from the very outset.

Selecting Basic Concepts for Describing and Classifying the Data

Having chosen a range of data for interest and some line of variability for explanation, the theorist must next generate a number of concepts for subdividing the data into appropriate categories so that the data can be analyzed. For example, the range of data in our political model is the political tactics of parties. The basic concepts we brought to bear on these data are (1) the subclassification of political tactics into criticizing policy, criticizing administrative incompetence, launching personal attacks on political figures, and so on, and (2) the subclassification of political parties into "ins" and "outs." To apply basic concepts to the data in this way is to slice up the range of data into parts that are appropriate for our purposes of generating a theoretical explanation for the problem we have posed.[2] A different problem might require a different set of concepts to break down the range of data.

One point to remember about the basic concepts in any sociological theory is that they do not have to be identical with the common-sense concepts that we use to think about the empirical world. For example, the first thought that often comes to mind about a political party is "what it stands for" in terms of its ideology or "whom it stands for" in terms of its constituency. In our particular model, we chose as the most important determinant of political tactics an aspect of political parties that might not be so close to common sense—that is, whether the parties did or did not hold office. A second caution is that the basic concepts of a sociological theory do not exhaust reality. They do not identify every aspect of the phenomena that we wish to explain. The styles of literature and history are much richer and more nearly complete as descriptions of "reality," considered in its most general sense. In social-scientific theorizing, however, the object is to select from reality particular aspects that are important for explaining the course of specified events. Scientific description is, in short, always selective, never exhaustive of reality.

Finally, it is important to ask which concepts, of the multiplicity of those available, we shall use for purposes of sociological description. Part of the answer to this question lies in the nature of the problem originally posed. For instance, in our model, it seems appropriate to choose the concepts "in" and "out" to explain the tactics of the parties, because tactics are the means a political party uses to try to gain power—

that is, to become an "in" party. If we changed the problem, and if we attempted to account for the concrete symbols in the party's ideology then the in or out status of the party would probably not be as important; we might wish to turn, instead, to the kind of political constituency from which the party typically draws its support. Another part of the answer depends on how well the model as a whole works. If our model had turned out to be unverified empirically—that is, if political tactics did not fluctuate in the way we predicted in the model—it may very well have been the case that the choice of in and out status as the major determinant was not the best one and that other aspects of political life should have been selected.

Specifying Indices or Measures for the Basic Concepts

Thus far we have been dealing mainly with a world of ideas, that is, specifying basic concepts that seem to be important in addressing a specific given problem. In addition, however, we must decide which phenomena in the empirical world constitute indices of these concepts. How do we recognize a political tactic when we see one? How do we recognize an "in" party when we see one? We answered these questions in a relatively simple way. We decided that a given political tactic—for example, an accusation that the party in power was corrupt—had been used when a panel of coders decided that the contents of political reports in *The New York Times* revealed such an accusation. And we decided that a party would be deemed in or out depending on whether or not it controlled the Presidency. These simple answers are certainly open to criticism. Nevertheless, it remains one of the central canons of theorizing that empirical indicators—or "operational definitions"—for the basic constructs must be sought. A theory is stronger or weaker according to how adequately this operation is performed.

Organizing the Basic Concepts Logically

To constitute a theory, the basic concepts we have chosen must be more than a simple list. They must be organized logically in relation to one another. Some may be represented as causes, others as effects; some may be represented as logical opposites to others; some may be represented as lying along a continuum. Once these concepts are so organized, a theory may be said to have a *logical structure*. In other words, the concepts may be said to constitute a *theoretical system*. Let me illustrate a few of the issues that arise in considering the logical structure of a theory.

The Problem of Logical Exhaustiveness

One of the canons that should be observed in constructing a theory is that the basic concepts should cover the entire range of data that are relevant to the scientific problem at hand. The encircled area in figure 6 represents the range of data, and the subdivisions represent concepts by which each datum is to be classified. The rule of logical exhaustiveness says that each datum should be classifiable in terms of the basic concepts. In our political model, for example, it is essential that the range of tactics available to a political party be exhausted by the classification scheme we have devised—attacks on policy, criticisms of administrative competence, and so on (indicated in the figure by the letters *a* through *e*). If this range is not exhaustive, we are likely to be confronted with many items of data on political tactics, the theoretical significance of which we cannot assess.

The Problem of Residual Categories

Sometimes the range of data is more complex than that presented in our theory, and while we acknowledge that some items of data fall within the basic range to be studied, we do not wish to treat these items as important. These items of data are assigned to a "residual category" represented as *x*, or non-*abcde*, in figure 6. An example can be provided

Figure 6. The range of data subdivided by basic concepts.

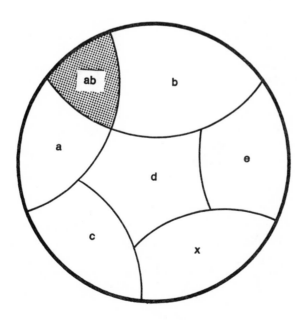

from our political model. In considering the in and out parties we restricted our attention to the two major parties—Republicans and Democrats. The world of political parties is, however, much more complicated than this. In every election there are a number of minor parties—for example, Vegetarian, Dixiecrat, or Peace and Freedom—that nominate candidates for the Presidency and that participate in the electoral campaign. These groups are clearly parties and fall into the range of data subsumed under the general heading "political parties." But for the purposes of our analysis we do not wish to consider them as important, so we create a miscellaneous, or residual, category of "other parties," and we consider this category to be nonproblematic for purposes of our model.

The use of residual categories sometimes presents thorny problems. Suppose that, in applying our model, we come across the campaigns of 1912 and 1968 in which the third party, headed by Theodore Roosevelt and George Wallace, respectively, played a significant role in the electoral process. Suppose further that our model of the sequence of tactics "fit" the data of the electoral campaign of 1968 but did not fit the data of the campaign of 1912. As investigators, we would be inclined to say that the campaign of 1912 turned out differently because of the presence of such a powerful third party. Such an interpretation certainly sounds plausible. But in making it, we are creating certain theoretical problems for ourselves. For one thing, we had already decided that "other parties" were theoretically residual—that is, did not play a role in our model—but we are now allowing them to be part of the theory. For another, we appealed to the importance of the third party *selectively*; that is, we pointed to its importance in 1912, when the data did not come out as predicted, but we ignored it for 1968, when it was as conspicuous in the campaign but did not appear to affect the basic sequence predicted by the model.

The selective use of residual categories is, in short, a way of having our cake and eating it too. On the one hand, we created a simplified and theoretically rigorous model of political tactics; on the other hand, we equipped it with a residual category which we can ignore when we choose and use as an explanation when we choose. It is certainly legitimate to treat "other parties" as an important variable in our theory, if we wish to do so; but if we do, it is necessary to incorporate the concept into the theoretical structure as logically and consistently as we did the other concepts, rather than rely on it in an ad hoc way. An important task for the theorist is to carve clearly defined concepts out of residual concepts and to integrate them logically into his theory [Parsons 1937, p. 18].

The Problem of Mutual Exclusiveness

The canon of mutual exclusiveness says that any item of data should be unequivocally classifiable as an instance of one of the basic concepts. Problems arise when items fall into more than one category—as in the shaded area *ab* in figure 6—because we do not know what kind of theoretical significance to assign them. Suppose, for instance, that in our political model, we made it a condition that, in order to be "in," a party had to control both the Presidency and the Congress. In the period 1956–1960 (Eisenhower's second term as President), however, the Republicans controlled the Presidency and the Democrats the Congress. Applying our criterion, we would have to say that neither party was in power—an absurd result in terms of our model (though perhaps not absurd from other standpoints). Or suppose that the condition for being "in" is that the party must control *either* the Presidency *or* Congress. Between 1956 and 1960 both parties would have been classified as in power, which is also absurd in terms of the model (though again, perhaps not absurd in all senses). Whatever its other merits, our original criterion—control of the Presidency alone—does have the advantage of preventing such absurdities from arising. The conclusion is that the basic concepts of a theory should not overlap logically. If a questionable instance of classification arises, there should be unambiguous rules for determining how the instance should be classified.

The Problem of Causal Relations

Perhaps most important, it is essential for the theorist to specify which of his concepts stand for causes and which for effects. (Effects are commonly called *dependent variables*, causes are called *independent variables*.) This distinction, above all, is what gives a theory its determinacy and permits the theorist to generate propositions from the theory. In our political model we were rather precise about identifying the effects— that is, the different kinds of political tactics. But we were less precise in identifying the causes that might determine the variation in the effects. The original model referred generally to the condition of being "out" as determining the pattern of tactics, but the exact causal mechanism was left rather vague. We attempted to remedy this flaw in the subsequent discussion by introducing some psychological generalizations regarding costs, gains, and risks of various political tactics. These generalizations made our model more determinate theoretically, and they permitted us to specify more nearly why the sequence should unfold in a definite pattern.

When we identify a cause, we must also identify the kind of cause that it is. Some causes may be represented as necessary conditions;

others as triggering mechanisms; others as inhibitors; and still others as intervening between a more remote cause and the ultimate effect. To specify the different kinds of causes and to set them into definite relations with one another gives a theory its causal structure.

156

The Problem of "Parameters" or "Givens"

Any theory must necessarily be selective with respect to both effects and causes. It cannot purport to explain everything in the world, and it cannot incorporate every conceivable cause of the phenomena to be explained. To attempt to do either would lead to an amorphous and unwieldy collection of thousands of variables and relations.

Because a theory selects out certain causes for emphasis, it necessarily makes certain assumptions about what are *not* to be regarded as causes. Consider our model of political tactics. One of the basic unspoken assumptions of that model is that political life takes place in a legal and constitutional structure, within which elections proceed more or less peacefully and by definite procedures. Furthermore, if a constitutional crisis should arise—a constitutional crisis that would jeopardize the entire electoral process—the crisis would certainly have to be reckoned with as a cause that would influence political tactics. But, for purposes of our model, we assumed that there would be no such crisis; we assumed the continuing existence of the constitutional and legal procedures that regulate the electoral process. In short, we assumed them to be "given." This assumption that certain potential causes are not operative—that is, that they are "constant" or "given"—is often described as specifying the *parameters* of the theory. Parameters are causes that are known to be potentially important if they vary, but that are assumed, for purposes of constructing a theory, not to vary. As we shall see, we often learn as much about a theory by examining its parameters as we do by examining its operative causes.

Deriving Propositions

Once the logical structure of a theory has been specified, it is possible to generate propositions about the phenomena to be explained by drawing out the logical implications of this structure. This operation is known as *derivation*. Derivation works in the following way: if we make certain assumptions about the parameters and other assumptions about the operative causes and if we organize these causes in a certain way, it follows that the effects will unfold in a certain way. As you will remember, our original model of political tactics lacked a very definite logical structure, so that we were unable to derive propositions. Our propositions seemed to be drawn out of thin air. It helped the model—from the standpoint of being able to derive propositions—to supplement it with postulates regarding cost, gain, and risk, because these postulates gave us reasons to predict that the political tactics would unfold in a definite pattern.

Making the Propositions Testable

It is not enough to generate propositions from theory. It is necessary to return once again to the world of facts and to devise ways of discovering whether our propositions are empirically valid. In our own model, we had to translate the hypothetical sequence of tactics into empirical terms. We had to say how long, in chronological time, a "phase" lasted; we had to specify rules by which changes in tactics could be measured over time; and we had to employ statistical tests to make sure that the changes in the tactics we uncovered could not have happened by chance alone.

One of the most familiar ways of making propositions testable in science is to conduct an experiment. The essence of an experiment is to devise a situation in which all the parameters are held constant, then systematically to vary the causes that are suspected to be operative, in an effort to create the predicted effect. If that effect is created, the proposition is judged to be conditionally verified. Unfortunately, much of the empirical data that are available to social scientists are not experimental data. Ethical and practical considerations prohibit experimenting with some aspects of life; for example, it is not possible to create experimentally a genuine panic in which people might be hurt or killed. In addition, much of the data available to social scientists are in the form of historical records, which were recorded, not for purposes of scientific research, but for other purposes. For this reason, in testing propositions, the social scientist has to rely on methods that only approximate the experimental method. For example, he has to hold potential causes constant by means of statistical manipulation or by means of comparative illustration. As we shall see, the theorists we have chosen for examination vary greatly in the manner in which they attempt to make their general propositions empirically testable.

Testing the Propositions

The final question to be asked of a theory is whether the specified empirical data conform to the propositions generated from the conceptual structure of the theory. If they conform—as we made our data do in the model of political tactics—the appropriate scientific strategy is to accept tentatively the proposition as valid and to attempt to extend the theory empirically and conceptually.

Suppose, however, that the data do not conform to theoretical expectations. In this case a number of strategies are available to us. We may reexamine the data to make sure that we have measured and coded them properly. We may invent new indices for the theory and attempt to test it on them. We may change our rules for locating operational definitions for the basic concepts. Or, alternatively, we may decide that the data are perfectly adequate, reliable, and valid, but that the theory is inadequate. We may suspect that we have identified the wrong variables as causes and that we should create a new model with different fundamental causes. Or it may be that we had created an inappropriate causal structure and that it is necessary to reconceptualize the nature of the causal relations in the theory. Finally, it may be that certain of our parametric assumptions were erroneous and that it is necessary to modify some of these. One way of putting the matter is this: there is only one way for a theory to be right—if and only if all the issues involved in generating and testing it have been effectively met—but there are many ways in which a theory can be wrong.

One bad habit that frequently tempts theorists when the data do not conform to theoretical expectations is to fall back on residual categories to account for apparent exceptions. In testing the model of political tactics, for example, suppose that I found that in the 1936–1940 electoral period personal attacks on the President ran very high throughout all four years of the electoral campaign. This would appear to disconfirm our prediction that these attacks would cluster just before the election. Faced with this discrepancy, suppose that I had attempted to account for it by asserting that President Roosevelt's personality was such that it provoked especially strong reactions. To fall back on this new variable—"the President's personality"—as an explanation is to resort to a factor that was not originally incorporated in the theory. To do this, furthermore, is to fail to confront the fact that the theory, as originally formulated, did not fit the data. It is a way of letting a theory bend without forcing it to break. By relying on residual categories in this way, the theorist is likely to give the impression that the theory simultaneously covers a great range of data *and* has a rigorous logical structure. But in reality this habit involves a sacrifice of logical structure, because the special, or residual, category involved has not been incorporated into the logical structure in the first place. To put it another way, a theory should be able to be falsified; but if it is surrounded by a number of residual categories which can be called upon whenever the theory appears to be embarrassed by data that do not fit it, the theory cannot be proved wrong. I mention this habit in particular because we shall find it practiced in various ways by the several theorists whose work we are going to examine.

Concluding Remarks

Many controversies have arisen in the history of philosophy and in the history of science around the issue of deduction versus induction as the proper way to generate knowledge. The preceding discussion of the issues that must be faced in theorizing suggests that some aspects of these controversies have not been fruitful. To my mind, the operations of moving from data to theories (induction) and from theories to data (deduction) are not competitors in the race for knowledge. The generation of scientific knowledge involves a constant interplay between both types of operations—a constant process of creating propositions from concepts and theories, and a constant process of rejecting, confirming, or modifying these propositions in the light of empirical data. It is possible to err in moving from theoretical concepts to empirical research, and it is possible to err in moving back again. But both activities are necessary for the generation of scientific explanations.

Having set forth the issues that are faced in the generation of theory, and having specified some of the desiderata for facing these issues, we are now prepared to turn to the work of several social theorists. We shall use the foregoing discussion as a scaffolding, as a framework for summarizing, criticizing, and in some cases reformulating the works of these theorists. I have chosen theorists who thought, at least implicitly, about many of these issues. Not all of them faced all the issues; and they did not face them equally well. Thus the several theories differ in the degree of their theoretical adequacy. By examining major sociological theories in this framework, we shall not only arrive at a notion of the adequacy of each, but also, it is hoped, sharpen our critical faculties in approaching other theories in the social sciences.

CHAPTER 10

Emile Durkheim's
Theory of Suicide

Durkheim's purposes in undertaking his classic work on *Suicide* [1897] were many. He was attempting to refute psychological, biological, and physical theories of social phenomena and to insist on the importance of distinctively social explanations for social facts, such as suicide rates.[3] And in insisting on the importance of social cohesion as an important determinant in social life (which he did in *Suicide* as well as in other works), he assumed a polemic position contrary to other sociological theories, such as the individualistic theory of Herbert Spencer and the materialistic theory of Karl Marx.[4] In this essay, however, we shall not consider these kinds of purposes in any detail, important though they may be; rather, we shall treat Durkheim's work as an effort to create a sociological theory of suicide and examine how he faced the problems that confronted him in this enterprise.

A Selective Summary of Durkheim's Theory

The Range of Data and the Problem

Put most simply, Durkheim was interested in accounting for variations in rates of suicide among different social groups, as these variations were revealed in the statistics available in the 1890s. Most of these statistics came from European countries, but he did have limited information on other societies as well. In one respect Durkheim's starting point was an advantageous one. His range of data was fairly well delimited, and the statistics, however unreliable they might have been, were available in the official records of many countries.

In identifying this problem, Durkheim insisted that he was not concerned with suicide as an individual phenomenon. Rather, he was concerned with differences in the rates of suicide—why the proportion of suicides among businessmen was higher than the proportion of suicides among workers, for example. Furthermore, in his search for causes of suicide, he emphasized the impact of social forces. While acknowledging a wide range of causes, he proposed not to concern himself with "the individual as such, his motives and his ideas," but to concentrate on the influences of "various social environments," such as religious congregations, family units, political societies, and occupational groups [p. 151].[5]

Durkheim was also careful to define his topic of interest clearly and to set it off from other, related phenomena. He defined suicide as "all cases of death resulting directly or indirectly from a positive or negative act of the victim himself which he knows will produce this result" [p. 44]. On the basis of this definition he excluded the suicides of animals because, he felt they could not know the consequences of their actions, and the suicides of the victims of hallucination. The definition also permitted him to draw at least an approximate line between suicide in its full sense and the deaths of alcoholics, of daredevils, and of scholars who work themselves to death. Durkheim felt it important to define suicide in this way, and not in terms of motives or ends, which were difficult to discover and assess.[6]

Basic Concepts

Before recounting Durkheim's social explanation of suicide, it is necessary to analyze in more detail his conception of suicide and its causes as *social facts*. He mobilized a variety of arguments to demonstrate the value of this conception.

First, arguing by elimination, he attempted to show that explanations relying on factors other than the social one are inadequate. For example, he ruled out individual insanity as a cause of suicides. In doing so, he used both definitional and empirical arguments. On definitional grounds he argued that there are many instances of types of suicide that do not display the same mental characteristics that insanity does [pp. 62–67]. On empirical grounds he sought to discredit in two different ways the possibility of a connection between the rates of suicide and those of insanity. First, more women than men are found among the populations of insane asylums, but in the society at large, more men than women are found to commit suicide. For this reason insanity appears not to be associated with suicide [pp. 71–72]. Second, insanity rates seem to reach a peak about age 35, they remain constant to about age 60, and they decline thereafter. But suicide "increases regularly from childhood to the most advanced old age" [p. 73], suggesting again that insanity is an unlikely cause of suicide.[7]

With respect to alcoholism as a possible cause, Durkheim compared maps of France, one showing the distribution of alcoholism and the other showing the distribution of suicide rates. Noting that the two phenomena clustered in very different ways, he concluded that alcoholism could not be regarded as an adequate explanation of suicide [pp. 77–78]. Using similar types of arguments, he attempted to push aside every nonsocial cause he could find—heredity, weather, race, and so forth—thus creating a presumption in favor of his preferred cause, the social factor.

To argue by elimination only, however, has inherent limitations, for no matter how effectively nonsocial causes were refuted, the positive importance of the social factor is not yet established by direct evidence. Durkheim was aware of this point, and he devoted most of his energy to a positive demonstration of the importance of social determinants. Initially, he developed a number of general arguments. He noted, for example, that suicide rates for any given society are almost invariant from year to year. He also noted that total mortality rates in a society fluctuate more than suicide rates from year to year. To Durkheim these two observations suggested that some general *social* feature of the society was responsible for the remarkable stability of suicide rates. And by comparing the large and persistent differences among countries such as Italy (low suicide rate) and Denmark (high suicide rate), he concluded that a definite suicide rate is "peculiar to each social group where it can be considered as a characteristic index" [p. 50]. On the basis of such arguments, Durkheim insisted that a new order of fact, a social fact, had to be brought to bear on our understanding of differences in suicide rates. This type of fact possesses a reality of its own, and its own distinctive characteristics.

So much for Durkheim's general case. But to insist on the *general* importance of the social factor does not generate very specific propositions about variations in suicide rates. To do this, Durkheim identified social cohesion as an especially salient factor in the etiology of suicide. As employed by Durkheim, the notion of cohesion refers to the ways in which individuals are attached to the collective values of the community and to the ways in which individual needs and desires are regulated by normative expectations.

Durkheim identified four types of social cohesion that are most relevant to the understanding of the causes of suicide:

1. Egoism. Normally, egoism refers to the gratification of self-interest, or selfishness. Durkheim preferred to give the term a primarily social meaning, though he did retain a thread of its psychological meaning. For him, *egoism* refers to the social condition in which individual activities take precedence over collective allegiances and obligations. Under this condition men become detached from the bonds of collective life and become the masters of their own destinies.

2. Altruism. As the opposite of egoism *altruism* refers to the condition in which man is insufficiently individuated from collective obligations and, as a result, has little control over his destiny. Altruism encompasses phenomena such as loyalty, honor, commitment, and self-sacrifice for the greater social good.

3. Anomie. The literal meaning of *anomie* is "rulelessness" or "without regulation." Normally, Durkheim argued, society plays an important regulative role in the life of an individual. Through normative systems of justice, equity, and distribution, the society controls and regulates his needs and desires. Under conditions of social stability, moreover, people's life experiences—their pleasures, their disappointments—conform more or less to the expectations established by the regulative norms of society. Under conditions of sudden crisis or drastic social change, however, individuals' life experiences diverge sharply from what the norms governing their lives have led them to expect, and this makes for a discontinuity in social regulation. The result is anomie.

4. Fatalism. Durkheim included the fourth type of suicide mainly for the sake of completeness and did not develop it. As the opposite of anomie, *fatalism* refers to excessive normative regulation and occurs when "futures [are] pitilessly blocked and passions violently choked by oppressive discipline" [p. 276].

Indices for the Basic Concepts

With respect to identifying his dependent variable—the rate of suicide —Durkheim referred to official statistics and to various impressionistic accounts of suicide for different societies. For several reasons such data are quite unreliable,[8] so the conclusions that Durkheim drew from them must be tempered with appropriate skepticism. Nevertheless, these were the only statistics available to Durkheim, and they were certainly better than no data at all.

With respect to empirical instances of the major types of social integration, Durkheim proceeded as follows:

1. Egoism. Durkheim found illustrations of egoistic integration in the religious, the familial, and the political spheres. Protestantism is an example of an egoistic religion, because of its antiauthoritarianism, its emphasis on the individual's direct relation to God, and its tradition of free inquiry—all of which detach men from their social environment. By contrast, Catholicism is less egoistic, because it has more common beliefs, a more doctrinaire approach, and a more authoritarian tradition [pp. 157–159]. Finally, Judaism ranks lowest on egoism, since it, "like all early religions, consists basically of a body of practices minutely governing all the details of life and leaving little free room to individual judgment" [p. 160].

For the familial sphere, Durkheim maintained that unmarried and widowed persons are more detached from domestic society than married persons, and that persons in small families are relatively more detached than those in large families.

Finally, for the political sphere, Durkheim argued that egoism decreases during episodes of political turmoil, such as war and revolutionary crisis:

Great social disturbances and great popular wars rouse collective sentiments, stimulate partisan spirit and patriotism, political and national faith, alike, and concentrating activity toward a single end, at least temporarily cause a stronger integration of society. . . . As they force men to close ranks and confront the common danger, the individual thinks less of himself and more of the common cause [p. 208].

2. Altruism. Most of Durkheim's illustrations of altruism were taken from travelers' and ethnographers' accounts of certain primitive societies, in which the burdens of custom were excessive, and from the histories of other societies noted for their high degree of social integration, such as classical Japan and classical India. But his most consistent and most thorough illustrations of altruism were found in the military systems, particularly those organized around values of honor, loyalty, and obedience.

3. Anomie. The illustrations of anomie came mainly from the economic and familial spheres. One feature of economic life that is particularly conducive to anomie is the business crisis. Even those of us who do not personally remember the Great Crash of 1929 still conjure up in

our minds the image of the businessman who took his life after being wiped out financially. For Durkheim, however, the business crash is anomic, not because the individual loses his fortune, but because he becomes disoriented: what he has come to expect is no longer available to him.

By the same token, Durkheim argued that a business boom creates a condition of anomie, because, like the crash, it upsets the relationship between man's expectations and his life experiences. It stimulates insatiable desires which remain unquenched even though a person's fortunes come to outstrip his expectations. Both crises of depression and crises of prosperity, in short, are "disturbances of the collective order" [p. 246]. Human activity is released from all restraint, and "nothing in the world can enjoy such a privilege" [p. 252].

In the familial sphere Durkheim considered divorce to be a prime example of anomie. Viewing marriage as "a regulation of sexual relations, including not merely the physical instincts which this intercourse involves but the feelings of every sort gradually engrafted by civilization on the foundation of physical desire" [p. 270], he regarded divorce as weakening this kind of regulation and, consequently, releasing unmanageable passions and desires.

4. Fatalism. Here Durkheim's illustrations are sparse. Perhaps the clearest example of fatalism would be the social condition of the slave, or of anyone else who lives under excessive and despotic rules, "against which there is no appeal" [p. 276].

Logical Relations Among the Basic Concepts

By now it is clear that Durkheim was not dealing with a simple, unorganized list of causes and effects in relation to suicide. The several types of cohesion (egoism, altruism, anomie, fatalism) are independent variables, the suicide rate dependent. Furthermore, the four types constitute two sets of paired opposites. Egoism is a condition of too great detachment of the individual from the community, altruism a condition of too little detachment; anomie is a condition of too little regulation by normative expectations, fatalism a condition of too great regulation. Such is the basic structure of Durkheim's theoretical system.

A number of additional variables—sometimes only implicit—arise when we consider the mechanisms that link the various types of cohesion with suicide. With respect to altruistic suicide, for example, suicide occurs as a result of conformity to group values:

Either death [has] to be imposed by society as a duty, or some question of honor [is] involved, or at least some disagreeable occurrence [has] to lower the value of life in the victim's eyes . . . it even happens that the individual kills himself purely for the joy of sacrifice, because, even with no particular reason, renunciation in itself is considered praiseworthy [p. 223].

With respect to egoistic religious suicide, however, another type of mechanism is involved. The individual is not directly encouraged to take his life. Indeed, as Durkheim noted, both Protestantism and Catholicism have strong taboos against suicide [p. 157]. The essential difference is that Protestantism encourages free inquiry, thus throwing the individual more on his own resources and protecting him less by group solidarity; by contrast, Catholicism puts less emphasis on individual conscience, encouraging, for example, the expiation of guilt through the participation of the community in the ritual of confession [pp. 157–158]. The mechanism whereby Protestantism encourages suicide is, then, a by-product, not a direct result, of conformity with the specific values of the Protestant religion.

The other types of egoistic suicide involve still other mechanisms. Speaking of the importance of large family size as a deterrent to suicide, Durkheim seemed to think that the "social density" as such was an important integrative mechanism:

Where collective sentiments are strong, it is because the force with which they affect each individual conscience is echoed in all the others, and reciprocally. The intensity they attain therefore depends on the number of consciences which react to them in common. For the same reason, the larger the crowd, the more capable of violence the passions vented by it. Consequently, in a family of small numbers, common sentiments and memories cannot be very intense; for there are not enough consciences in which they can be represented and reenforced by sharing them [p. 202].

In connection with egoism in the political sphere, Durkheim stressed the importance of a common foe in building solidarity and high morale, thus protecting the individual against the possibility of self-destruction. And finally, with respect to anomic suicide, he felt that lack of regulation had the psychological effect of confusing and disorienting the individual, thus making him more vulnerable to all kinds of passions and more prone to self-destruction.

Evidently, then, Durkheim acknowledged, sometimes explicitly and sometimes implicitly, that the social determinants of suicide excite psychological forces in the individual, which in turn manifest themselves in the act of suicide. At one point in his analysis he argued that the social factors do not act in the same way on all individuals: "Each victim of suicide gives his act a personal stamp which expresses his temperament, the special conditions in which he is involved, and which, consequently, cannot be explained by the social and general causes of the phenomenon" [p. 277–278]. Nevertheless, Durkheim was convinced that the social causes made a "collective mark" on individuals. The typical individual expression of the social state of egoism, for example, is a "loathness to act" and a "melancholy detachment." Egoistic suicides also have an "intellectual and meditative nature" because of the "high development of knowledge and reflective intelligence" in egoistic persons [278–283].

168

Thus, even though Durkheim insisted on constructing a relatively simple theoretical system of social variables to explain the suicide rate, he actually supplemented this by introducing a number of psychological assumptions that make the link between the different forms of cohesion and the social incidence of suicide intelligible. These psychological assumptions are, moreover, in the nature of "residual categories" because Durkheim did not incorporate them systematically into his theory.

Generation of Hypotheses

Our discussion of the logical structure of Durkheim's theoretical scheme has already revealed his master hypothesis: extremes of social cohesion—too much and too little—cause high suicide rates. Since he specified two dimensions of cohesion—integration and regulation—this master hypothesis breaks down into four versions. With respect to integration, egoism and altruism both make for high suicide rates, with a lower rate falling between the two extremes, where individual interests and collective interests are more or less evenly balanced. Figure 7 represents these relationships graphically. A similar set of hypotheses is generated for the dimension of regulation, with anomie and fatalism as the extremes that cause high suicide rates and with intermediate conditions making for lower rates.

Figure 7. Egoism, altruism, and the suicide rate.

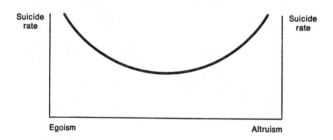

Making the Hypotheses Testable

If the relations among a number of theoretical variables have been specified, and if a number of empirical instances of these variables have been identified, the problem of testing the emergent hypotheses is a fairly straightforward matter. If the hypotheses are to be confirmed, Protestants should have higher rates of suicide than Catholics, and Catholics higher than Jews. Single persons should be more prone to suicide than married persons, and married persons without children more prone to suicide than married persons with children. The suicide rate should drop during revolutionary and wartime crises and rise as these crises come to a close. Military personnel should commit suicide at a higher rate than civilians. Economic crises of all sorts should show a rise in the suicide rate. Divorced persons should show higher suicide rates than those in other marital categories. And so on down the line for the various forms of social cohesion.

Testing the Hypotheses

To test the relations that emerge from his theory, Durkheim assembled the available data and attempted to demonstrate that the various social groupings and social categories he identified showed the kinds of differences in suicide rates that are predicted by the theory. Table 1, showing consistent differences between Protestants and Catholics, is a typical statistical presentation used by Durkheim. On the face of it, most of

Table 1. Suicides in different countries per million by religious persuasion.

		Protestants	*Catholics*
Austria	1852–1859	79.5	51.3
Prussia	1849–1855	159.9	49.6
Prussia	1869–1872	187.0	69.0
Prussia	1890	240.0	100.0
Baden	1852–1862	139.0	117.0
Baden	1870–1874	171.0	136.7
Baden	1878–1888	242.0	170.0
Bavaria	1844–1856	135.4	49.1
Bavaria	1884–1891	224.0	94.0
Wurttemberg	1846–1860	113.5	77.9
Wurttemberg	1873–1876	190.0	120.0
Wurttemberg	1881–1890	170.0	119.0

SOURCE: Adapted from Table XVII [Durkheim 1897, p. 154].

Durkheim's statistical information points in the directions suggested by his hypotheses. This is not to say, however, that his theory should be pronounced as empirically valid on the basis of this evidence alone. The following is a sample of the kinds of issues that Durkheim's critics have raised with respect to his data and the inferences he drew from them:

1. The data, drawn mainly from municipal and provincial archives, were irregularly recorded, and Durkheim had no way of knowing the ways in which they might have been biased in the recording process. For example, were Catholic suicides consistently underreported because of the especially strong stigma attached to suicide among Catholics?

2. While many of Durkheim's basic findings—concerning the relations between age, sex, marital status, and religion on the one side and suicide on the other—have stood quite well the test of subsequent research, more recent and improved data have indicated that some of the empirical relations posited by him do not hold. Andrew Henry and James F. Short, for example, compiled extensive—and more recent—statistics on the changes in the suicide rate in relation to business indices. They found that while suicide rates do rise during periods of economic slump, they drop—contrary to Durkheim's assertion—during periods of economic prosperity [Henry & Short 1954]. Such findings, if valid, raise questions, not only about Durkheim's data, but also about the psychological assumptions he incorporated into his explanation of anomic suicide.

3. Many of Durkheim's empirical associations involve the *ecological fallacy*. For example, to point out that the Bavarian provinces with Protestant majorities have a higher suicide rate than Bavarian provinces with Catholic majorities [p. 153] in no way demonstrates that Protestants commit suicide in the former and Catholics commit suicide in the latter. In other words, the fact that a province has a Protestant majority cannot be taken to mean that its greater number of suicides are perpetrated solely by Protestants. To confirm the relation, Durkheim would have had to demonstrate an association between religious preference and suicide at the level of individual persons, not simply at the province level. The general point is this: on the basis of ecological associations between two characteristics in the larger units (between religion and suicide on the province level), it is not possible to infer causal relations between the characteristics for smaller units (between religion and suicide on the individual level).[9]

In some cases an empirical claim made by Durkheim is not actually evident in the statistics on which he based the claim. For example, in one statistical table, comparing the suicide rates of Protestants, Catholics, and Jews in different countries for different periods, Jews showed *higher* suicide rates than Catholics in six of twelve cases [p. 154]. Such a finding should cast some doubt on the posited relation between the two religious groups with respect to suicide, but Durkheim continued to maintain that "the aptitude of Jews for suicide is . . . in a very general way . . . though to a lesser degree, lower than that of Catholics" [p. 155]. True, Durkheim did attempt to adduce reasons why the differences between Catholics and Jews were not greater than the statistics showed—for example, that Jews live in cities, are in intellectual occupations, and are therefore inclined to suicide for reasons other than their religion [p. 155]. But in many instances the reasons seem either forced or unsubstantiated except by seemingly plausible argumentation.[10]

In fairness to Durkheim, it should be pointed out that he sometimes used relatively sophisticated methods to isolate causal forces. For example, he frequently undertook further analysis to establish the validity of a suspected association. On examining the countries for which religious data were available, Durkheim noticed that in most cases Catholics were in the minority. Could it not be, he asked, that minority status rather than religious tradition is the operative variable in the genesis of lower suicide rates among Catholics? To throw light on this question, he examined regions such as Austria and Bavaria, where Catholics are in the majority; in these regions he discovered some diminution of the religious differences between Protestants and Catholics, but he found that Protestant rates were still higher. On the basis of this examination, he concluded that "Catholicism does not . . . owe [its protective influence] solely to its minority status" [p. 157]. In this operation Durkheim was making minority status into a constant in order to isolate the distinctive influence of the religious variable. In comparing military and civilian suicides, and in comparing suicides of married and single persons, Durkheim frequently held age and sex constant in order better to isolate the effect of military and marital status.

Another device that Durkheim used to strengthen his inferences was to replicate general findings at different levels. With respect to altruistic suicide, he predicted higher rates of suicide among military personnel than among civilians, and the available suicide statistics tended to support this hypothesis. It might be argued, however, that on the basis of this gross comparison alone it is not clear that Durkheim had isolated the salient differences between military and civilian personnel; after all, they differed in many other circumstances than in degree of commitment to a code of honor. To support his interpretation, Durkheim turned to the analysis of *intramilitary* differences in suicide rates. First, he compared those with limited terms of service with those of longer duration, finding that the latter—presumably more imbued with the military spirit than the former—showed higher suicide rates. Next, he compared officers and noncommissioned officers with private soldiers, finding the former—again more involved in the military life—showing higher rates. Finally, he found a greater tendency for suicide among volunteers and reenlisted men (those who chose the military life freely) than among conscripts. Summarizing these findings, Durkheim concluded that "the members of the army most stricken by suicide are also those who are most inclined to this career . . ." [p. 233]. By this replication *within* the military Durkheim rendered more plausible the relation *between* military and civilian personnel.[11]

Some Conceptual and Theoretical Problems

From our hasty examination of Durkheim's use of empirical data, we may conclude that while he exercised care and ingenuity in interpreting his statistical data, the quality of the data and the quality of his own inferences call for caution in accepting his results as definitive. We shall not pursue this conclusion further, mainly because we are concerned more with the logic of theorizing than with research design and empirical inference in this essay. Let us turn, then, to a number of theoretical problems in Durkheim's work.

A Definitional Problem

As indicated, Durkheim approached suicide from a positivistic point of view. He wanted to conceptualize suicide, not in terms of a mental state, but as a tangible act, which could be identified and measured. For this reason he eschewed defining it by reference to motives or "ends sought by the actor." His positivism also is expressed in his own definition of suicide: "all cases of death resulting directly or indirectly from a positive or negative act of the victim himself, which he knows will produce this result."

While Durkheim's definition appears to be relatively straightforward, closer examination raises a number of questions. First, it is not clear that Durkheim actually avoided reference to "internal states" of the individual, as much as he desired to do so. In fact his definition requires that the victim "know that the act will produce this result." Even though this is a cognitive criterion, it is no less "internal" to the actor than a motive. Moreover, such knowledge is often very difficult to establish,[12] especially since the victim cannot report on his state of mind after the act of suicide. It appears, then, that Durkheim's own definition is not entirely consistent with his positivistic stance.

Some Ambiguities in Durkheim's Basic Categories

While our earlier discussion indicated that egoism, altruism, anomie, and fatalism could be represented as two sets of paired opposites on the dimensions of integration and regulation, a closer examination of the ways in which Durkheim employed these variables suggests that their relations to one another are fraught with ambiguity.

Consider egoism first. Its essence appears to lie in the degree of detachment from group life. But as Durkheim's discussion developed, a number of different possible meanings arose. With respect to religious egoism, he referred to the commitment to values of individualism and freedom that isolate the individual from the group; with respect to familial egoism, he referred to a kind of quantitative social density, or frequency of interaction among numbers of persons; and with respect to political egoism, he referred to closeness arising from common commitment to a collectivity facing an external threat.

This multiplicity of meanings of egoism raises the question of whether that concept should stand in paired opposition to altruism. Altruism appears to be opposite only to the first, religious meaning of egoism; religious egoism is primarily a lack of commitment to dogma, whereas altruism is unquestioning faith. Altruism may also stand in opposition to "lack of common commitment under external threat." But it is difficult to ascertain the sense in which altruism is opposite to "lack of social density" in some quantitative sense.

Even Durkheim's discussion of religious egoism is ambiguous. In contrasting Protestantism and Catholicism, two possible readings of religious egoism emerge. The first, stemming from Durkheim's argument that Protestantism is not a doctrinaire religion, suggests that egoism means that individuals are less collectively bound to values and thus are more detached from society. But a second meaning of Protestantism is that individuals are strongly bound to values such as free inquiry; in fact, the more strongly they adhere to these values, the more likely they are to pursue their individual ends. On the one hand, Durkheim appears to argue that the weakness of attachment to values encourages high suicide rates among Protestants. In this case egoism would be the opposite of altruism. Yet on the other hand he appears to argue that strong attachment to certain *kinds* of values—such as liberty, free inquiry, and the like—encourages suicide. In this case egoism and altruism would not be all that different.

Thus egoism and altruism, as defined and used by Durkheim, do not seem to be paired opposites on the dimension of social integration, but instead conceal a more complicated series of dimensions, the exact relations among which are not specified. Even if a satisfactory opposition between the two could be established, another fundamental problem remains. In Durkheim's discussion of egoism, he ranked Protestantism, Catholicism, and Judaism in diminishing levels of egoism, with Judaism, "like all early religions," the most integrated of all, and hence the most protected against suicide. But in discussing altruistic suicide, he argued that other early religions, such as the Japanese, the Indian, and various primitive religions, were so demanding of the individual that they encouraged altruistic suicide. These assertions leave Judaism with an ambiguous theoretical status. Should it be considered "unegoistic" in contrast to Protestantism and therefore protective against individual self-destruction, or should it be considered "altruistic," like other early religions, and thus encouraging suicide? Or, to put the question more generally, where does the diminishing egoism end and where does increasing altruism begin? Unless the dimension of integration is represented as a scale, with definite intervals to which cases can be assigned, it is possible to characterize almost any empirical instance as either egoistic or altruistic, depending on the other empirical instances with which it is being compared.

With respect to anomie, too, Durkheim's analysis is ambiguous. On the one hand, he characterized anomie as a sudden discontinuity between life experiences and established normative expectations, as in the cases of business crises and divorce. On the other hand, he characterized anomie as a "regular, constant factor," indeed a "chronic state" in trade and industry [p. 254], which he regarded as relatively unregulated by traditional religious and political norms. Out of this chronic lack of regulation arises a kind of chronic state of crisis, restlessness, unbounded ambitiousness, and futility [p. 256].

Given the multiplicity of meanings of both egoism and anomie, the differences between these two concepts also become unclear. Durkheim himself recognized the overlap in meaning when he acknowledged that "both [anomic and egoistic suicide] spring from society's insufficient presence in individuals. But he also insisted that the two differ on both the social and individual level. For egoistic suicide, society is "deficient in truly collective activity, thus depriving the latter of object and meaning"; for anomic suicide, "society's influence is lacking in the basically individual passions, thus leaving them without a check-rein" [p. 258]. On the individual level,

Suicides of both [egoistic and anomic] types suffer from what has been called the disease of the infinite. But the disease does not assume the same form in both cases. In [egoistic suicide], reflective intelligence is affected and immoderately overnourished; in [anomic suicide], emotion is overexcited and freed from all restraint. In one, thought, by dint of falling back upon itself, has no object left;

in the other, passion, no longer recognizing bounds, has no goal left. The former is lost in the infinity of dreams, the second in the infinity of desires [p. 287].

Despite his insistence on their independence, his descriptions are so **175** vague and general that it becomes difficult to know whether to classify a given social situation as egoistic, as anomic, or as both.[13]

The implication of these criticisms is that, although Durkheim presented his theory of suicide as a simple, compact, and logically coherent theoretical scheme, it is in fact something of a jumble of ambiguous and only partially interrelated variables. It is wanting in logical structure and, as a consequence, wanting in the ability to generate consistent propositions. It is as though Durkheim, presented with a great array of empirical differences in suicide rates among a number of social groups and social categories, subtly changed the meaning of a number of general terms—egoism and anomie in particular—in order to render those empirical results plausible and consistent. But in doing so he damaged his theory by sacrificing some of its logical structure.

Durkheim's Use of "Floating" and Residual Categories

To loosen the logical structure of a theory renders it less able to generate propositions, since the relations among the basic categories are no longer fixed. For the same reason, to loosen the logical structure also permits the investigator to use variables in a number of ad hoc ways to account for apparent exceptions to the theory. Durkheim sometimes used his major categories in a somewhat arbitrary or "floating" way and tended also to rely on a number of residual categories that were not "officially" incorporated in his theory.

For instance, consider Durkheim's discussion of the role of education in the etiology of suicide. In contrasting suicide rates among various religious groupings, he argued that free inquiry, as nourished by Protestantism, gives rise to an emphasis on education. "When irrational beliefs or practices have lost their hold [as among Protestants], appeal must be made, in the search for others, to the enlightened consciousness of which knowledge is only the highest form." Thus, he continued, the decline of religious doctrine and the valuation of education "are one and spring from the same source" [p. 162]. He then proceeded to show in varying ways that level of education is positively correlated with suicide rates.

At this point, however, Durkheim noted "one case . . . in which our law [relating education to suicide] might seem not to be verified." This case was Judaism, which "counts the fewest suicides, yet in none other is education so general" [p. 167]. In fact, Durkheim identified precisely the opposite correlation between education and suicide for

Jews from that which he found among the Protestants. How did he interpret this apparent exception? He argued that the Jew, who has lived as a member of an embattled minority for centuries, "seeks to learn, not in order to replace his collective prejudices by reflective thought, but merely to be better armed for the struggle" [p. 168]. He maintained, in short, that the *significance* of education is different for Protestants and for Jews.

In this assertion Durkheim may have been empirically correct. But his shifting of ground underscores the looseness of his theoretical scheme. Explaining education among Protestants as a manifestation of free inquiry—one meaning of egoism—he shifted his argument for Jews, maintaining that the emphasis on education it is in fact a manifestation of *another* facet of egoism, namely, the degree to which a group is in a state of political crisis. The Jews, argued Durkheim, have been in a kind of chronic state of political crisis, and this has affected both their interest in education and their low rate of suicide. But the fact that egoism has a number of meanings permitted Durkheim to appeal to one facet of the variable when the statistics fell one way, and to another facet when they fell another way. To shift from meaning to meaning in this way permits the investigator to be right all the time, but at the same time his theory begins to develop another shortcoming, the lack of falsifiability.[14]

In other instances, Durkheim appealed to variables foreign to his main theoretical framework. The impact of sex on the propensity to suicide is a conspicuous example. In a long and somewhat tortured passage on egoistic suicide, Durkheim attempted to sort out some apparently contradictory statistics on the effect of marriage and widowhood on suicide by arguing that the "most favored sex" in each society is more protected from suicide by marriage and widowhood [pp. 178–189]. In another passage, in which he was attempting to account for the fact that men seem more adversely affected by divorce in societies in which divorce is common, he posed the following, somewhat quaint explanation:

Woman's sexual needs have less of a mental character [than man's] because generally speaking, her mental life is less developed. These needs are more closely related to the needs of the organism, following rather than leading them, and consequently find in them an efficient restraint. Being a more instinctive creature than man, woman has only to follow her instincts to find calmness and peace [p. 272].

Perhaps we should generously write off the substance of Durkheim's observation on sexual differences as reflecting the late Victorian prejudices of his day. From the standpoint of his theoretical account of suicide, however, it is apparent that Durkheim was appealing to a factor—innate sexual differences—that was extraneous to his main explanatory framework to account for facts on which the basic variables themselves threw little or no light. The apparently arbitrary use of categories such as these contributes further to the looseness of Durkheim's theoretical structure and further decreases the level of generality of his explanations.

The Unsatisfactory Status of Psychological Variables in Durkheim's Theory

As we have seen, one of Durkheim's objectives was to create a *sociological* theory, dealing with social facts (such as aggregated suicide rates) that are to be explained by reference to other social facts (such as various states of social integration or cohesion). He maintained that he was not concerned with variables other than social ones; in particular he eschewed an interest in psychological causes. He did acknowledge that there are individual determinants of suicide, but he presumed that they are not important enough to influence the social suicide rate. "They may perhaps cause this or that separate individual to kill himself, but not give society as a whole a greater or lesser tendency to suicide." Since these psychological factors "have no social repercussions," he argued further, "they concern the psychologist, not the sociologist" [p. 51]. Here Durkheim was arguing that psychological causes should be treated as variables that are *separate* in their operation from social causes and that they are sufficiently unimportant that they may be ignored.

As we have seen, however, Durkheim also spoke of the "collective mark" that egoism, altruism, and anomie stamp on individuals and of a definite "personality type" associated with each social type of suicide. In this formulation he was treating the individual as a kind of vessel through which suicidogenic social forces flow. This formulation definitely rests on psychological generalizations, for example, that the social condition of anomie creates feelings of disorientation, irritation, and disgust and that these feelings are especially conducive to self-destruction. In this case psychological processes are treated as factors that *intervene* between the social facts (integration) and behavioral outcomes (suicide).

At this point, however, a disquieting series of questions arise. If the individual is to be treated as the vessel through which social forces flow, why don't *all* Protestants commit suicide, if they are affected by the condition of egoism generated by their religion? And why do *any* Catholics or Jews commit suicide? Or, alternatively, how do we account for those Protestants who do *not* commit suicide? One sympathetic to Durk heim would respond by asserting that other social forces—for example, the character of his family situation or the presence or absence of anomic conditions in his life—would augment or inhibit the religious influences. There is some merit in this response, but we should also ask whether there are not independent psychological factors as well that interact with these social factors to influence not only individual suicides but also social suicide rates.

I have in mind two possible kinds of psychological factors: variables complementary to the social and variables independent of the social. It might well be, for example, that exposure to Protestantism generates an excessively strong conscience and a corresponding tendency to express aggression in an inward rather than an outward direction. But this does not tell the whole story of suicide. Individuals are also equipped with a vast array of defense mechanisms and coping capacities, so that we would expect *on psychological grounds* that some individuals would be better able to withstand such self-destructive tendencies and to turn them into other lines of activity. In this case we would be treating various psychological variables as *complementing* the social forces in their impact on suicide and presumably contributing to a more refined causal statement based only on the social forces.

A final possibility is that psychological factors are responsible *both* for membership in certain social groups (such as the Protestant church) *and* for self-destructive tendencies. According to psychoanalytic explanations of suicide associated with Sigmund Freud [1917, 1924] and with Karl Abraham [1924], suicide is closely linked to a state of personal melancholy, which is in turn based on the loss of a significant object in early periods of childhood, on anger with the lost object, on identification with the lost object, and on the turning of the anger inward in an act that is simultaneously self-punitive and hostile. Might not this constellation of motivational forces predispose an individual to accept a religion that stresses individual conscience, self-discipline, and perhaps even masochism? If so, both commitment to a religious belief and a tendency to self-destruction would be effects of a set of *independent* psychological variables.

The upshot of these remarks is that the psychological parameters[15] in Durkheim's theory are unsatisfactory because they raise a number of unresolved issues and involve him in a number of questionable psychological formulations. Refinement of these parameters along the lines suggested would not only make his theory more realistic psychologically but would also create the possibility of generating a more nearly complete explanation of both individual suicides and aggregated suicide rates.

CHAPTER 11

Talcott Parsons' Theory of Deviance and Social Control

Though Durkheim's analysis of suicide was tied to a general theory of social integration, his explanation rested at a "middle range" of generality. It was directed toward a fairly restricted range of data—suicide rates—and attempted to explain variations in these data by referring to differences in social integration and regulation.

The theoretical focus of Talcott Parsons is much more general. Working to create a "general theory of action," Parsons anticipates that his framework will form a basis for explaining *all* behavior; in fact, he has worked out theoretical statements on many analytical levels—the personality, the social, the cultural, and the biological. Even his theoretical perspective on deviance and social control—on which we shall concentrate—is pitched at an abstract level. Parsons, then, has consistently been a "general" or "grand" theorist.[16]

Transition from Durkheim to Parsons: Merton's Deviance Paradigm

In order to shift from Durkheim's to Parsons' theoretical style, I shall summarize briefly Robert Merton's paradigm on deviance. It is broader in scope than Durkheim's theory of suicide in that it attempts to account for a *variety of types* of deviance; at the same time it is less abstract than Parsons' formulation. To mention Merton makes sense for another reason as well, since Parsons argues that Merton's paradigm on deviance is consistent with—indeed, is a "special case" of—his own theory of deviance [pp. 257–258].[17] We shall not analyze Merton's paradigm in great detail, however, nor shall we subject it to the same kinds of criticisms that are leveled at our four major theorists.[18]

Whereas Durkheim was interested in explaining different rates of suicide, Merton focuses on all "nonconforming rather than conforming conduct" [1968, p. 186]. Despite his broader range of data, Merton's approach is similar to Durkheim's in several respects. First, he emphasizes the social genesis of deviance in contrast to explanations grounded in biological impulses or personality disorders, although he is not as thorough as Durkheim in attempting to demolish these explanations. In any case, Merton's focus is on the "normal reaction of normal people to abnormal [social] conditions." Also like Durkheim, Merton is interested in *rates* of behavior—the aggregated features of deviance— not in individual cases. Finally, Merton shares Durkheim's concern with a specific kind of social determinant—a lack of integration.

Merton selects *anomie* as his fundamental independent variable, but he differs somewhat from Durkheim in the meaning assigned to this concept. Durkheim defined anomie as a lack of regulation by the normative order. Merton defines it, however, as a disjunctive relationship between cultural goals and institutionalized norms in society. As his principal example of anomie Merton chooses the American cultural goal of monetary success and asks how well this goal can be attained within the scope of institutionalized norms for doing so. Merton's answer is that the goal is not readily attainable within accepted norms, and for that reason a variety of types of deviant behavior can be expected to develop in American society.

Merton classifies the major deviant responses in terms of whether the individual accepts or rejects the cultural goals or the institutionalized norms, or both. First, *conformity* involves accepting both society's goals and its legitimately institutionalized norms. An example is the boy who wants to get rich and works hard at it by educating himself, getting a job, and making his way up the occupational ladder. Second, *innovation* involves accepting the cultural goals but rejecting the institutionalized means of attaining them. The innovator relies on new, illegitimate means such as racketeering, vice, or perhaps white-collar crime. Third, *ritualism* rejects the cultural goals while continuing to accept, indeed to overemphasize, the institutionalized norms. A familiar type of ritualist is the bureaucrat who insists on following every rule to the letter, thus choking the system with red tape and defeating organizational aims. Fourth, *retreatism* involves the rejection of both cultural goals and the institutionalized means of realizing them; here Merton has in mind society's outcasts—hobos, psychotics, alcoholics, and drug addicts. And finally, *rebellion*, also, involves the rejection of both cultural goals and institutionalized norms but substitutes new goals and means in their place. The rebel develops an ideology, perhaps a revolutionary one, that creates new values and norms, which are regarded as more legitimate than the existing ones.

Schematically, Merton's paradigm of deviant responses can be represented as follows:

Modes of Adaptation	Cultural Goals	Institutionalized Means
1 Conformity	+	+
2 Innovation	+	−
3 Ritualism	−	+
4 Retreatism	−	−
5 Rebellion	±	±

There is an important difference between Durkheim's and Merton's methods of classifying variables. Durkheim defined suicide in general terms at the outset of his analysis. He subdivided this dependent variable in two ways—first in terms of its social causes (egoism, altruism, and so on), and second in terms of its individual psychological manifestations (here again he characterized the psychological traits of the egoistic suicide, altruistic suicide, and so on). Merton's procedure is different. Having identified the basic cause of deviance in anomie—a discontinuity between cultural goals and institutionalized norms—he classified individual responses to anomie *in terms of their modifications of the basic independent variables (goals and norms)*. Merton, in short, used the same set of concepts to classify both his independent and his dependent variables.

Merton's hypotheses about the social incidence of deviant behavior are not strictly derived from, but they are consistent with, his classification of causes and outcomes. We have already indicated his most general hypothesis: that deviant behavior "may be regarded sociologically as a symptom of dissociation between culturally prescribed aspirations and socially structured avenues for realizing these aspirations" [1968, p. 188]. One type of such dissociation occurs in a "society in which there is an exceptionally strong emphasis upon specific goals without a corresponding emphasis upon institutional procedures." The particular form of frustration in such a society—and Merton clearly has in mind the United States, where monetary success is overvalued and the means of attaining it undervalued—is that society arouses hopes in its populace but does not provide adequate opportunities to realize them.

These general propositions say little about the *differential* incidence of the several types of deviant behavior. To specify this, Merton suggests that people in different locations in the class structure will deviate in different ways. Leaving conformity aside, Merton argues that a great dissociation between goals and institutionalized procedures occurs among the lower but not the lowest members of the working classes. The goal of monetary success is remote from them, and legitimate means of attaining it are largely unavailable. Consequently, Merton argues, they are the most likely types of persons to reject societal means and to adopt illegitimate innovations, such as crime, as a mode of deviant behavior [1968, pp. 198–199]. Ritualism, by contrast, is the mode of adaptation most common in the lower middle classes. Clerks and bookkeepers are perhaps closer to the opportunities for monetary success, but if they are to make it they have to avoid risk and stick closely to the rules [1968, pp. 204–205]. Retreatism is a manifestation of the hopelessness of the very lowest orders of society, who are so far from realizing the cultural goals that they reject both the goals themselves and the means of attaining them [1968, pp. 207–208]. Finally, though Merton did not analyze rebellion very thoroughly, he suggests that rebellion is likely to be the dominant response in a social class that is rising, but not fast enough to realize its aspirations. As these illustrations show, the variable of "degree of remoteness from cultural goals and means" is an important variable in leading Merton to generate predictions about what kinds of people will choose what kinds of deviant responses.

Merton's paradigm of deviance is very much in the Durkheimian tradition. Even though it is more comprehensive in its range of data, it is still "middle range" in that it produces a series of fairly definite hypotheses. While these hypotheses are not put to the test by Merton, he did bring them to a point that was sufficiently specific to guide other investigators in concrete empirical research that would test their validity.

182

Parsons: A General Perspective

In studying Parsons, we shall focus on the same topic analyzed by Durkheim and Merton—social deviance. Given the character of Parsons' analysis, however, it is not possible to plunge directly into that topic; his analysis of deviance is so closely tied to his general theoretical formulations that we must sketch a few rudiments of "general action theory" as an introduction to his theory of deviance.

The Ingredients of "Action"

In much of Parsons' work, the starting point for analysis is the concept of an *actor*, who is represented as a motivated, goal-seeking individual. It is convenient to identify the actor as a person, although Parsons considers it also possible to treat groups and collectivities as actors. Because the actor is represented as goal seeking, he seeks to establish certain relations with objects in his environment. Thus the second element in the definition of action is the *end* toward which the actor strives.

The actor, however, does not choose his ends randomly, nor does he attain them automatically. Various other factors intervene as the actor strives to maximize his satisfaction. In the first place, action takes place in a *situation*, which is significant for the actor in two respects. First, in order to attain ends, he must have *means*, such as facilities, tools, or resources; and second, he must overcome *conditions*, or obstacles to the attainment of ends. A final element of action arises from the fact that the choice of ends, the means for attaining them, and the means for overcoming obstacles are all regulated by *normative standards*. These standards underscore the fact that all action is basically social in character. It is continuously influenced by norms that arise in the interaction among individuals.

Formally defined, then, action includes the following characteristics: (1) It is "behavior [of an organism] . . . oriented toward the attainment of ends or goals or other anticipated states of affairs. (2) It takes place in situations. (3) It is normatively regulated; and (4) it involves the expenditure of energy, or effort, in 'motivation' " [Parsons & Shils 1951, p. 53]. Its several ingredients are represented graphically in figure 8.

There are three types of objects in the actor's environment. The first type comprises *physical* objects, which are important to the actor as ends, means, or conditions, but with which he does not actually interact. The second type includes *social* objects—other actors—with which he does interact. The third type includes cultural objects—such as ideas, beliefs, and symbols—which regulate and lend meaning to action.

Figure 8. Elements of action [after Parsons 1937, p. 44].

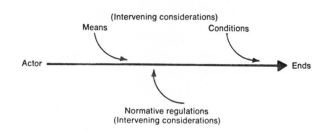

Systems of Action

Parsons argues that all the ingredients of action have to be taken into consideration in analyzing any discrete "unit act." He also argues, however, that action does not occur in isolated bits, unconnected with one another. Rather, every unit act is implicated in *systems of action*, which maintain patterns over periods of time and give structure to action. These systems of action are organized at several levels of generality. For purposes of understanding his theory of deviance, the three most important systems are the personality system, the social system, and the cultural system. These three systems are linked with one another in complex relations, but we shall concentrate especially on the relations between the personality and social systems.

The focus of organization of the personality system is the individual actor, and the important units of the personality are drives, attitudes, skills, conceptions of self, and so on. The academic discipline of psychology concentrates on the analysis of this system.

Social systems lie on a different level of abstraction from the personality. A social system is that set of relations arising from selected aspects of the interaction among persons. These aspects of interaction are *roles*, such as the role of husband, student, or church member. A role is only a part of a person's interaction system. For example, a student in his role as student has certain relations with instructors, deans, and other students. However, the role of student does not exhaust all the aspects of his other interactions; he is also a child to his parents, a husband to his wife if he is married, a citizen of the nation, and a resident of a locality. Nor is a role—or even the sum of all significant roles—equivalent to the personality. Personality involves the organization of action at a different analytic level. It is important to keep in mind, furthermore, that the basic units of social systems are roles, not personalities.

The central ingredient of the concept of role is the *expectation* that the actor will perform in certain ways. Roles involve normative relations; they consist of a cluster of expectations about how people should behave toward one another. Perhaps the clearest examples of expectations are found in legal codes and contracts, which spell out explicitly certain prohibitions and obligations. Criminal law explicitly prohibits physical assault; contracts stipulate when and where deliveries of goods and payments for goods are to be made. Other normative expectations—such as subtle rules of etiquette—are not so explicit, but their influence on social conduct can nevertheless be very strong.

The concept of *sanctions* refers to the means by which people attempt to secure compliance with role expectations. Sanctions, too, may be formal and explicit, such as paying a person a salary for continuing to perform his occupational role or restraining him physically if he commits a crime; but they also may be informal and subtle, such as letting a person know by a chilly silence that he is doing the wrong thing.

Having reviewed the concepts of expectation, performance, and sanction, we may now note Parsons' formal definition of a social system: "a system of interaction of a plurality of actors, in which the action is oriented by rules which are complexes of complementary expectations concerning roles and sanctions" [Parsons & Shils 1951, p. 195]. A social system is a network of interactive relationships. Furthermore, if any one of these relationships is modified or disturbed, a series of processes is set off in the system, by means of which it readjusts or undergoes certain types of change.

Figure 9 represents a simple social system, with two actors, whom Parsons labels "ego" and "alter" for convenience of reference. The social system is constituted by the interactive relationship between ego and alter. But it is also important to remember that while each actor is involved in his relationship with the other, he has as well his own particular situation, consisting in part of his other role involvements.

Finally, a word should be added about cultural systems, even though they will not figure significantly in the subsequent discussion. As indicated, they are made up of ideas, values, expressive symbols, and the like; in short, a cultural system is a system of meanings. Concrete illustrations of cultural systems are languages, religious belief systems, and organized sets of mathematical relations. Cultural systems, like personality and social systems, are abstractions from behavior in general and are conceived as analytically independent from other systems of action. Empirically, however, cultural systems shape behavior in the other two

Figure 9. A simple social system.

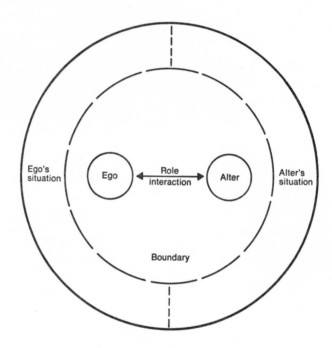

types of systems, mainly by becoming internalized in personalities and institutionalized in social systems.

A Summary of Parsons' Theory of Deviance and Social Control

In discussing Parsons' theory of deviance, we shall follow the same approach that we took to Durkheim's theory of suicide: we shall give a general summary of Parsons' analysis, raising a few critical points and elaborations along the way, and we shall reserve the central theoretical criticisms until the end.

Definitions of Deviance

Parsons' general definition of deviance arises from his conception of interaction, which involves two or more actors whose behavior is continuously regulated by role expectation and sanctions and continuously monitored by communication. The starting point for defining deviance is the pattern of normative expectations that regulate behavior. If behavior is to be deviant, it has to deviate *from* some specific set of expectations. Delinquent behavior by juveniles is regarded as deviant by most members of a community but is conforming behavior from the standpoint of the norms governing the delinquent gang itself. School segregation by race is officially illegal and therefore deviant from the standpoint of the law of the land, but from the standpoint of many localities that resist integration, *de*segregation is the deviant behavior. Deviance, then, is not a particular kind of behavior; it is behavior assessed in relation to some normative reference point [pp. 250–251].

Parsons defines *deviance* as "the processes by which resistances to conformity with social expectations develop, and the mechanisms by which these tendencies are or tend to be counteracted in social systems" [p. 249]. This definition, like Merton's, focuses on nonconforming behavior in general. In addition, however, Parsons includes social control as an integral part of his definition, an aspect generally not considered by Merton.

Both Durkheim and Merton insisted on the distinctively social character of deviance. Parsons shares this emphasis but, in addition, considers deviance as a *relation* between individual behavior and social norms. Accordingly, we can find two additional, somewhat more specific definitions of deviance in his work, one referring to the social system, the other to the personality system. Viewed from the perspective of the social system, deviance is "the tendency on the part of one or more of the component actors to behave in such a way as to disturb the equilibrium of the interactive process" [p. 250]. According to this formulation, it is the system of interaction that is disturbed by deviant behavior. Viewed from the perspective of the person, deviance is "a motivated tendency for an actor to behave in contravention of one or more institutionalized normative patterns." While norms are mentioned in this case, the primary focus is on the actor's motivation.

The several definitions of deviance offered by Parsons may appear to contradict one another, but this is not the case. They identify different facets of the same general phenomenon, a phenomenon that is necessarily multifaceted because it has links to both the social and the personality systems. Nevertheless, if an investigator chooses one of these facets as the primary one, he predisposes himself to raise certain kinds of questions and not others. For example, Parsons chooses to emphasize two facets: the motivational orientation of the person who deviates and the system's definition of role expectations. These emphases suggest an interest in what motivates the deviant and in the processes of social control that remotivate him to return to a conforming relation with the system's norms.

Consider, however, an alternative focus. Suppose that deviance is regarded in terms of neither the personality of the deviant nor the system's norms, but rather as a result of the assessment of those who have the power to wield sanctions and enforce norms as they interpret them. This definition of deviance from the perspective of the enforcer has been advanced by sociologists such as Goffman [1962] and Becker [1963]. Goffman, for example, considers that "mental illness" is not so much a matter of the motivational state of the individual "patient" as it is of certain acts of labeling people as "sick" and of certain administrative decisions on the part of persons in authority—lawyers, judges, psychiatrists, and hospital officials. Such an approach raises questions that are different from those suggested by Parsons' definition. The motivational genesis of deviant behavior becomes relatively unimportant for a sociologist like Goffman, because the "deviant" may well be a victim of rule-making and rule application by those in authority, no matter what his motivation. Parsons tends to view agents in social control more as "responding" to actions that do not conform to role expectations. Hence he is led more to ask why the expectations were violated. By the same token, Goffman is less likely to consider these aspects. This is not to say that Parsons' theory precludes analysis of the power relations between "enforcer" and "deviant," or that Goffman's theory precludes an analysis of the "deviant's" motivation. Their initial definitions, however, do not single out and highlight these respective aspects. In any case, the example should underscore the intimate link between a theorist's general perspective on a subject and the kinds of questions that he may be led to pursue.

Before moving on, let us raise one set of complications regarding the concept of normative expectations, which is Parsons' reference point for defining deviance. Parsons' definition suggests that norms are relatively precise in their specification of deviant behavior (for example, "thou shalt not kill"), and as a result, behavior that is deviant in relation to these norms (killing) is readily identifiable. In examining several characteristics of social norms, however, it becomes apparent that the identification of deviant acts is sometimes a very ambiguous matter. Consider the following distinctions:

1. Explicit versus vague normative expectations. An important dimension of role expectations is the degree to which they are explicit or vague in their reference to expected performances. An explicit expectation is, for example, that a university professor is expected to meet his classes. If he does not, he is judged deviant by the university administration unless he has an acceptable excuse, such as a death in the immediate family. Another expectation is that he should publish books and

articles; this expectation is somewhat vague, however, and one has difficulty determining exactly when it is being violated. If a professor publishes one article in five years, it is generally agreed that this is too little and that he has not lived up to the expectations regarding publication. On the other hand, it is sometimes asserted that a professor publishes too much, which suggests that he is sacrificing quality for quantity. But there is no precise measure either in terms of quantity (pages or pounds of published materials) or of quality, to determine whether he has met the expectation adequately. This kind of loose, open expectation makes conformity and deviance difficult to identify, even though the distinction is extremely important in determining the rewards and punishments received by an individual professor.

2. Required versus optional behavior. By and large, both meeting classes and writing scholarly works are required features of the role of university professor. But an additional range of other behavior—attending ceremonials such as graduations, giving public speeches in the community, and the like—is frequently specified as "expected" somewhere in the university handbook. The expectation is a weak one, however, and while by strict interpretation nonperformance constitutes a case of deviance, few people become concerned about nonperformance, and no particular sanctions are applied against the nonperformer. Thus, deviant behavior becomes more difficult to define and identify as we move from required normative expectations toward optional ones.

3. Required versus prohibited behavior. A third dimension of role expectations concerns whether they require or prohibit the performance of an act. Most criminal laws enjoin us not to do something; they are prohibitive. Some criminal laws, however, call for positive actions. The legal codes of some states specify a crime known as misprision of felony; these laws state that if an individual knows that a felony is going to occur, he is in criminal violation if he does not report this to the authorities. Yet such a law is seldom enforced, and failure to comply is often more difficult to specify than actions that are in defiance of prohibitive laws.

Parsons' definition of deviance seems to apply most readily to certain types of norms: to those that specify explicit and required performances and prohibitions, instances of which are identifiable. But such norms constitute only part of the normative order, and we would expect a different set of processes of deviance and social control to operate in the gray, borderline areas of vague and optional norms. For example, when norms are vague and optional, we would not expect processes involving simple "deviance" and "social control" so much as we would expect processes of argument and negotiation between parties as to what the norms really are and whether deviance is occurring. These areas of ambiguity in the social world make the phenomenon of deviance ever more relative and contingent than Parsons' definition suggests.

The Organization of Central Concepts

Parsons' presentation of his theory of deviance is extraordinarily complex. He moves rapidly from extremely abstract concepts to very detailed empirical illustrations. He brings many variables to bear in his discussion of deviance, but he does not always place these variables in specific relationship to one another. Giving Parsons a sympathetic reading and at the risk of oversimplifying and distorting his theory, I shall extract what appear to be the central theoretical variables, break them into component parts, and make explicit the implicit logical relations among them. In short, my summary aims to recapitulate and perhaps to make more systematic the theory of deviance.

There appear to be four main types of variables in Parsons' theory: (1) strain, which is the major factor in the genesis of deviant behavior; (2) the directions of deviant behavior, an analysis of which provides a typology of deviant tendencies; (3) the structuring of deviant tendencies, which rises the question of the opportunities for deviant behavior, and (4) social control, or the tendencies that arise in reaction to deviance. We shall consider these variables in the order listed.

1. Strain. The starting point for Parsons' analysis is the interactive system, which is characterized by the presence of role expectations, by the mutual interplay of sanctions, and above all, by the anticipation that the behavior and attitudes of each actor will conform with the expectations of the other.

The stage for the development of deviant behavior is set when, "from whatever source, a disturbance is introduced into the system [of interaction], of such character that what alter does leads to a frustration, in some important respects, of ego's expectation-system vis-à-vis alter's" [p. 252]. This disturbance constitutes "strain," because there has been a breakdown in the relationship between expectation and behavior. The concept of strain is not identical with the concept of deviance; it constitutes one of the main conditions giving rise to deviant responses. The distinction between the two may be confusing, because on some occasions deviance in one part of a social system may create strain elsewhere in the system, but still it is necessary to keep the two concepts of strain and deviance analytically separate.

As the phrase "from whatever source" indicates, Parsons is not initially concerned with the origin of disequilibrium, or strain, which initially upsets the system of interaction. It may come from any concrete source—an earthquake, the death of a leader, or the imperfect socialization of an individual into a role. The main idea is that strain creates a frustration of expectations.

Although Parsons' theory is thus "open" with respect to the sources of strain, he does identify several sources in his discussion. One source of strain lies in the *specific pattern of role expectations themselves:* "the ways in which 'pressure' is exerted on the motivational system of the actor will vary as a function of the kind of pattern with which he is expected to conform" [p. 267]. For example, Parsons argues that roles that are characterized by a high degree of specialization and impersonality and by high expectations of achievement are likely to frustrate the immediate gratification of impulses and, consequently, are more likely to create strain than other types of social roles. By way of illustration, Parsons argues that the expectations governing the occupational roles for American adult males frustrate dependency needs, because these cannot normally be gratified in most occupational roles. Indeed, "this seems to be one of the focal points of strain in American society" [p. 269]. The institutionalization of certain types of role requirements, then, creates a predisposition toward strain in the system.

Another kind of strain arises from *role ambiguities,* in which the expectations for roles are not clear. In this connection Parsons employs a distinction noted earlier, the distinction between explicit and vague role expectations. In some roles it is difficult to know what constitutes conformity; once again, in the achievement-oriented system of American occupational roles, it is difficult to know when a person is finally to be judged a "success."

A third source of strain is *role conflict,* by which is meant "the exposure of the actors to conflicting sets of legitimized role expectations such that complete fulfillment of both is realistically impossible" [p. 280]. For example, a husband is subject to role conflict if his wife expects him to act like a man and exercise initiative, while his mother expects him to act as an obedient son. Or, a student may be subject to conflict between his anticipated future role as a scholar, which requires hard study, and his role as a member of a peer group, which requires that one not be a "grind."

Strain, then, some sources of which we have just mentioned, is one of the necessary conditions for deviant behavior. However, Parsons qualifies this causal relation in two ways: by specifying several ways to reduce strain, thereby "heading off" tendencies of deviant behavior; and by indicating several responses to strain other than deviance.

A common way of minimizing potential strain is to give greater weight to one role expectation than to another. In our society, for example, the demands of occupation and family are quite important, and often super-sede other role obligations. Thus, upon receiving a dinner invitation, a parent might say, "We'd love to accept but the children are ill and I wouldn't want to leave them with a babysitter," or "We'd love to come, but I have to attend a special meeting at the office." In such a case, a hierarchy is invoked to resolve any potential role conflict and minimize any strain that might arise.

Another way is to schedule potentially conflicting role performances at different times. A straightforward example is segregating the role obligations of the job from the role obligations of the home by institutionalizing a nine-to-five job. In this way types of behavior that might be appropriate to the family setting but inappropriate to the job setting, and vice versa, are structurally segregated from one another.

A third mechanism for reducing role conflict is to conceal the activities associated with one role from those associated with another. Thus, our student who is ambitious and who desires popularity as well studies in secret, away from his peers. To mention another example, adolescent peer groups are typically eager to keep their activities separate from parental surveillance, thus avoiding the role conflicts that would arise if both peers and parents were present.

A final mechanism for reducing role conflict is to develop certain rationalizations, whereby a set of role expectations is believed to hold in one context but not in another. A person might argue that it is acceptable for blacks to work in the same shop or belong to the same labor union as whites but not live in a white neighborhood. Many potential rationalizations are found in a culture's proverbs, which often contradict one another but which are uttered on separate occasions as if they held for all occasions. For example, the proverb "he who hesitates is lost," seems to be difficult to reconcile with the proverb "look before you leap." Yet each enjoys a kind of separate and absolute existence, and each is singled out to justify behavior in a situation that might involve some role conflict. Again, the cliché "business is business" is a way of saying that an actor is engaging in some behavior that might be deviant from one perspective but that the business role is such that this behavior ought not to be considered so.

Parsons also mentions a number of responses to strain other than deviance. For example, a person subject to role conflict may simply withdraw from one role. Our ambitious student may decide to ignore the social pressures exerted by his peers and thus avoid role conflict. He is not exactly engaging in deviant behavior but withdrawing from the interactive system that would pose conflict for him. Or he may decide that certain gratifications are not important for him or seek to gratify his needs in other (nondeviant) ways that do not produce so much conflict.

Thus strain is not a single variable but a system of variables—conditions that give rise to strain, strain itself, and mechanisms to reduce strain. Furthermore, strain gives rise to a number of responses, only one of which is deviant behavior. The concept of strain contains a miniature model of tendencies and countertendencies to strain, even though Parsons develops this model only embryonically. Further refinement of the model would require a a systematic classification of the types of sources of strain, of the means of reducing strain, and of the alternate responses to strain. This refinement would include as well an indication of the conditions under which strain would give rise to deviance rather than to some other kind of response.

2. Directions of deviance. Let us suppose that the level of strain in an interactive situation is relatively high and that it is neither contained nor drained off in responses other than deviant behavior. We may now analyze the ways in which strain develops into deviance and the directions that deviant behavior takes.

The psychological responses to strain are complicated, involving a combination of anxiety, hostility, and fantasy. But the response most consistently emphasized by Parsons is *ambivalence*. Under conditions of strain an actor does not simply become hostile, but he responds with mixed positive and negative affects toward alter, who, after all, has been the object of gratification in the interactive system. Thus, the response to a situation of strain calls forth both a tendency for continuing conformity as well as a tendency for alienation.

In this concept of ambivalence Parsons finds his first dimension for analyzing the directions of deviance. If the alienative side of the ambivalence is dominant, the response is *compulsive alienation*; if the conformative aspect of the ambivalent response is dominant, the response is *compulsive conformity*. These two distinctions are similar to Merton's concepts of rejection and acceptance.

A second dimension for classifying the directions of deviant response is the differentiation between activity and passivity, which, Parsons notes, is "of generally recognized psychological significance" [pp. 256–257]. This is the issue in "fight versus flight," or whether the individual will attack or withdraw in the interactive situation.

Combining these two dimensions, we produce four types of deviant response, shown in figure 10. Parsons comments on the similarity of his classification scheme to Merton's four types of deviance. Compulsive

193

**Figure 10. Four directions of deviant response
[from Parsons 1951, p. 257].**

	Activity	Passivity
Conformative Dominance	Compulsive performance orientation	Compulsive acquiescence in status expectations
Alienative Dominance	Rebelliousness	Withdrawal

performance corresponds to "innovation," compulsive acquiescence to "ritualism," withdrawal to "retreatism," and rebelliousness to "rebellion" [p. 258].

Parsons adds yet another dimension to his classification. The social system comprised of a number of actors, interacting according to a series of normative role expectations. The deviant response of an actor, whether conformative or alienative, whether active or passive, may focus either on other *actors* (social objects) or on *norms*. Subdividing each of the four deviant responses according to this distinction, we produce eight separate directions of deviant behavior, as shown in figure 11.

The following examples illustrate each of these eight types. (1) The compulsively active conformist with an emphasis on social objects is the "bossy" character who pushes others around. (2) The compulsively active conformist with an emphasis on norms is the rigid enforcer of rules, the taskmaster, who goes by the book. (3) The compulsively passive conformist who focuses on social objects is the meek type who puts himself in the position of continuously submitting to others. (4) The compulsively passive conformist who focuses on norms also lives by the book, but instead of demanding exacting performance from others, falls into the role of the functionary who lives by the letter of the rules. (5) The compulsively active alienated person who focuses on social objects moves through the world with a chip on his shoulder, always trying to pick a fight, whatever the cause. (6) The compulsively active alienated person who focuses on norms is the individual who breaks rules for the sake of breaking rules, perhaps a "rebel without a cause." For this person the very presence of a rule excites the impulse to flaunt it. (7) The compulsively passive alienated person who focuses on social objects becomes independent; he distrusts others, but he prefers to go his own way rather than pick a fight. (8) And finally, the compulsively passive alienated person who focuses on norms does not flaunt the rules but breaks them through various strategies of evasion.

3. The empirical structuring of deviant behavior. Figure 11 is an analytic classification of tendencies toward deviant behavior. Parsons is careful to distinguish between these analytically "pure" tendencies and the concrete ways in which these tendencies become "structured" in patterns of behavior [p. 283]. Structuring involves the actual behavior of persons and groups in situations. Parsons speaks of three distinct levels of structuring of deviant tendencies—one individual and two collective. The first level of collective structuring occurs when deviants join in some sort of collectivity; the second level of collective structuring involves a threat to the legitimacy of the normative regulations themselves and an effort to replace them.[19] Let us illustrate each level:

(a) Individual deviance. Parsons speaks of the actively alienated person's predisposition toward individualized crime, and the passively alienated person's predisposition toward hoboism, bohemianism, and schizophrenia. Illness, in general, is a passive and alienative response, but Parsons points out that the person who defines himself as ill does set himself off from the social structure, but also asks to be taken care of and made well, thereby being drawn back into social interaction.

As for the compulsively active conformist, Parsons finds it difficult to find concrete examples of deviant behavior, but he does single out the "compulsive achiever who places excessive demands on himself and on others, and who may also show his alienative motives by excessive competitiveness, and incapacity to tolerate normal challenges to his security and adequacy" [p. 286]. Finally, the passive conformist is the perfectionist who evades fulfillment of expectations by never "sticking his neck out."

(b) The collectivization of deviance. Parsons next takes up the "possi-

Figure 11. Eight directions of deviant behavior [from Parsons 1951, p. 259].

	Compulsive Performance Orientation (Activity)		Compulsive Acquiescence Orientation (Passivity)	
	Focus on Social Objects	Focus on Norms	Focus on Social Objects	Focus on Norms
Conformative Dominance	1. Dominance	2 Compulsive enforcement	3 Submission	4 Perfectionist observance
	Rebelliousness		Withdrawal	
Alienative Dominance	5 Aggressiveness toward social objects	6 Incorrigibility	7. Compulsive independence	8 Evasion

bility that ego can team up with one or more alters" in deviant behavior [p. 286]. By introducing this possibility, Parsons opens the topic of the "opportunity" for deviance. He considers that the presence of like-minded deviant personalities provides an additional incentive or opportunity for acting on deviant tendencies. What does the deviant gain by joining others? First, there is an increase in numbers and ability to resist sanctions. Organized crime is more effective in evading and corrupting the law than the criminal who goes it alone. Second, the deviant is more comfortable in his own alienation if he can have it approved and reinforced by others who feel the same way.

Third, and perhaps most important, the collectivization of deviant tendencies allows for the emergence of the initially *ambivalent* quality of deviant behavior. By joining a collectivity of deviants, the deviant is "enabled to act out *both* the conformative and the alienative components of his ambivalent motivational structure" [p. 286]. He can gratify his alienative tendencies by defying authority and simultaneously gratify his conformative tendencies by subordinating himself to the norms of the deviant collectivity. Familiar examples of this are "honor among thieves," the notable conformity within bohemian groups, and the strict discipline among alienated political groups, often matched only by their alienation from the dominant political system. In many respects, then, the collectivization of deviant behavior is a way of having one's cake (deviance) and eating it too (conformity).[20]

Parsons also treats certain types of group prejudice as a way of coming to terms with ambivalence. The anti-Semite, for example, holds that he, the conformist, is respectful of the ethics of fairness and honesty in the occupational world but that the Jew is the shrewd, sneaky, unfairly competitive deviant. In this case the psychological mechanism of projection plays an important role in splitting the ambivalence. The anti-Semite projects the alienative side of his ambivalence outside, while retaining the conformative side for himself. For this reason, prejudice is characteristically accompanied by feelings of moral righteousness.

(c) The collectivization of deviance that challenges legitimacy. This type of deviance involves not only breaking existing norms but challenging the system as a whole, and perhaps substituting new norms and values. It, too, is characterized by ambivalence. Many revolutionary movements attempt to legitimize themselves by pointing out that they are the "true" representatives of the fundamental value system of the society in question, thus adopting a position of wishing to destroy the system (alienative), but in the name of the system's own values (conformative). Members of revolutionary movements may also be ambivalent toward the norms of the society they are attacking. Parsons gives the following example:

> The Communists certainly often quite self-consciously exploit the patterns of freedom of speech and the like in liberal societies, but certainly in the rank and file there is widespread feeling that in justice they have a right to expect every "consideration" from the law. But, at the same time that they insist on this right they indulge in wholesale denunciation of the "system" of which it is an institutionalized part . . . it scarcely seems possible, considering the processes of recruitment of the position of such a movement in our society, that very many of its members should be anything but deeply ambivalent about the position they have taken [pp. 294–295].

4. Social control. Thus far we have been dealing only with the tendencies toward deviance in an interactive system. The final major variable in Parsons' theory is social control or "the forestalling of . . . deviant tendencies . . . and the processes by which once under way, these [tendencies] can be counteracted and the system brought back in the relevant respects to the old equilibrium state" [p. 298].

In the passage just quoted, Parsons distinguishes between the prevention of deviance—"forestalling"—on the one hand, and the containment and control of deviance on the other. The line between these two types of control is not always easy to draw, but the distinction provides a convenient basis for discussing the arguments developed by Parsons.

With respect to the prevention of deviance, we have already mentioned a number of ways of "easing" frustrating situations, especially role conflict—hierarchical priorities among roles, time scheduling of activities, concealment, and rationalization. By reducing strain these strategies lessen the probability of deviant behavior and may therefore be considered as a very general type of control over deviant behavior. In addition, Parsons identifies a number of institutionalized possibilities for "acting out" deviant tendencies in legitimate or quasi-legitimate settings, so that these tendencies are not "dammed up," only to emerge as deviant behavior elsewhere. Parsons provides two examples: (a) the ritualized expression of tension at times of great stress, such as the funeral ritual, which is supported socially and which "serves to organize the reaction system in a positive manner and to put a check on the disruptive tendencies" [p. 304]; (b) various "secondary institutions," such as "youth culture," which are relatively permissive. Youth culture may be regarded as a "safety valve" that allows people to "raise hell" in a tension-generating period of life. Activities such as reunions, celebrations, and athletic events often serve the same function. Parsons treats secondary institutions mainly as drain-off mechanisms to control deviant behavior, but he also notes that they border on deviance themselves and may pass over the line. Gambling, for example, is a control in the sense that it "relieves the strains by permitting a good deal of [deviant] behavior, and yet keeping it sufficiently within bounds so that it is not too disruptive in the opposite direction" [p. 307]. Carried to excess, however, gambling comes to be treated as a case of full-fledged deviance.

With respect to the *containment* and *control* of deviance Parsons also mentions several different mechanisms. We shall consider isolation, insulation, and the paradigm of social control processes, the last of which restores rather than merely contains deviant tendencies.

The prototypical case of isolation is the incarceration of the criminal who, in the extreme case, is simply kept apart from others, without any effort at rehabilitation. A similar case would be the removal of the mentally ill to "insane asylums" in order to put them out of the way. In recent times, the relations between isolation and rehabilitation have become blurred, as some reforms have led to treating the criminal and the insane as "sick" and "possibly to be helped" as well as "dangerous."

The line between isolation and insulation is not always clear. In general, however, insulation does not involve such deliberate "structuring out" of the deviant from the system, is not so complete in its prevention of interactions between deviant and dominant culture, and allows for the voluntary return of the deviant from the insulated sector of the larger society. An example of insulation would be placing the ill into hospitals for a temporary stay. The self-imposed insulation of deviant subgroups in geographical areas such as Greenwich Village and the Left Bank of Paris may also serve the function of minimizing day-by-day contact between the deviant group and the larger society. Of course, publicizing these groups in the mass media tends to counteract these insulative mechanisms and partially reintroduces the groups back into the social order.

Finally, Parsons outlines a paradigm of social control processes. These may be combined with other mechanisms such as insulation, but they also involve a more or less deliberate effort to return the deviant to acceptable behavior as defined by the dominant culture. This paradigm of social control can be illustrated by the religious confessional, by criminal rehabilitation, or by Alcoholics Anonymous, but I shall use Parsons' most developed example, psychotherapy, as a form of restorative social control.

Parsons considers that mental illness is *motivated* deviance. In this assertion he is completely in line with the psychoanalytic tradition,

198

which treats mental illness as rooted in neurotic conflict of the individual. Parsons suggests that psychotherapeutic settings involve a number of processes that increase the probability that the patient will be motivated to return to conformity with various role expectations—particularly familial and occupational ones—from which his illness had permitted him to withdraw.

The first ingredient of psychotherapy is the *generalized support* that is given to the person who is ill. He is not simply rejected. In the psychotherapeutic relationship the establishment of a basic trust between the therapist and the patient is essential to the relearning of various types of motivation, commitments, and role expectations. This support reincorporates the mentally disturbed person into a meaningful social relationship and reduces the chances that he will withdraw from interaction altogether.

The second condition is *permissiveness*. In the psychotherapeutic setting the patient is permitted to bring to the surface various deviant tendencies, but the psychotherapist typically does not take a moralistic or blaming attitude toward the patient. Such a stance permits the patient to gain a new level of understanding of the deviant behavior.

A third condition, closely related to permissiveness, is that the therapist *refuses to reciprocate* or gratify the patient's demands. If the patient expresses anger, the therapist does not fight back; if the patient is seductive, the therapist does not join him in collectively acting out the deviant tendencies. This frustration of deviant tendencies is an important ingredient of the situation in which motivational relearning can take place.

Finally, the psychotherapist is in the position to *manipulate rewards*. He is able to reward insights and corrective emotional relearning on the part of the patient and thus "to bring him back," as it were, to greater mental health and to restore his ability to conform to role expectations. Such, in capsule, is Parsons' theory of restorative social control as illustrated by psychotherapy.

Thus the social system is equipped with a variety of controls—drain-off mechanisms, buffers, isolation, insulation, and social structures specializing in restorative social control—all of which are counter-determinants to deviant tendencies. Parsons treats these as ways of restoring the social system to the kind of equilibrium state that existed prior to the introduction of strain into the system. It should be clear, however, that this model of restorative equilibrium is presented by Parsons as an analytic model, not as an unqualified empirical generalization. He does not maintain that deviant tendencies always are controlled and the social system thereby returned to normal functioning.

In fact, he links his analysis of deviance with his theory of social change—developed elsewhere in his writings—with the following concluding sentence in his chapter on deviance: "Structured deviant behavior tendencies, which are not successfully coped with by the control mechanisms of the social system, constitute one of the principal sources of change in the structure in the social system" [p. 321].

Summary

We have reviewed four major classes of variables in the development of Parsons' theory of deviance—the genesis of strain, the directions and types of deviance itself, the structuring of deviance, and social control. The review has indicated an implicit logical ordering among the four classes of variables. Each can be considered as logically prior to the other. Strain, for example, is a necessary condition for the development of a deviant tendency. A deviant tendency is a necessary condition for the empirical structuring of deviance. And finally, the presence of some sort of deviant behavior is a necessary condition for the activation of processes of social control. Parsons himself does not make these priorities explicit, but his discussion reveals this cumulative sequence of variables that constitute the model of deviance and control.

Some Criticisms Regarding the Logic and Testability of Parsons' Theory

A Specific Criticism: The Correspondence with Merton's Paradigm

Earlier we noted Parsons' claim that fourfold classification of deviance constituted a generalization of Merton's paradigm or, to put it another way, that Merton's paradigm "is a very important special case" of (Parsons') classification. According to Parsons, the correspondences are as follows:

Parsons	*Merton*
"Equilibrated condition of the interactive system" [p. 258]	Conformity
Compulsive performance (active conformity)	Innovation
Compulsive acquiescence (passive conformity)	Ritualism
Rebelliousness (active alienation)	Rebellion
Withdrawal (passive alienation)	Retreatism

The cases of equilibrated condition and conformity, compulsive acquiescence and ritualism, and withdrawal and retreatism appear to be relatively straightforward instances of logical parallelism, and justify Parsons' claim. The cases of compulsive performance and innovation, as
well as rebelliousness and rebellion, are more questionable. It will
be recalled that Merton cites several types of criminal activity as the
main examples of innovation. Immediately a question arises: is it appropriate to consider crime an instance of "active conformity"? If we
follow the logical parallel proposed by Parsons, it should be considered
so. Subsequently, however, Parsons himself observes that it is the "actively *alienated* [that is, rebellious] person [who] is predisposed toward
individualized crime" [p. 284, emphasis added]. Whether directly or indirectly, Parsons thus assigns criminal activity to both the conformative
and the alienative mode. With respect to the parallel between rebelliousness and rebellion, Parsons considers rebelliousness to be a case of
active alienation, whereas Merton considers it to be alienation from
goals and means, *plus* a substitution of and attraction to a new system
of goals and means. These kinds of asymmetries between Parsons' and
Merton's classificatory schemes suggest that Parsons' claim of the
"special case" is overextended and that the two schemes should be
regarded as similar in some but not all respects.

A More General Criticism:
The Problem of Derivation

One of the statements made by Parsons about the classification of directions of deviance concerns "its direct derivation from the analysis of the
interaction paradigm" [p. 257]. The precise reference of the phrase
"the interaction paradigm" is not entirely clear in this passage, but we
may assume that it involves the main components of action (actors,
means, condition, ends, norms), as well as the fundamentals of interaction (ego, alter, expectations, roles, sanctions). A classification of
deviance derived from this paradigm would presumably involve the
same concepts that denote the interaction paradigm itself—over-
conformity with expectations, underconformity with expectations, over-
sanctioning, undersanctioning, overemphasis on ends, overemphasis on
means, and so on.[21]

In what sense does Parsons "derive" from the interaction paradigm
the categories of compulsive performance, compulsive acquiescence,
rebelliousness, and withdrawal? The first dimension on which the classification is built is ambivalence, which is not derived from the categories of the interaction paradigm but is posited as a typical response
when an ego's relations with alter are disturbed or frustrated under conditions of strain. But hostility—and the resulting ambivalence—is not a

consequence that follows necessarily from the categories of the inter-action paradigm, nor is it the only empirical consequence of strain on the interaction system.[22] We might ask, then, why only one of several possible, nonderived psychological reactions to strain on the interaction system was chosen as a primary dimension for the classification of direc-tions of deviance.

The second dimension on which the classification is built is *activity-passivity*, another dimension relating to the actor's orientation to action. Parsons argues that this is "a direct derivative of the fundamental para-digm of interaction itself." He considers it as "one primary aspect of the mutual orientation of ego and alter to each other as objects" [p. 257n]. Activity is a derivation whereby an actor takes "a larger degree of con-trol over the interaction process, than the role-expectations call for"; passivity is the opposite. Once again, while such a distinction is con-sistent with the interaction paradigm, it is not developed elsewhere as a fundamental or logically necessary feature of the paradigm; further-more, the sense in which it is logically derived from the interaction paradigm is not clear. Parsons' "derivations" leave unanswered the question as to why these two types of individual reactions to institution-alized role expectations, rather than others, were chosen as the basis for the theoretical classification of deviant tendencies.

The Most General Criticism: The Incompleteness of the Theory of Deviance and Social Control

In our summary of Parsons' theory of deviance and control, we at-tempted to make explicit the logical ordering among the major variables that constitute the theory—strain, directions of deviance, the empirical structuring of deviance, and social control. Each prior variable may be conceived as a necessary condition for the following one, with the out-come—social deviance—being a product of the cumulation and inter-action among the several variables.

This implied logical ordering, however, is very loose. With respect to strain, Parsons lists a variety of sources, each of which may give rise to strain or to a number of other responses. Strain, in turn, is a neces-sary condition for the development of deviant tendencies, but it is not a sufficient condition; other responses are envisioned, but the conditions under which they, rather than deviant tendencies, will occur are not specified. Furthermore, the various tendencies to deviance may become structured empirically in a variety of ways. Finally, once deviance has arisen, it may be completely controlled or partially controlled, or it may spill over into processes of change in the social system. In these ways

Parsons' theory of deviance is characterized by a kind of openness or indeterminacy with respect to specific outcomes.

Parsons' theory thus contrasts with Durkheim's theory of suicide in that it is less able to produce precise propositions. Durkheim attempted to associate *specific* kinds of integration and regulation with suicide rates in *specific* social groups. While his classification of different types of social integration and regulation posed serious ambiguities, his propositions were relatively precise and lent themselves in principle to direct empirical confirmation or disconfirmation.[23] By contrast, the type of propositions emerging from Parsons' analysis is that a *general class* of independent variables (for example, the several types of strain) are causally linked to a *general class* of dependent variables (for example, the several directions of deviance). Because of this looseness of theoretical structure, it is not possible to relate a specific type of strain (for example, role conflict) to a specific type of deviance (for example, compulsive conformity). For the same reason, the "propositions" or "laws" in Parsons' theory take on a correspondingly indeterminate form. Consider, for example, Parsons' citation of a "law of motivational process":

Strain, defined as some combination of one or more of the factors of withdrawal of support, interference with permissiveness, contravention of internalized norms and refusal of approval for value performance, results in such reactions as anxiety, fantasy, hostile impulses, and resort to the defensive-adjustment mechanism . . . [p. 485].

The indefiniteness of this "law" arises from the fact that there are many classes of variables on both the independent and the dependent variable side and that the relations among the variables on each side are unclear.

Arising from this theoretical incompleteness is a corresponding methodological and empirical incompleteness. Because Parsons' theory of deviance and social control is indeterminate and because it does not produce specific hypotheses, a detailed methodology or research design by which it might be tested cannot be proposed. For example, because strain is not a sufficient condition for deviance, strain may exist without producing deviant behavior; for this reason, it is impossible to know what strength of empirical association between "strain" and deviance" is required to be significant. Furthermore, while Parsons does illustrate the various categories in his theory empirically—withdrawal by hoboism or by schizophrenia, for example, and the process of social control by the therapeutic process—it is impossible to ascertain what kinds of data would be required to confirm the theory. The theory's propositions are not definite enough to call for specific relations among empirical indicators.

Parsons' theory, then, appears to be less complete than Durkheim's with respect to facing the main criteria of theoretical adequacy. Although Parsons's theory is a comprehensive set of classifications and partial empirical connections, it fails to specify the conditions under which empirical associations should be expected or the canons for testing such relationships. While Durkheim's empirical methodology leaves much to be desired, while his results are far from convincing, and while his interpretations of data are vulnerable, he was nevertheless able to bring his theoretically related propositions to a level of specificity that allowed him to conduct primitive empirical tests and that permitted the critic to assess these tests. Parsons' theory falls short of this specificity and therefore does not permit such detailed criticism. For this reason we have pitched our main criticisms at a more general level, corresponding to the more general level of his formulations.

These observations suggest that what Parsons' theory needs most is a greater specification—of the conditions under which strain leads to deviance; of the conditions under which one type of deviance tends to excite one type of social control; and of the conditions under which social control tends to be effective or ineffective. Such specification would give his paradigm greater theoretical adequacy and bring it closer to direct testability.

Karl Marx's Theory of Economic Organization and Class Conflict

In discussing the work of Karl Marx, we move back in time considerably: Marx published *Das Kapital* in 1867, thirty years before Durkheim published *Suicide* and about seventy years before Parsons developed his theory on deviance. Marx's work, moreover, contrasts sharply with that of Durkheim and Parsons in several substantive respects. First, that part of Marxist theory chosen for discussion here deals with large-scale societal forces, as well as with the evolution of societies from one form to another; the focus of Parsons and Durkheim was more on the relations between the individual and his social environment and on the kinds of individual behavior that were produced by these relations. (We should not push this contrast too far, however. Durkheim also had a vision of long-term historical evolution [Bellah 1959], and elsewhere in Parsons' work we find analyses of the systematic qualities of entire societies, as well as considerations of their evolution over the centuries [Parsons 1966].) Second, both Durkheim and Parsons took social integration as their starting point and treated their respective dependent variables—suicide and deviant behavior—as manifestations of the failure of integration. Moreover, in the segments of Durkheim's and Parsons' theories that we considered, individual and group conflict arises as a by-product of the failures in the integration of a system. By contrast, Marx regarded social conflict as a necessary and endemic feature of all known societies in human history. While the integration and conflict perspectives may well be reconcilable in principle,[24] integration occupies a more central place in the work of Durkheim and Parsons, whereas conflict holds a more central place in the work of Marx. Third, the authors differ in their treatment of values and ideas as determinants of social action. Durkheim stressed the importance of moral principles as integrative forces, and Parsons identifies normative expectations as important determinants of social action. Marx conceived of values, norms, and ideas primarily as by-products of more fundamental economic and social forces. His position is summarized in the following well-known statement:

In the social production which men carry on, they enter into definite relations that are indispensable and independent of their will; these relations of production correspond to a definite stage of development of their material powers of production. The sum total of these relations of production constitutes the economic structure of society—the real foundation, on which rise legal and political superstructures and to which correspond definite forms of social consciousness. The mode of production in material life determines the general character of the social, political, and spiritual processes of life. It is not the consciousness of men that determines their existence, but, on the contrary, their social existence determines their consciousness [Marx 1859, p. 11].

Despite these differences in perspective, we shall ask the same questions of Marx as we did of Durkheim and Parsons. We shall ask how he organized his ideas and how he applied them to historical data; on the basis of our answers, we shall attempt to assess the scientific adequacy of Marx's effort. In one respect it is difficult to approach Marx in this way. Marx led a most diversified life as a scholar, journalist, ideologue, and revolutionary. His work reflects this diversity. A book like *Capital* is a work that belongs simultaneously to economics, sociology, political science, philosophy, and ideology. Therefore it is difficult, if not outright unfair, to attempt to select the theoretical or scientific aspect of Marx's work for special treatment.[25] It should be noted, however, that Marx himself conceived the "ultimate aim" of *Capital* to be a scientific one—"to lay bare the economic law of motion of modern society" [p. xix].[26] Furthermore, he welcomed "every opinion [of his work] based on scientific criticism" [p. xx].

Our treatment of Marx will be selective in still another sense. Only *Capital* will be considered. This means that many differences between *Capital* and his other works will be disregarded. Furthermore, we shall not consider the subsequent fate of the ideas found in *Capital*—for example, the discrediting of the labor theory of value, on which *Capital* is founded, and the various efforts of socialist scholars to reshape Marxist thought in the past century. In short, we shall be treating *Capital* as a self-contained enterprise, as Marx's most mature effort to explain the workings of the capitalist system.

A Selective Summary of Marx's Analysis

Marx's Starting Point: The Labor Theory of Value

Marx began his analysis with a treatment of the concept of *commodity*, which he defined as an "object outside us, a thing that by its properties satisfies human wants of some sort or another" [p. 1]. As an economist, he asked first what makes a commodity valuable, or wherein lies its source of value. Marx worked toward an answer to this question in an essentially analytic way, by breaking up what we usually think of as a physical commodity—a sack of sugar, a kitchen table, a car, and so on— into its different aspects for purposes of his analysis. In the first instance a commodity is valuable because it is useful in the process of consumption. We eat corn, we build tools with iron, and we use automobiles to move ourselves from place to place. Marx argued that this use value of a commodity has nothing to do with how much human labor has gone into producing it. Water is very useful, indeed necessary, for human survival, but it takes little or no human labor to produce it. Furthermore, use values become real only as the commodity is actually consumed.

A second important aspect of a commodity's value is its exchange value, what it will bring in the market or what it can be exchanged for. Marx noted that at first sight exchange values are very evasive, because they change continuously from time to time, from place to place, and from market to market. Nevertheless, he continued to pursue the question of why two commodities—for example, two pounds of sugar and one pound of iron—exchange for one another. Because they do exchange, he reasoned, the two commodities necessarily have something in common. What is this "something"? First, he indicated what this something is *not*—it is not "either a geometrical, a chemical, or any other natural property of commodities" [p. 4]. These features make up the *use* value of a commodity, and these uses are qualitatively different from one another; it is thus impossible to compare or consider as equivalent the different uses of a sack of sugar and a piece of iron. With this argument, Marx eliminated use value as the determinant of exchange value.[27]

If use values does not determine what a commodity will bring in the market, what does? Marx answered as follows: "if . . . we leave out of consideration the use-value of commodities, they have only one common property left, that of being products of labor" [p. 4]. The exchange values of all commodities are thereby reduced to "one and the same sort of labor, human labor in the abstract" [p. 5]. Simply stated, Marx's position is that the exchange value of an object is determined by the amount of human labor that has gone into its production. Figure 12 summarizes this position.

Basically, then, use value and exchange value are independent. As Adam Smith's famous example shows, the exchange value of diamonds is greater than that of water, but the use value of water is greater than that of diamonds. At the same time, Marx noted some peculiarities in the relationship between the two types of value. Some commodities, such as "air, virgin soil, natural meadows, etc." [p. 7] can have use value without any exchange value. Also, some things are useful products of human labor but do not have exchange value as a commodity—for example, human labor devoted to one's own satisfaction. In order for a thing to be a commodity, it has to have *some* use value for others, or social use value. And finally, if a person puts a great deal of labor into something of no use value at all, it has no exchange value. Aside

Figure 12. Labor equivalents in commodities.

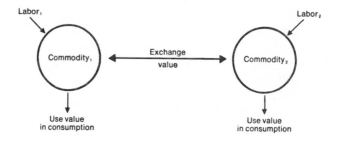

Note: Labor₁ = Labor₂

from these qualifications, however, Marx maintained that the relationship between use value and exchange value is indeterminate and that exchange value depends only on the amount of human labor incorporated into commodities.

Such, in outline, is the labor theory of value. It is the kernel of Marx's theory of capitalism. Step by systematic step he moved from this simple conception to more and more complicated formulations, bringing new considerations and assumptions to bear, until he created a model of an entire economic system. Let us now retrace his steps in that logical journey.

Extensions and Qualifications on the Simple Labor Theory of Value

The essence of the labor theory of value is contained in the following statement: "As values, all commodities are only definite masses of congealed labor-time" [p. 6]. Soon after formulating this principle, Marx qualified and extended it in several ways.

Recall that Marx distinguished between a qualitative and a quantitative aspect of commodities. The qualitative aspect is found in use values, which differ from commodity to commodity. The quantitative aspect, or that which all commodities have in common, is found in the exchange value. Marx made a similar distinction between the qualitative and quantitative aspects of the labor embodied in commodities. Labor devoted to producing particular use values is called "useful labor." This type of labor differs from one product to another. "As the coat and the linen are two qualitatively different use values, so also are the two forms of labor that produce them, tailoring and weaving" [p. 8]. Different types of useful labor are not comparable with one another.

How, then, is labor quantitatively comparable? Marx left aside the useful character of labor and argued that what is left is a simple "expenditure of human labor-power," or the productive "expenditure of human brains, nerves, and muscles" [p. 11]. This conception assumes that work drains the potential for effort from the worker at a certain rate. How do we measure this simple, abstract labor? Simply by counting the amount of time spent in working. This quantitative aspect of labor—which Marx termed "simple average labor"—is what he used as the basis for the labor theory of value. In any concrete situation both useful labor and simple average labor are intermingled; Marx simply discarded the useful form analytically and retained the simple quantity of labor, which is measured in terms of the hours, days, and weeks worked.

A problem immediately arises, however. If we rely on simple average labor, do we measure the labor of the skilled violinmaker—which is measured by hours to be sure—by the same units as that of the common laborer? How do we handle the problem of divergent skills? Marx solved this problem by a simple sort of reduction. He argued that "skilled labor counts only as simple labor intensified, or rather, as multiplied simple labor, a given quantity of skill being considered equal to a greater quantity of simple labor" [p. 11]. He added, "Experience shows that this reduction is constantly being made."

The labor of the violinmaker should thus be considered as some multiple of that of the common laborer. In the last analysis, however, and "for simplicity's sake," Marx decided that "we shall henceforth account for every kind of labor to be unskilled, simple labor; by this we do no more than save ourselves the trouble of making the reduction [from skilled to unskilled]" [p. 12].

Marx also noted that the value of a commodity should not be calculated by counting the number of hours taken to produce it under all conditions, but by counting the hours of what he calls *socially necessary labor time*. By this he meant that the exchange value of a commodity is determined by the amount of labor time "required to produce an article under normal conditions of production, and with the average degree of skill and intensity prevalent at the time" [p. 6]. In this way Marx introduced the level of technology as a variable to qualify the simple labor theory of value. It is not possible to apply the theory both to a piece of cloth woven by a handloom and to another cloth woven by a machine operative. The former spends more time in producing his commodity, but its exchange value is not as great as that made by the machine operative, who spends less time. In order to apply the labor theory of value strictly, technology, or socially necessary labor, must be held constant. If labor is to be compared under different technological conditions, appropriate modifications of the measuring procedure must be made.

Marx's most important qualification of the labor theory of value is that labor power itself can be treated as a commodity that can be bought and sold. In other words, the value of labor itself is determined by the labor theory of value. Consider first an analogy. We buy a refrigerator new and lay out a certain amount of money for it. But in order to keep it running, we have to consume a certain amount of electricity, and we have to repair it now and then. All this costs time and money. The case is similar with labor power. It takes time, money, food, and effort to train the laborer in his skill. It also takes a day-to-day maintenance in the form of food, shelter, opportunities for relaxation, and so forth, to guarantee his continuous appearance in the market. To provide these things requires other people's labor. Furthermore, "[the] value of labor-power is determined, as in the case of every other commodity, by the labor time necessary for the production, and consequently also the reproduction, of this special article" [p. 149]. Thus the laborer's power, having an exchange value, can be bought and sold on the market like any other commodity. As we shall see, this formulation is central to Marx's entire theory of the creation of capital.

Marx expressed his basic labor theory of value—that the relationship among commodities is an expression of the relative amounts of abstract labor congealed in the commodities—in a variety of ways. For example, he identified the "relative form of value," in which one commodity, such as a coat, is made equal to twenty yards of linen. In stating this, we are equating "the labor embodied in the former to that in the latter" [p. 18]. He also identified the "total or expanded form of value," in which a series of commodity equivalencies are stated in relation to one another. This formulation is simply an expansion of the relative form and shows the total list of relative values of commodities, each expressing the amount of labor congealed in it. Finally, Marx stated the "general form of value," which expresses *all* the commodity values in terms of one commodity. Marx chose linen as the illustrative commodity [p. 35], but it proved a simple step to move from linen to money as the common commodity [pp. 39–41]. In these ways Marx extended the basic theory in various directions, yielding a more complete picture of possibilities and complications. But in the end, all these extensions rest on, and can be traced back to, the simple labor theory of value.

Extension of the Labor Theory of Value to Exchange

As commodities with different use values come to be produced in larger quantities, and as exchange grows and becomes a normal social act, "some portion at least of the products of labor must be produced with a special view to exchange" [p. 60]. Furthermore, as exchange increases, there arises the necessity for a more or less universal measure of value and standard of price to facilitate exchange. Such is Marx's theory of the origin of money.

The development of a money system, however, does not modify the labor theory of value, which still stands as the foundation of the economy. Early in his discussion of the exchange process, Marx reminded his readers that "every commodity is a symbol, since, in so far as it is value it is only the material envelope of the human labor spent upon it" [p. 63]. Likewise, money is also a symbol, once removed from the ultimate standard, human labor.

Marx's general formula for what happens when exchange occurs is this:

$$Commodity \text{——} Money \text{——} Commodity$$

or

$$C \text{——} M \text{——} C$$

A weaver sells his linen for money then purchases a Bible with the money.

The result of the whole transaction, as regards the weaver is this, that instead of being in possession of the linen, he now has the Bible; instead of his original commodity, he now possesses another of the same value but of different utility. In like manner he procures his other means of subsistence and means of production. From his point of view, the whole process effectuates nothing more than the exchange of the product of his labor for the product of someone else's, nothing more than an exchange of products [p. 78].

The prices in these transactions are nothing more than the "money-name of the labor realized in a commodity" [p. 74]. Of course, the exchange relationship and the price rest on the notion of socially necessary labor time. If weaving technology changes—for example, if a power loom is introduced to take the place of a hand loom—the exchange ratio of the prices changes accordingly, because under the new technology the weaver spends less labor time on his particular product than before.

It is possible to complicate this basic formula of exchange by introducing rents and taxes and other types of payments, each of which is a special aspect of money, and each of which, by reduction, can be treated as a representation of commodities with certain values. It is even possible to generalize the formula to international exchange and to show how money develops as a complicated international standard. Any exchange system, whether simple or complex, emerges in the following form:

The total circulation of commodities in a given country during a given period is made up on the one hand of numerous isolated and simultaneous partial metamorphoses, sales which are at the same time purchases, in which each coin changes its place only once, or makes only one move; on the other hand of numerous distinct series of metamorphoses, partly running side by side, and partly coalescing with each other, in each of which series each coin makes a number of moves, the number being greater or less according to circumstances [p. 95].

The Nature of Capital and the Riddle

Up to this point we have created a picture of society with men devoting their labor to commodities and thereby imparting value to them—and exchanging them by using coin, money, and other standards of value. This picture, however reveals nothing about either capital or capitalism, which were the prime objects of Marx's analysis. In fact, we have not mentioned the word *capital* at all. Marx went on to derive the concept of capitalist society by introducing a series of new notions, especially that of surplus value. Let us first outline his general concept of capital.

The basic formula for the circulation of commodities is

$$C——M——C$$

In such an exchange the individual obtains a variety of different commodities in order to use them. The weaver gives up his linen for others to use and receives his Bible and other commodities to put them to his own use. Commodities continuously drop out of circulation as they are used. Money serves as a generalized medium, a standard of price, and a measure of value; it lubricates the process of exchange.

The basic formula for capital is different:

$$M——C——M$$

In this case the object is to buy a commodity in order to sell it for money; the purchaser's interest is not in the use of the commodity but in the process of exchange itself.

At first sight it appears nonsensical for an individual to purchase a commodity with money and then purchase money with that commodity. It is as if he bought linen with corn and then used the linen to buy back the same corn. Given this apparent absurdity, Marx argued that the transaction for capital was not simply $M——C——M$ but rather:

$$M——C——M'$$

with M' being *larger* than M. The capital transaction, therefore, must be devoted to the increase of money, "the increment or excess over the original value." Marx called this increment "surplus-value" [p. 128].

Marx's technical definition of surplus value, then, is buying cheaper in order to sell dearer. Furthermore, the creation of capital—or surplus value—is part of the very process of circulation. The capitalist, however, unlike the consumer, is not interested in the use value of commodities. "The restless never-ending process of profit-making alone is what he aims at" [p. 130]. The capitalist is a "rational miser," because he continuously increases his supply of money "by constantly throwing it afresh into circulation" [p. 131]. He pursues "value in process, money in process, and, as such, capital" [p. 132].

214 Having defined capital, Marx then presented his readers with a riddle. By his definition capital originates in the circulation of commodities. But how, he asked, can *new* value, or surplus value, be created in the process of circulation? After all, the origin of value is in labor, and the process of circulation itself involves no new labor. Marx considered a number of possible answers to this riddle, such as selling at prices deviating from their values, speculation, and so on, but he concluded that these practices could create no new value but could only redistribute existing value. After a long and somewhat tortured series of arguments, Marx concluded: "[turn] and twist then as we may, the fact remains unaltered. If equivalents are exchanged, no surplus-value results, and if non-equivalents are exchanged, still no surplus-value. Circulation, or the exchange of commodities, begets no value" [p. 141]. On the verge of discovering the secret of capital, Marx apparently concluded both that it is impossible for capital to be produced in circulation and that it is equally impossible to have it originate apart from circulation. Marx's famous "double result" is that capital "must have its origin both in circulation and not in circulation" [p. 144]. How, then, can capital be created?

The Nature of the Commodity of Labor

Marx did not leave his readers long to contemplate the riddle. Immediately after posing it, he revealed its answer. The capitalist is able to locate and create capital in the commodity of labor. This commodity alone possesses characteristics that permit the build-up and drain-off of surplus value and the creation of capital and a capitalist class.

Labor power, Marx argued, is a unique type of commodity. It is a "commodity, whose use-value possesses the peculiar property of being a source of value, whose actual consumption, therefore, is itself an embodiment of labor, and consequently, the creation of values" [p. 145]. As the value of labor is used or consumed, new value is created. Furthermore, labor power, like any other commodity, must be continuously renewed if it is to be used in production. Furthermore, this process of renewal can be defined in terms of the quantity of labor that is required to keep labor power producing. Marx formally defined labor power as "the aggregate of those mental and physical capabilities existing in a human being, which he exercises whenever he produces a use-value of any description" [p. 145]. The value of these capabilities, moreover, is reducible to "the labor-time necessary for the production, and conse-

quently also the reproduction, of this special article [of labor power]"
[p. 149].

How is the value of labor power measured? First, Marx argued that we
would have to know the value of the means of subsistence—food, cloth- **215**
ing, fuel, and housing—that are required to maintain a laboring individual. In addition, however, Marx also recognized that a distinctive cultural factor influences the needs of workers:

> The number and extent of [the worker's] so-called necessary wants, as also the
> modes of satisfying them, are themselves the product of historical development,
> and depend therefore to a great extent on the degree of civilization of a country,
> more particularly on the conditions under which, and consequently on the habits
> and degree of comfort in which, the class of free laborers has been formed. In
> contradistinction therefore to the case of commodities, there enters into the
> determination of the value of labor-power a *historical and moral element* [p. 150
> (emphasis added)].

Despite the difficulties of measuring the value of labor power, Marx concluded that "in a given country, at a given period, the average quantity
of the means of subsistence necessary for the laborer is practically
known" [p. 150]. The value of labor power is a sum of the labor of others
required to keep the laborer continuously appearing in the market and
of the labor required to train and maintain his children, who are his
future substitutes.

How much labor of others is required to reproduce the laborer from
day to day? Marx speculated that it would take six hours of others' labor
to do this. In monetary terms, this would come to three shillings of payment to them. This means that the wage for the work of the laborer is
also three shillings, because that is the equivalent of the amount of labor
that has gone into producing him. Marx treated the laborer strictly as a
commodity, and the wages he receives are calculated in the same way
as prices are calculated for any commodity—in terms of the labor congealed in them. The purchaser of labor power must pay three shillings,
or else the labor power will deteriorate and cannot produce commodities
with use values.

In this peculiar commodity of labor power Marx found the secret of
capital, profits, exploitation, and class warfare.

The Production of Absolute Surplus Value

Marx first considered what he called absolute surplus value, or that type
of capital that is produced *within* a given technological framework. Thus
he assumed economic organization and technology to remain constant.

He also made a number of other assumptions about the conditions of capitalist production and marketing. First, the worker sells his labor power, as any other commodity would be sold; the worker has no other commodity than his labor to sell; he sells it to the potential capitalist; and the product of his labors is the property of the potential capitalist.

To observe how surplus value is extracted from the worker, Marx reviewed the factors that enter into the production of a given commodity, for example, cotton yarn. Pursuing a hypothetical example, he noted that the wear and tear of the spindles and other machinery, as well as the raw material that goes into the yarn, are not without value. Certain types of labor must have gone into them in order to make them useful for spinning cotton yarn. Marx calculated the value of the fixed and working capital hypothetically as two days' labor, or twelve shillings. Marx was counting capital as stored-up labor, which is consumed in the process of production.

In addition to the fixed and working capital, the laborer, too, expends energy, and it is necessary to calculate how much labor has to go into him to make him reproducible for the following day. Again, Marx calculated hypothetically that six hours, or three shillings, would be required. If we add the cost of maintaining the spindles, the raw cotton, and the worker for six hours, the cotton yarn is worth fifteen shillings, and this represents the value of the labor that went into the product.

At this point the capitalist sees some possibilities. The worker requires three shillings per day to keep himself alive and reappearing in the market, and the capitalist must pay this amount. But this does not prevent the capitalist from working the laborer *more* than six hours but still paying him three shillings. The capitalist proceeds to work the worker *twelve* hours, paying him only the necessary three shillings in twelve hours. In a twelve-hour period, the capitalist pays twenty-four shillings for spindles and raw cotton, three shillings for necessary labor, but retains the three shillings that the laborer has created in use values during his excess six hours. In this way the capitalist has created three shillings of *surplus value* for himself. This is the key to the production of absolute surplus value—working the worker for more hours than is necessary to keep him reappearing in the market.

To calculate the rate of surplus value, Marx made a number of formal definitions. First, he defined the spindles, machinery, building, raw cotton, as *constant capital* (*c*): "that part of capital which is represented by the means of production, by the raw material, auxiliary material, the instruments of labor, and does not in the process of production, undergo any quantitative alteration of value" [p. 191]. The stored-up labor in capital is transferred without modification to the final product of cotton yarn. Second, the production process also involves *variable capital* (*v*), which is "represented by labor power, and which does, in the process of production, undergo an alteration of value. It produces the equivalent of its own value [that necessary to keep the laborer appearing in the market] and also produces a surplus-value" [pp. 191–192]. To calculate the rate of surplus value, *c* is ignored, for it simply transfers its value to the final product. The remaining value of the final product contains a certain amount of variable capital (*v*) *and* a certain amount of surplus value (*s*). The rate of production of surplus value is the ratio of the surplus value to the variable capital:

$$\frac{s}{v}$$

In the hypothetical example above, the rate of surplus value would be arrived at by dividing three shillings (surplus value) by three shillings (variable capital); the rate of surplus value would be 1.0.[28]

On the basis of this calculation, Marx arrived at a technical definition of exploitation: "[the] rate of surplus-value is . . . an exact expression for the degree of exploitation of labor-power by capital, or of the laborer by the capitalist" [pp. 200–201]. For Marx, therefore, exploitation is not simply a general form of economic injustice. It is a technically defined process, derived from a view of the economy based on the labor theory of value. The social classes that emerge from the process of producing surplus value are also technically defined. Those classes accruing surplus value are the capitalists, or the bourgeoisie; those being exploited are the workers, or the proletariat.

Thus far, Marx's examples of surplus value have been purely hypothetical; they have been given meaning only in terms of the formal structure of his theory. How, in practice, does the capitalist acquire absolute surplus value?

Marx answered by arguing that under a given system of technology the capitalist extends the working day to extract the maximum surplus value from the worker in the minimum time. He stops short of killing the laborer by overwork, because he has an interest in seeing that the worker continues to appear in the market; but this is the only limit on the capitalist. Under the capitalist system there is an inherent tendency to extend the workday as far as possible. This tendency is to be found, moreover, wherever capitalism is found. The production of absolute surplus-value proves "to be independent of any change in the mode of production itself . . . it was not less active in the old-fashioned bakeries than in the modern cotton factories" [p. 297]. The production of absolute surplus value does not require any growth or expansion of capitalism to realize itself.

The tendency of exploitation is counteracted by the tendency of the laboring classes to resist the exploitation: "the laborer maintains his right as seller when he wishes to reduce the working day to one of definite normal duration" [p. 218]. The history of capitalist production, then, can be read as a struggle between the exploiters and the exploited. "[The] determination of what is a working day presents itself as the result of a struggle, a struggle between collective capital, i.e., the class of capitalists, and collective labor, i.e., the working class."

Having given his theory of the production of absolute value some empirical reference, Marx then turned to the facts of capitalist history and interpreted them in the light of this theory. Chapter 10 of *Capital* is devoted to an extensive documentation of the capitalists' strategies of lengthening the working day. Marx interpreted the history of labor under capitalism as a complicated interplay among three historical tendencies: (1) The tendency of capitalism "to appropriate labor during all the 24 hours of the day" [p. 241]. (2) The limitation imposed by the need to keep labor at a bare survival level in order that it continue to be available for capitalist exploitation. "[The] limiting of factory labor was dictated by the same necessity which spread guano over the English fields. The same blind eagerness for plunder that in the one case exhausted the soil, had, in the other, torn up by the roots the living force of the nation" [p. 222]. (3) The power of "the working class movement that daily grew more threatening." A major part of the history of capitalism, then, is the story of the struggle for a normal working day.

Summary and Recapitulation

We have now concluded the long journey from the definition of a commodity to the explanation of some of the basic facts of capitalist production. Marx first defined the nature of a commodity in terms of value, which was found in human labor. Next, he determined the nature of capital, which is systematically extracted in the form of surplus labor from the process of circulation of commodities of labor. He then equated the rate of creation of surplus value with the rate of exploitation of workers by capitalists. Next, he identified one major form of exploitation as the extension of the working day by capitalists. He next argued, by further specification, that many critical historical events in capitalism can be interpreted as a working out of this struggle between the exploiters and the exploited. Finally, he interpreted, at great length, events such as the imposition of night work, the relay system, and the workers' mobilization to agitate for a normal working day as the historical manifestation of this struggle.

I have not summarized Marx's theory in terms of the seven components of scientific inquiry outlined at the beginning of this essay. The exposition of that theory is complicated enough as it is, and such a summary would have encumbered the presentation. Nevertheless, it is possible to recapitulate his theory in terms of those components.

1. The basic problems that Marx faced were to identify the laws governing the production, exchange, and distribution of commodities (labor included) under the capitalist system and to specify the relations among the various agents in this process. His range of data thus included a vast array of economic and social characteristics of the capitalist system.

2. His basic concepts were "commodity" and "labor." From these basic concepts he proceeded logically to the concepts of exchange, surplus value, exploitation, profits, and the conflict among classes.

3. The structure of Marx's theory involves the logical relationship between labor, surplus value, exploitation, and the other basic concepts. Marx's theory is especially impressive in its systematic transitions from one basic concept to the next. It closely approaches derivation, because each new basic concept is defined explicitly in terms of the foregoing ones.

5. The propositions emerging from the theory are many, but the master proposition is that the capitalists, or extractors of surplus value, maximize their position by accumulating as much value (profits) as they can without actually destroying the working population. Correspondingly, the workers resist this exploitation and demand the normal working day, which represents the true value of their labor.

6. Empirically these propositions translate into historical statements that the classes will behave as if in conflict—the capitalists to extend hours, the workers to shorten them. The result will be a series of struggles emerging from the basically antipathetic positions of the classes.

7. Marx attempted to verify these historical statements by detailed historical investigation of working conditions under the capitalist mode of production.

The Production of Relative Surplus Value

In this analysis of absolute surplus value, Marx noted that he was not considering "changes in the method of production." His analysis of the working day related only to "given conditions of production" and to "a given stage in the economical development of society" [p. 300]. After considering absolute surplus value, Marx relaxed these assumptions.

The production of *absolute* surplus value depends on the establishment of a ratio between surplus value and variable capital, and absolute surplus value can be expressed in the formula s/v. Furthermore, absolute surplus value is produced by lengthening the working day and thereby making s larger.

The production of *relative* surplus value also involves increasing the ratio between s and v, but it does so by making v smaller. Marx defined relative surplus value as "arising from the curtailment of the necessary labor-time, and from the corresponding alteration in the respective lengths of the two components of the working day [that is, necessary and surplus labor-time]" [p. 304].

How can necessary labor time (variable capital) be reduced? Marx found the answer in technological change, which cuts down the variable capital or necessary labor time to produce a commodity. Pursuing a hypothetical example, Marx argued that by saving labor through the use of a mechanical invention, the capitalist lowers the cost of his commodity from one shilling to nine pence, thus giving himself three pence more surplus value. Of course, the capitalist lowers his price somewhat, say to ten pence, which means that he acquires two pence less in the market for his product, but he gains a marked advantage over his competitors and still retains one pence more of surplus value than his competitors. The production of relative surplus value means that the capitalist attains surplus value relative to other capitalists operating under less advanced technological conditions. On the basis of this reasoning, Marx concluded that "there is a motive for each individual capitalist to cheapen his commodities by increasing the productiveness of labor" [p. 307].

Of course, the innovating capitalist's advantage is likely to be temporary. As a new method of production becomes widely known, other capitalists pick it up, and the relative difference between the innovator's profits and the profits of the others begins to diminish. The capitalist system thus coerces competitors to adopt new methods and coerces prospective innovators to seek continuously for new ways to improve their relative position once again.

By improving technology and reducing the necessary part of the working day, the capitalist is simultaneously reducing the amount of labor time necessary to keep his laborers on the job. This should not suggest, however, that the capitalist actually reduces the length of the working day. In fact, Marx argued that the capitalist attempts to maximize both absolute and relative surplus value. He lengthens the working day and cuts the necessary working time at the same time. Both strategies work toward the maximization of surplus value, exploitation, and profits. The production of absolute surplus value and the production of relative surplus value are simply two different ways for the capitalist to attain his objectives.

By introducing the notion of relative surplus value, Marx made his view of the capitalist system dynamic. The capitalist innovates to gain an advantage over his competitors, because he is motivated to increase his surplus value. Furthermore, innovation is necessarily temporary, because competitors continuously copy new advances and reduce the relative advantage of the innovators. Capitalists are thus motivated to change the system of production at an increasingly furious rate. Insofar as this process of change increases the level of relative surplus value, exploitation becomes more and more severe as the capitalist system moves ahead.

What are the specific mechanisms by which the capitalist increases relative surplus value? Marx identified three such mechanisms: the introduction of cooperation among laborers; the introduction of a division of labor; and the introduction of machinery.

1. Cooperation. Marx argued that the bringing together of laborers into cooperative relationships made an enterprise more productive (and thereby increased relative surplus value). First, in cooperating, many workers use capital in common, and this cheapens commodities and brings about a decrease in necessary labor. It is more economical to use twenty weavers in one building than one weaver in one building. Second, working cooperatively increases the morale of each worker. Third, an urgent project (for example, the harvesting of wheat) can be completed more effectively if many cooperate. Fourth, work over an extended space can be completed more effectively through cooperation. Finally, Marx noted that increased cooperation gives rise to the possibility of an increased division of labor. Each of these effects augments relative surplus value.

As might be expected, Marx regarded cooperation as one of the manifestations of the capitalist's motive "to extract the greatest possible amount of surplus-value from the workers" [p. 321]. At the same time, he noted that cooperation and increasing productivity set the stage for a more effective resistance to this kind of exploitation on the part of the laborers.

As the number of the cooperating laborers increases, so too does their resistance to the domination of capital, and with it, the necessity for capital to overcome this resistance by counter-pressure [discipline and control]. The control exercised by the capitalist is not only a special function, due to the nature of the social labor-process, and peculiar to that process, but it is, at the same time, a function of the exploitation of a social labor-process, and is consequently rooted in the unavoidable antagonism between the exploiter and the living and laboring raw material he exploits [p. 321].

Innovation increases exploitation, which in turn increases the antagonism of the laborers toward the capitalists. This in turn increases the efforts on the part of the capitalists to overcome this antagonism.

222

2. Manufacturing, or the division of labor. Marx saw a similar advantage accruing to the capitalist who has workers assemble different objects into a single commodity or has them progressively modify a commodity into its final form. The economic effect of an increasing division of labor is to simplify the tasks of any one laborer, to integrate the efforts of all, to make work more efficient, and thereby to increase the surplus value for the capitalist. Furthermore, because of the increased efficiency of labor, manufacturing imparts to the capitalist system a tendency to grow larger and larger, to expand its capital, and to concentrate it in fewer hands [pp. 353–354]. The social effect of the increasing division of labor is to begin the process of dividing society into two groups— a small group of intelligent persons and a large group of detailed laborers, whose relationship to the productive process becomes more and more remote. Manufacturing decomposes the handicrafts and begins to form a large army of detailed laborers. This process of destroying skill is not completed, however, until the onset of machinery [p. 362].

3. Machinery. The introduction of machinery has a much greater impact on the worker than cooperation or manufacturing, but it resembles these more modest innovations in that it is yet another way of maximizing relative surplus value for the capitalist.

For Marx, the essence of machinery consists of the substitution of natural power for human power and the application of science—as opposed to the rule of thumb—to manufacturing. The result is that manufacturing is removed from the control of the workman. Machinery forces a pattern of cooperation on labor, but it is different from the kind that existed before machinery. "[The] cooperative character of the labor-process [under machinery] is a technical necessity, dictated by the instrument of labor itself" [p. 382].

To calculate the value of the final product under conditions of machine production, it is necessary to count the amount of labor that goes into the manufacture of the machine and to compare this with the amount of current labor it saves. If the total labor entering the product is less, the capitalist has increased productivity and thereby increased his profit.

Marx specified a number of mechanisms by which machinery leads to greater exploitation and, thereby, to greater antagonism among the classes. The first effect of machinery is to appropriate supplementary labor, mainly in the form of women and children, as adjuncts to the machinery. This becomes possible because of the minor cleaning, tending, and other ancillary, low-skill operations necessary for the operation of machinery.

How does the employment of women and children provide the capitalist with more surplus value? It will be recalled that the labor necessary to sustain a worker in the market also includes the labor necessary to support his family so that tomorrow's labor force can be produced. In any case the capitalist has to pay the laborer sufficient wages to support his family. If the capitalist employs the worker, his wife, and his two children at the same time, he gains the work of four for the cost of supplying a single family's subsistence.

The economic effect of appropriating supplementary labor is to multiply the amount of relative surplus value available to the capitalist. The social effects are equally profound. The workman becomes a slave dealer. "Previously, [he] sold his own labor-power, which he disposed of nominally as a free agent. Now he sells wife and child" [p. 393]. Factory labor leads to the physical deterioration and the moral degradation of women and children. And finally, the capitalist uses women and children as weapons in his war against male workers. "By the excessive addition of women and children to the ranks of the workers, machinery at last breaks down the resistance which the male operatives in the manufacturing period continued to oppose, the despotism of capital" [p. 400].

The second effect of machinery is to give the capitalist a new advantage in his effort to lengthen the working day. If the machine is used continuously, it can be replaced more quickly. Furthermore, most of its depreciation comes through use rather than rust and decay. In addition, the extension of the working day means more intensive use of the land, buildings, and other fixed capital. Finally, the working day can be extended, because the worker is now paced to the machine, not to his own work habits.

The further extension of the working day unfolds by two stages. First, when the entrepreneur introduces a new machine, he has a temporary monopoly, since his competitors are still producing on the old basis. During the period when profits are exceptional, the innovator attempts to build these profits as rapidly as possible, by prolonging the working day. Second, when profits begin to drop as others adopt the new technology, the capitalist lengthens the working day even more, in order to slow the decline of his profits. By such means, Marx argued, "machinery sweeps away almost every moral and natural restriction on the length of the working day" [p. 406].

The third effect of machinery is to permit the capitalist to intensify labor in his factor by speeding up the machines. This strategy was adopted by capitalists, Marx argued, especially when, in the nineteenth century, the working class movement succeeded in reducing the absolute length of the working day.

Fourth, the introduction of machinery revolutionizes those branches that continue under old systems of production. As machinery invades capitalist production, the domestic and handicraft industries must either become departments of factories or be forced into increasing misery because of their inability to compete with factory-made goods. Furthermore, because of their dispersion and isolation, workers in these industries cannot resist exploitation. For these and other reasons, Marx felt that the conditions of exploitation and human degradation were at their very worst in the transitional domestic and handicraft industries [pp. 464ff.].

Finally, the introduction of machinery initiates increasingly severe crises of capitalist production. The introduction of a new method of machine production is typically followed by a brief period of extraordinarily high profits for the innovator, because of his great advantage over his competitors. As they discover his market advantage, however, they rush in great numbers to share in it. Thus capitalism grows furiously, but by fits and starts, and by recurrent crises of expansion and overproduction:

The enormous power, inherent in the factory system, of expanding by jumps, and the dependence of that system on the markets of the world, necessarily beget feverish production, followed by overfilling of the markets, whereupon contraction of the markets brings on crippling of production. The life of modern industry becomes a series of periods of moderate activity, prosperity, overproduction, crisis and stagnation [p. 455].

The effect of these crises on the working classes is alternately to attract and to repel them from employment, generally rendering their relationship to the capitalist system more precarious. "The work-people are . . . continuously both repelled and attracted, hustled from pillar to post . . ." [p. 456].

The capitalist, then, possesses a whole arsenal of tactics to increase exploitation—such as lengthening the working day, bringing workers into cooperation with one another, dividing their labor into specialized tasks, appropriating female and child labor, or speeding up machinery. Moreover, the worker may be expected to resist this exploitation in whatever form he finds it. The history of class relations is therefore one of constant warfare; "[the] contest between the capitalist and the wage-laborer dates back to the very origin of capital" [p. 427]. And while Marx did not actually spell out a fixed evolution of stages of worker resistance, the development of resistance tended to parallel the development of capitalist industry.

Thus, while the class struggle "raged on throughout the whole manufacturing period" [p. 427], it took a new form with the introduction of machinery, which forcibly displaces workmen. With the introduction of machinery, the workers' attacks turned against "the instruments of labor itself," and the early history of machinery was marked by violent attacks upon new machinery [pp. 427–429].

As the excesses of exploitation by machinery multiplied in the late eighteenth century in England, and as "the workpeople learnt to distinguish between machinery and its employment by capital" [p. 429], they began to direct their attacks not so much toward the machines themselves but toward the exploitative tactics associated with them. Thus, in the early and middle nineteenth century, the workers fought to reduce the length of the working day, to reduce the labor of women and children, and to check the tendency to speed up machinery. Marx argued that these reactions on the part of the workers were as inevitable as the introduction of machinery itself:

Factory legislation, that first conscious and methodical reaction of society against the spontaneously developed form of the process of production is . . . just as much the necessary product of modern industry as cotton yarn, self-actors, and the electric telegraph [pp. 485–486].

Finally, as workers develop a greater consciousness and ability to mobilize against capital, they gradually forge a revolutionary organization that is destined ultimately to overthrow the capitalist system by violence and to usher in a socialist system free from the contradictions bred by the system of capitalist production.

Some Criticisms of Marx's Theoretical Foundations of Capitalist Society

One of the remarkable features of Marx's theory, as developed in *Capital*, is its systematic series of transitions from general principles to specific historical interpretations. The first and most fundamental ingredient of his theory is the *labor theory of value*, by which he attempted to demonstrate that the value of—as well as the rates of exchange among—commodities can be explained by calculating the quantity of labor that has entered into them. In accord with this general principle, Marx defined the commodity of labor and deduced that by buying and selling labor power it is possible to create *surplus value*, or the accumulation of value above and beyond that imparted to commodities. To define surplus value, moreover, is to provide the definitions of *capital, exploitation,* and *profits*, all of which are direct expressions of the process of extracting surplus value from the working population. Next, by introducing a notion of the organization of production, Marx was able to identify the *specific means* of augmenting surplus value and exploitation—means such as extending the working day, introducing machinery, recruiting women and children, and so forth. By further specification, he argued that the intensity of *class antagonism* and *class struggle* would also be a direct expression of the level of exploitation inflicted by the capitalist class, though the form of the struggle would depend on the maturity of the working-class movement as well. Having arrived at this level of specificity, Marx had produced a series of statements about how capitalists and workers behave—the capitalists to maximize profits, surplus value, and exploitation, and the workers to resist in a variety of ways—and he could write the history of capitalism in terms of these tendencies.

We shall develop two lines of criticism of this elaborate theoretical structure. First, we shall raise a number of questions about the basic concepts Marx employed in erecting his theoretical scaffolding—concepts such as value, socially necessary labor time, and simple average labor. This line of criticism will focus on the conceptual aspects of his theory. Second, we shall raise a number of critical observations concerning the power of his concepts to predict the future of capitalism and to account for the behavior of the working classes, particularly in the period of British history that commanded Marx's attention. This line of criticism will focus on some of the empirical, or historical, aspects of his theory.

The Labor Theory of Value

Toward the end of the nineteenth century the Austrian economist Eugen von Böhm-Bawerk published a book entitled *Karl Marx and the Close of His System*, in which he raised a number of objections to Marx's logic in establishing the labor theory of value. In the first place, he questioned Marx's assumption that if commodities are to exchange they must have something in common. Böhm-Bawerk remarked that it seemed more logical to assume that some inequality between commodities would induce the exchange; "[where] equality and exact equilibrium obtain, no change is likely to disturb the balance" [1949, p. 68]. Marx himself seemed to be aware of this point, since he did qualify his concept of value by acknowledging that in order to exchange at all, commodities have to have some use value, that is, a qualitatively unique property.

According to Böhm-Bawerk, Marx erred further in moving from this questionable philosophical starting point to his search for the common factor. Marx used the argument by elimination: he excluded all "geometrical, physical, chemical, or other natural properties of the commodities" that makes up their use value (even though, in the qualification just noted, these properties could not be excluded altogether). Leaving use value aside, Marx argued that "there remains in [commodities] only one other property, that of being products of labor." Böhm-Bawerk reacted sharply to this argument:

> Is it so? I ask . . . is there only one other property? Is not the property of being scarce in proportion to demand also common to all exchangeable goods? Or that they are the subjects of demand and supply? Or that they are appropriated? Or that they are natural products? . . . Or is not the property that they cause expense to their producers . . . common to exchangeable goods [1949, p. 75]?

Finally, Böhm-Bawerk criticized Marx for his discrepancy in the treatment of labor and all other commodities. Marx argued that values-in-use of all commodities are qualitatively different and cannot be compared; but with respect to labor he was prepared to separate a quantitative value-in-use (that is, the wearing down of "human brains, nerves, and muscles") from its qualitative aspect. Why could not the same distinction be made for other commodities, whose value-in-use could then be made a quantitatively comparable basis for exchange [1949, pp. 76–77]?

Böhm-Bawerk's general philosophical criticisms themselves have not gone unchallenged [Hilferding 1949], and, even if correct, do not necessarily undermine completely Marx's conclusions about the functioning of the capitalist system, which may be *empirically* valid even if not properly derived from Marx's first principles. Nevertheless, criticisms of the sort advanced by Böhm-Bawerk do raise questions about the soundness of the *logical* basis Marx advanced for accepting the fundamental premises of his theory.

Marx's Equivocations on Several Central Concepts

Equally serious—though different—logical problems arise in connection with two of Marx's attempted refinements of the labor theory of value: his concept of simple average labor and his concept of socially necessary labor time.

1. Simple average labor. Marx arrived at his notion of simple average labor by disregarding the qualitative element of labor and considering the remaining quantitative "expenditure of human brains, nerves, and muscles." The problem of diverse skills—the violinmaker and the common laborer—is handled by assuming that a reduction is made, whereby the value of the labor of the violinmaker is some multiple of that of the laborer.

How is simple average labor to be measured? By what formula should the various multiples of simple labor be calculated empirically? Marx never gave a satisfactory answer. Simple average labor cannot be calculated by observing a laborer at work and counting the absolute hours he works, because he is working with a certain level of skill and within a certain technological level. Nor can it be found in the actual level of wages paid to a laborer.[29] Simple average labor is something concealed: "[the] different proportions in which different sorts of labor are reduced to unskilled labor as their standard, are established by a social process that goes on behind the backs of the producers, and consequently, appear to be fixed by custom" [p. 12]. Nonetheless, Marx argued that experience shows that this reduction is constantly being made.

Given this formulation, it is difficult to know how to determine simple average labor in commodities other than by observing the ratios at which commodities actually exchange. But that exchange ratio is presumably what is to be explained by referring to the amount of labor. Marx seemed to place himself in a circle, whereby he argued that the exchange ratios are determined by the amount of simple average labor and that we know the amount of simple average labor by looking at the exchange ratios. The presumed cause is likely to be identified only by its presumed effects. Furthermore, if the amount of simple average labor cannot be identified empirically aside from exchange ratios, it tends to become simply another way of renaming whatever exchange ratios happen to exist at any given time. The concept of simple average labor is, in short, an evasive concept. Marx supplied no operations by which it might be identified empirically, and insofar as he hinted that it is to be discovered in the exchange process itself, he approached the danger of circular reasoning.

2. Socially necessary labor time. Marx qualified his concept of labor by arguing that absolute hours of labor can be considered comparable only under a given state of technology. The amount of labor time necessary to produce an article changes as technology changes. But as in the case of simple average labor, Marx provided no hints as to how the amount of socially necessary labor time could be calculated in practice. This omission is a particularly serious one, since the concept plays such a crucial role in his theory of surplus value. Surplus value, as well as exploitation, is represented as a ratio between surplus labor time and necessary labor time. But in his own demonstration of how suplus value is created, Marx relied not on any *empirical* measure of necessary labor time, but instead on a purely *hypothetical* representation of six hours of labor time, without defending his choice of this particular number. His entire calculation rested on this hypothetical figure. Moreover, his con-

cept of the rate of surplus value would have been drastically affected if he had chosen some number of hours—for example, twelve or thirteen—for necessary labor time, a number that could not be readily lengthened on an absolute basis. Marx did note that necessary labor includes food, fuel, housing, and other necessary wants, but that it also contains a "historical and moral element"—a complex package of inputs that appears to defy accurate measurement and calculation. In short, Marx's failure to provide empirical clues to the calculation of necessary labor time weakens his derivation of surplus value, capital, profits, and exploitation.

To summarize this line of criticism, it appears that Marx enfeebled his theory by making a number of important equivocations. First, he equivocated with respect to the principle that only labor determines exchange value by acknowledging that a minimum of use value is necessary. Second, he qualified the labor theory of value by saying that the amount of labor has to be both "simple average" and "socially necessary" in form. But in indicating how such labor might be empirically identified, he further equivocated by falling back on phrases such as "experience shows" or "it can be practically known." Such equivocations prompted E. H. Carr to venture the following harsh judgment:

Instead of the concrete proposition that "the value of a commodity is determined by the labor-time requisite to produce it," we are now asked to believe that a certain abstract property called value, which belongs to any labor-produced commodity, and which, though purporting to be its exchange-value, does not in fact coincide with its price . . . is determined by the amount embodied in the said commodity of another abstract property called "simple average labor." Stated in such terms, the labor theory of value becomes a pure abstraction. It may be believed in as a matter of faith; but it cannot be proved or disproved by logic. It may possess a moral or philosophical meaning; but whether true or false, it has ceased to have any validity in the world of economics [1934, p. 264].

Such a judgment is overstated. It is not necessary to demand that abstract concepts correspond to reality, for concepts are meant, not simply to reflect reality, but to enhance our understanding of reality by giving us reasons to expect certain empirical outcomes under specified conditions.[30] Nevertheless, the judgment has some merit, since it indicates that Marx, by making a number of serious equivocations in defining his basic concepts, reduced his theory's ability to predict the specific values of a number of variables—such as surplus value and exploitation—that are essential to his entire theoretical structure.

Some Problems in Prediction and Historical Explanation

Predicting the Future of Capitalism

One strong feature of Marx's theory is that, despite the fact that it may rest on wobbly logical foundations, its conceptual ingredients are so organized that Marx was able to make definite predictions about the future of capitalism—that exploitation would intensify, that workers would be driven into increasing misery, and that they would eventually coalesce into a successful revolutionary movement. Marx's theory, then, appears to measure up well on the criterion of potential verifiability and falsifiability when compared, for example, with Parsons' theory of deviance.[31] In this section I shall review Marx's technical basis for predicting the future of capitalism, indicate a few of the ways in which his predictions proved vulnerable, and suggest a modification within Marx's theory that might improve its predictive potential.

Toward the end of the first volume of *Capital*, Marx turned to the analysis of the laws of capitalist growth and accumulation. The most important factor in this analysis is "the composition of capital and the changes it undergoes" [p. 208]. Marx defined this as the ratio between the constant capital, or the value of the means of production (c), and the variable capital, or value of labor power (v). These two concepts were employed in arriving at the original definition of surplus value.

If the composition of capital remains the same, an expansion of constant capital will automatically expand the variable capital by a fixed, corresponding amount. The impact of this type of expansion on class relations, Marx argued, is simply that "the sphere of capital's exploitation and rule merely extends with its own dimensions and the number of its subjects" [p. 631]. Under conditions of competition, however, capitalists begin to innovate and to accumulate more surplus value by reducing the amount of variable capital (v), thus increasing the composition ratio c/v. This process of "development of the productivity of social labor becomes the most powerful lever of accumulation" [p. 635]. By thus making fewer laborers produce more work, the capitalist alters the rate of relative surplus value. This leads in turn to the further concentration of capital, or the transformation of capital into fewer hands controlling more. As productivity increases, the number of laborers "falls in proportion to the mass of the means of production worked up by them" [p. 641].

Under these conditions of the changing composition of capital, an accelerating process of change is generated. Furthermore, since the variable part of capital (necessary labor) is continuously being reduced, the process begins to create a "relatively redundant population of laborers, a population of greater extent than suffices for the average needs of self-expansion of capital, and therefore a surplus-population" [pp. 643–644]. It is the essence of capitalism to form "a disposable industrial reserve army, that belongs to capital; it creates, for the changing needs of the self-expansion of capital, a mass of human material always ready for exploitation" [p. 646]. This accelerating vicious circle associated with continuing increases in productivity leads to a deterioration of the labor force and permits the continuing use of supplementary labor, the replacement of skilled by unskilled workers, and so on. In the long run the contradictions bred by this law of capitalist accumulation lead to the deterioration of the entire system:

Within the capitalist system all methods for raising the social productiveness of labor are brought about at the cost of the individual laborer; all means for the development of production transform themselves into means of domination over, and exploitation of, the producers; they mutilate the laborer into a fragment of a man, degrade him to the level of an appendage of a machine, destroy every remnant of charm in his work, and turn it into a hated toil; they estrange from him the intellectual potentialities of the labor-process in the same proportion as science is incorporated in it as an independent power; they distort the conditions under which he works, subject him during the labor-process to a despotism more hateful for its meanness; they transform his life-time into working-time and drag his wife and child beneath the wheels of the juggernaut of capital. But all methods for the production of surplus-value are at the same time methods of accumulation; and every extension of accumulation becomes again a means for the development of those methods. It follows therefore that in proportion as capital accumulates, the lot of the laborer, be his payment high or low, must grow worse. The law, finally, that always equilibrates the relative surplus-population, or industrial reserve army, to the extent and energy of accumulation, this law rivets the laborer . . . firmly to capital . . . . It establishes an accumulation of misery, corresponding with accumulation of capital. Accumulation of wealth at one pole is, therefore, at the same time accumulation of misery, agony of toil, slavery, ignorance, brutality, mental degradation, at the opposite pole . . . [pp. 660–661].

Many of the criticisms of Marx in the century since *Capital* was written have argued that Marx was mistaken in his predictions: that capital has not centralized at the rate anticipated by Marx; that the industrial reserve army has not increased at an accelerated rate; that technology has wiped out unskilled jobs more than skilled ones; that the diversification of "proletarian" jobs has prevented the emergence of a unified working class; that gradual diminution of worker exploitation through reform instead of violent revolution has been the hallmark of the subsequent development of capitalist societies; that class conflict has been successfully institutionalized; and so on.[32]

In so far as these generalizations about the past century of the history of capitalism are accurate, they constitute important objections to Marx's theory. However, instead of concluding simply that "Marx was wrong" or instead of examining in detail each prediction emanating from his theory, I am going to argue that many of the valid parts of Marx' theory of capital accumulation can be accepted, despite the fact that they led to erroneous predictions. The method of making them acceptable, moreover, is to modify one critical assumption in his formulation of the law of accumulation, thereby permitting different lines of prediction to emerge from his theory.

The critical assumption has to do with a key qualification in *Capital:* that the "necessary wants" of a laborer—that is, those things that must be satisfied if a laborer is to continue to appear in the market—*are themselves subject to historical variation.* Marx explicitly acknowledged this when he said that wants "depend to a great extent on the degree of civilization of a country," and thus depend on "a historical and moral element" [p. 150]. Yet in his own formulation of the basic law of capital accumulation—which involves an accelerating process of reducing necessary labor time—Marx implicitly held the "necessary wants" of workers constant. In fact, however, many of the struggles of social groups in the past century have concerned the degree to which subordinated groups in Western societies "deserve" various social benefits such as education, decent housing, exposure to culture, and so on. Such struggles, which have brought about significant social changes, have concerned the cultural definitions of what is socially necessary for workers and other groups. As such, these changes have slowed down the pace at which technological innovation has reduced necessary labor by changing the cultural criteria of what is necessary for labor.

If Marx had envisioned a substantial change in the cultural definition of a worker's "needs" or "wants"—that is, if he had allowed for a substantial modification in the social definition of necessary labor time—he might well have softened his predictions concerning the rate at which surplus value and profits are created, the rate at which capital is centralized, the rate at which an industrial reserve army grows, and so on. The corresponding predictions concerning the class struggle also would have been broadened to include the possibility that the bourgeoisie and the proletariat would engage in political struggles over worker's "rights"—that is, the proper social definitions of their necessary and legitimate wants and needs—as well as in life-and-death revolutionary struggles involving the fate of the whole capitalist system.

232

What I am suggesting is that Marx's predictions about the future of capitalism were incorrect in part because he envisioned the entire evolution of capitalism as depending only on changes in one fundamental factor: the changing composition of capital. I am suggesting further that it would be fruitful to modify this vision by permitting the possibility of variation in certain historical and moral conditions that Marx himself acknowledged as variable in principle. This theoretical modification would appear to make Marx's predictions more realistic historically and would, at the same time, preserve the basically valid relations between the components of capital as analyzed by Marx.

Some Problems in Using "Exploitation" and "Class Consciousness" as Explanatory Concepts

One of the central principles in Marx's interpretation of capitalist history is that capitalists and workers are ranged in opposition to one another and that workers will fight exploitation when they find it oppressing them.

Basing his interpretations on this principle, Marx advanced an interpretation of the behavior of the British workers in the eighteenth and nineteenth centuries in relation to the length of the working day. He described the last third of the eighteenth century as "a violent encroachment like that of an avalanche in its intensity and extent. All bounds of morals and nature, age and sex, day and night, were broken down. . . . Capital celebrated its orgies" [p. 264]. Exploitation was at its highest. Marx asserted further that "as soon as the working class, stunned at first by the noise and turmoil of the new system of production, recovered, in some measure, its senses, its resistance began." Exploitation was met by working-class resistance.

In my own research on the working classes during the British industrial revolution, however, a number of historical events appeared incongruent with the supposed relationship between exploitation and its resistance. Working-class agitation to shorten hours and improve conditions did not appear until several decades after the bitterest exploitation of the early factory system. Furthermore, when the antagonism between capitalists and workers flared over the question of hours in the 1830s and 1840s, the conditions of exploitation—hours, wages, health, and so on—were improving. Finally, after the Factory Act of 1833 was passed, *both* workers and capitalists cooperated to evade the act, lengthen hours, overwork children, and thereby to increase the level of worker exploitation. The workers' agitations throughout the 1830s display this same interest in perpetuating the system of child labor [Smelser 1959, pp. 214, 238–244].

How might Marx have accounted for these instances of increasing exploitation unaccompanied by worker resistance and diminishing exploitation accompanied by a good deal of worker opposition? One possibility, suggested by Marx's observation that the working class was "stunned" and required time to "recover its senses," is that workers were for a time unconscious of their position and their interests. This is a famous phenomenon of "false consciousness," or, perhaps more accurately in this case, "delayed consciousness." This kind of explanation, which takes both time and experience into account, appears to throw light on the timing of the British workers' reactions to exploitation. As general theoretical categories, however, the conceptions of "consciousness" and "false consciousness" create certain problems. Unless they are specifically related to the objective conditions of exploitation, they do not reveal precisely what kind of time lag might obtain between exploitation and resistance. These concepts themselves do not indicate why the workers waited until the 1830s to agitate, or why they did not agitate in 1800, or why they did not delay until 1850, or 1890, or even until the present. Furthermore, such categories are likely to be used with such flexibility that they are able to help account *both* for occasions on which exploited workers revolt ("because they were exploited") *and* for occasions on which they do not ("because they have not become conscious of their position"). The categories of consciousness, delayed consciousness, and false consciousness, in short, can become elastic "residual categories" that sacrifice the explanatory power of the theory of exploitation by making it nonfalsifiable.

A second possibility, suggested by Marx's observation that workers become "slave dealers" in the labor of their wives and children under conditions of machine production, is that workers are so badly exploited that they turn to the exploitation of their dependents. Like the former, this possibility is probably documentable historically, but also like the former, it requires formal theoretical incorporation to avoid becoming a convenient explanatory "out" to be used when workers do not resist capitalist exploitation according to theoretical expectations.

In addition, the Marxian concept of exploitation itself poses certain explanatory problems. Using his own definitions of exploitative tactics, it is possible to discover clear cases of exploitation as a backdrop for British worker agitation in the 1820s and 1830s—the increase of productivity by the introduction of superior machines and the displacement of adult male laborers (the increase of relative surplus value). At the same time, however, other kinds of exploitation were apparently diminishing. The production of absolute surplus value was decreasing with the gradual diminution of hours, and real wages were rising. Which kind of exploitation do we choose to explain the agitation among the workers? And why was not the greater absolute exploitation through long hours the cause of a similar agitation earlier? Such questions arise because the Marxist conception of exploitation has many components—long hours, displacement of adult labor, overworking of females and children, and so on—the relations among which are only partially specified. It is possible to discover *some* type of exploitation at *all* times in the late eighteenth and early nineteenth centuries in Great Britain. Yet the workers engaged in class warfare only irregularly and on specific occasions. In short, the concept of exploitation is perhaps too general and inclusive to explain the specifics of worker protests.[33]

Robert Michels' Theory of Organizational Structure

As we have just seen, one of Marx's most conspicuous characteristics was his profound antagonism toward industrial capitalism. He regarded it as an economic system that set classes in conflict with one another and that generated the conditions for its own downfall by means of revolutionary overthrow. Marx's sympathies, moreover, lay with the proletarian class, which would overturn the political and economic structure of capitalist society and build the foundations for the communism of the future.

Robert Michels, born in 1876—shortly after the publication of *Das Kapital*—was thoroughly exposed to Marxism, and he shared many of the revolutionary ideals of Marxist socialism. His great contribution to sociology, *Political Parties*, clearly shows the influence of Marx. Michels was preoccupied with the class struggle and with the kinds of organizations—trade unions, socialist political parties, cooperative societies—that represent the efforts of the workers to protest against the oppressive system of industrial capitalism.

Michels shared another characteristic with Marx. Both men tended to minimize the importance of ideas as moving forces in history. For Marx, human consciousness reflects more fundamental economic forces in society and men's ideas are determined in large part by their position in the economic system. Michels, too, regarded ideas and ideologies as rationalizations, or efforts to preserve a position of power in a social organization. The real basis for action, according to Michels, lies in the political relations among persons.

Even though Michels thus took up many aspects of Marxian thought, there are a number of important differences between the two men. First, Michels never intended to develop a grand, deductive theory with a full exposition of its philosophical foundations. In fact, he explicitly disavowed an interest in such theories. In the preface to *Political Parties*, he stated that

the present study makes no attempt to offer a "new system." It is not the principal aim of science to create systems, but rather to promote understanding. It is not the purpose of sociological science to discover, or rediscover solutions, since numerous problems of the individual life and the life of social groups are not capable of "solution" at all, but must ever remain "open." The sociologist should aim rather at the dispassionate exposition of tendencies and counter-operating forces, of reasons and opposing reasons, at the display, in a word, of the warp and the woof of social life. Precise diagnosis is the logical and indispensible preliminary to any possible prognosis [1911, p. viii].[34]

By adopting this position Michels clearly eschewed the creation of a grand theoretical and ethical system, to which Marx devoted so much of his energy. Nevertheless, as we shall see, most of the components of a theory are to be found in Michels' work; and in fact he did generate a highly organized explanation of the origins of oligarchy in social life. Second, Michels' focus was narrower than that of Marx. In particular, he was concerned with the political aspects of Marxian theory—expecially class conflict between the bourgeoisie and proletariat. Michels, however, took class conflict as his starting point, whereas Marx analyzed the economic relations that give rise to class conflict. Michels concentrated on the political fate of revolutionary movements and organizations, whereas Marx built a theory that would encompass all of social life. Third, while Marx felt that industrial capitalism—as well as all preceding economic systems—rendered social democracy impossible, he did predict that when the economic conditions of capitalism were destroyed and when a socialist society was created, genuine social democracy would emerge. Michels was more pessimistic. He felt that certain fundamental sociological laws prohibited the attainment of social equality, no matter what the economic or political system. In sharp opposition to Marx, Michels argued that a socialist revolution could not substantially modify the conditions of social inequality. "The socialists might conquer, but not socialism, which would perish in the moment of its adherents' triumph. We are tempted to speak of this process as a tragi-comedy in which the masses are content to devote all their energies to affecting a change of masters" [p. 391].

Why did Michels lack faith in the ability of a revolutionary movement to establish a society based on social equality? To ask this question is to go to the heart of Michels' theory. Let us now recapitulate his main arguments.

A Selective Summary of Michels' Theory

The Range of Data and the Problem

Michels' fundamental range of data can be identified empirically with two branches of the working-class movement in Europe in the late nineteenth and early twentieth centuries—socialist political parties and left-wing labor unions. He posed two sorts of questions about these organizations: (1) Why were these working class organizations ineffective in class warfare; why had they lost their militancy? (2) Why had these organizations become less democratic; why had leaders consolidated their positions of power? These two sets of questions were intimately connected, for in answering them Michels felt that the disappearance of democracy was one of the main factors in making such groups less militant and therefore less effective in fighting the class war.

Why did Michels choose revolutionary groups as his main object of analysis? He felt that it would be too easy to choose organizations committed to oligarchic ideologies to demonstrate the universality of his new law that oligarchy arises in all organizations. He felt that revolutionary parties, committed to an ideal of egalitarianism, would provide the best settings for demonstrating his law, because in such organizations it would hold *in spite of* their ideologies. "The appearance of oligarchical phenomena in the very bosom of the revolutionary parties is a conclusive proof of the existence of immanent oligarchical tendencies in every kind of human organization which strives for the attainment of definite ends" [p. 11]. Just as Durkheim chose what might appear to common sense to be the *least* social of all activities—suicide—to prove the importance of the social factor, so Michels chose the type of organization apparently *least* committed to an oligarchic ideology to demonstrate the tendency for oligarchy to develop in organizations.

Central Concepts

Michels' central interest is in the paired and opposing concepts of oligarchy and democracy. In the history of political thought a great many meanings have been assigned to these terms, but Michels did not clearly indicate which meanings he intended to stress. Oligarchy, for example, can refer to differential participation in decision making; differential placement in power positions; differential consolidation of power over long periods of time; or exploitation of a group that does not hold power by a group that does. Michels referred to all of these meanings, and possibly more, as he developed his argument. As we shall see, a number of criticisms arise from ambiguities in his conceptualization of oligarchy and of its opposite, democracy.

Michels set for himself the task of analyzing the antidemocratic tendencies in social life. Among these tendencies he singled out for special attention what he called "the nature of organization" and "the nature of the human individual" [p. viii].

Michels was also vague about the exact meaning of "organization." The term was never formally defined, and in fact Michels did not go beyond identifying certain empirical characteristics of the organization of the groups that he was studying. Several salient characteristics of organization occupied his attention. The first is size. On the whole, Michels was interested in analyzing the structure of large groups, numbering perhaps from 1,000 to 10,000 members. The second is the complexity of organization—the number of functions or the degree of specialization. Third, Michels considered the coordination of group activities to be an important feature of organization. In these three characteristics of organization lie those tendencies that Michels believed to operate against democracy.

Michels also felt that certain psychological tendencies on the part of leaders and followers are important in the creation of oligarchic structures. He referred to age, experience, and training as important factors in leadership, and he also employed certain psychological generalizations relating to the susceptibility of the masses to persuasion and manipulation.

Operationalization

At present we shall say only a word about how Michels identified his basic concepts empirically. Like Parsons and Marx, he referred in a somewhat unsystematic way to available historical and institutional data. Michels assembled as much material as was available to him on the political parties and trade unions of his day and interpreted this information as evidence for his basic propositions. As we have seen from previous critiques, however, selective illustration is a method that may have severe limitations. We shall take up some special problems in Michels later.

Logical Structure

In identifying the main tendencies that bear on democracy and oligarchy, we have already indicated a certain causal priority in Michels' concepts. To formalize this priority, it is helpful to employ the language of dependent and independent variables.

The basic dependent variable in Michels' system is the degree of democracy or of its opposite, oligarchy, that exists in an organization. In particular, Michels was interested in analyzing why organizations with a fighting spirit and a democratic structure gradually develop oligarchical structures over time.

All the other variables in Michels' theory can be considered as independent, and all work toward the same result. The most important independent variables are to be found in the phenomenon of organization itself. Michels referred to the "mechanical and technical impossibility of direct government by the masses" in the kinds of organizations he was analyzing [p. 226]. Several features of large organizations prevent such democratic participation. For example, large numbers of persons cannot deliberate and arrive at any sort of resolution or direct action. In addition, the masses cannot possibly participate equally in day-to-day activities of large organizations. The difficulties of maintaining adequate communication and coordination prevent the involvement of all members equally. As a result of this necessarily differential level of participation. Michels concluded that "the technical specialization that inevitably results from all extensive organization renders necessary what is called expert leadership" [p. 31]. Such are the origins of centralized power and oligarchy.

Furthermore, when a revolutionary organization begins to engage in a struggle, a hierarchical chain of command is required to mobilize the participants for action. If leaders had to consult with the rank and file on every question of action, "an enormous loss of time" would be involved, "and the opinion thus obtained would, moreover, be summary and vague" [p. 42]. Democracy is a luxury a fighting organization cannot afford.

The problems of the hour need a speedy decision and this is why democracy can no longer function in its primitive and genuine form, unless the policy pursued is to be temporizing, involving a loss of the most favorable opportunities for action. Under such guidance, the party becomes incapable of acting in alliance with others and loses its political elasticity. A fighting party needs a hierarchical structure [p. 42].

The very act of entering into a struggle, then, sets in motion tendencies that undermine democracy in a fighting group.

Michels also considered that the psychological characteristics of the masses contribute to oligarchy. He spoke of "the need for leadership felt by the masses" [p. 49], of the "gratitude felt by the crowd for those who speak and write on their behalf" [p. 60], and of the "childish character of proletarian psychology" [p. 67]. The masses are hypnotized by a speaker's power and momentarily see in him a magnified image of their own egos. They want to have a leader they can admire and worship. "Though it grumbles occasionally, the majority is really delighted to find persons who will take the trouble to look after its affairs. In the mass, and even in the organized mass of labor parties, there is an immense need for direction and guidance" [p. 53].

Michels identified two additional peculiarities of the masses that contribute to their passivity. First, most trade union members appeared to be between the ages of 25 and 39 years [p. 78]. Michels concluded from these data that the very young men, who would supply passion to the movement, are slow to join and that men over 40 often become "weary and disillusioned" and resign their membership. "Consequently, there is lacking in the organization the force of control of ardent and irreverent youth and also that of experienced maturity." Second, the rank and file in trade unions has a more fluctuating membership than leaders, and consequently, leaders "constitute a more stable, and more constant element of the organized membership" [p. 79].

The third set of factors contributing to the development and consolidation of oligarchy comprises the qualities of individuals who become leaders. In the early stages of organization, oratorical skill is especially important; the masses are hypnotized by it. Other qualities that facilitate leaders include

force of will which reduces to obedience less powerful wills; . . . a wider extent of knowledge which impresses the members of the leaders' environment; a catonian strength of conviction of force of ideas often verging on its very intensity; self-sufficiency, even if it is accompanied by an arrogant pride, so long as the leader knows how to make the crowd share his own pride in himself; in exceptional cases, finally, goodness of heart and disinterestedness, qualities which recall in the minds of the crowd the figure of Christ, and reawaken religious sentiments which are decayed but not extinct [p. 72].

All three sets of independent variables work in one direction: to establish an oligarchical structure. Furthermore, once an oligarchy is established, it manifests similar consequences. In particular, Michels pointed out the tendency for leaders to become superior in education, wealth, and cultural skills, once they had attained the advantages of office. In addition, leaders come to think of themselves as indispensable and regard their right to office as necessary and sacred. These by-products of oligarchical leadership feed back and further consolidate the original tendencies for power to become centralized.

The system of variables summarized in figure 13 shows how oligarchy is "overdetermined" in Michels' analysis. Everything operates in the same direction. There are no other possible outcomes; there are no important countertendencies. Given large organizations, the inevitable result is oligarchy.

Concluding his analysis, Michels simplified his explanation even more. In reflecting on the various forces working toward oligarchy, he observed that "if we leave out of consideration the tendency of the leaders, and the general immobility and passivity of the masses, we are led to conclude that the principal cause of oligarchy in the democratic parties is to be found in the technical indispensability of leadership" [p. 400]. In other words, Michels' opinion was that even if we ignore the psychological characteristics of the leaders and the led, the technical and practical features of organization are still sufficient to produce oligarchy.

Figure 13. Causal relations among Michels' major variables.

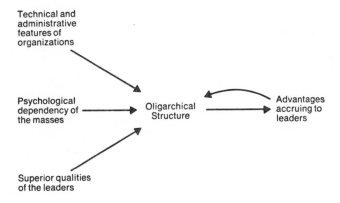

Generation of Hypotheses

Michels' central proposition—the iron law of oligarchy—emerges from his analysis almost as an anticlimax. Given the overdetermined explanatory scheme, there can be no other result than oligarchy. It is not surprising he called it an iron law. As Michels stated the law, "it is organization which gives birth to the dominion of the elected over the electors, of the mandataries over the mandators, of the delegates over the delegators. Who says organization, says oligarchy" [p. 401]. Michels also concluded that this law is devastating in its consequences for revolutionary movements. Only in the beginning stages can protest movements be truly fighting, democratic units. In time, however, power is consolidated, oligarchy emerges, the "embourgeoisement" of the leaders occurs, and the movements become conservative.

Empirical Aspects of the Study

Most of Michels' book is an effort to document his iron law by reference to the history of left-wing parties and trade unions in Europe. Basically, his method is that of selective historical comparison, not unlike the method employed by Marx. In addition, Michels devoted much attention to certain facts that might have appeared to be exceptions or contradictions to his iron law. For example, he noted that proletarian leaders are sometimes substituted for bourgeois leaders in the working-class movement. But he discarded this phenomenon as offering "no guarantee, either in theory or practice, against the political or moral infidelity of the leaders" [p. 307].

In a similar spirit, Michels also developed a brief analysis of the referendum. On first glance, the referendum would appear to be a means by which the masses exercise some control over the legislation of their leaders. Yet Michels stressed the futility of the referendum and the impotence of those who try to utilize it as a political weapon. In fact, he concluded that "the history of the referendum as a democratic expedient utilized by the social parties may be summed up by saying that its application has been rare, and that its results have been unfortunate" [p. 335].

Again, on the face of it, the phenomenon of the resignation of leaders in times of crisis would seem to present evidence that the leader's power can be diminished. Michels disagreed. He argued that we should not take seriously the reasons given by leaders who resign. Rather, he interpreted the threat to resign as the leader's attempt to consolidate his own power; it is an invitation for a new mandate. The leader emphasizes his indispensability by resigning or threatening to do so, and his followers reinstate him in recognition of his indispensability. Resignation is, then, an instrument for bullying the masses and reconsolidating power.

Finally, Michels continually reiterated his position that ideology has no effect on the iron law of oligarchy. Those espousing radical syndicalist ideologies, for example, are not "immunized against the action of sociological laws of universal validity" [p. 347]. Anarchism, too, "succumbs . . . to the law of authoritarianism as soon as it abandons the region of pure thought and as soon as its adherents unite to form associations aiming at any sort of political activity" [p. 360].

In these efforts to discount possibly contrary evidence or arguments, Michels was employing a strategy that is by now familiar to us: argument by elimination. His particular method of pressing this strategy was to acknowledge the existence of apparently contrary facts, but to deny their significance by endowing them with a meaning different from their apparent one. Michels went behind the scenes in an attempt to discover other, more fundamental mechanisms that render the superficially democratic features of organized life unimportant.

Concluding Note

At the end of his analysis, Michels found himself facing a troublesome dilemma. He was a man committed to the ideals of socialist democracy, yet his discoveries seemed to have led him to the conclusion that socialist democracy is impossible. Even the class struggle would "invariably culminate in the creation of new oligarchies which undergo fusion with the old" [p. 390]. Such a discovery was no doubt extremely disquieting.

At the very end of the book Michels made an effort to restore some of his old faith. He reminded the reader that he did not wish to deny that "every revolutionary working class movement, and every movement sincerely inspired by the democratic spirit, may have a certain value as contributing to the enfeeblement of oligarchic tendencies" [p. 405]. He then related a fable: "A peasant when on his death bed tells his sons that a treasure is buried in the field. After his death they dig everywhere looking for the treasure. They did not succeed in finding it, but their indefatigable labor so improves the soil that it secures for them a comparative well-being." Michels continued: "The treasure in the fable may well symbolize democracy. Democracy is a treasure which no one will ever discover by deliberate search, but in continuing the search, in laboring indefatigably to discover the indiscoverable, we shall perform a work which will have fertile results in the democratic sense" [p. 405]. Such an ending strikes a note of pathos; it seems neither realistic nor satisfactory. It is difficult to imagine a socialist party with the motto "We shall prevail, indirectly." Yet the fable and the moral that Michels drew from it perhaps constitute his own effort to reconcile his discovery of the iron law with his commitment to socialist ideals.

Some Unresolved Problems in Michels' Analysis

The Conception of Democracy

The model of democracy that Michels adopted is an extreme one: the model of equal participation by all individuals in the decisions and binding actions of the group. Let us, however, consider another notion of democracy, one that does involve the influence of the rank and file on decision making but that does not necessarily imply equal participation by all individuals in all decisions. This alternative conception of democracy involves a plurality of organized groups, each possessing something like an oligarchical structure itself, to be sure, but each capable of exerting some power on the political center, thus representing the several groups of constituents in decision making. There is not equal participation by all, but democracy exists in the sense that the desires, grievances, and influence of the masses are taken into account when decisions are made. I am suggesting that because Michels began with an extremely individualistic notion of democracy he made his task of demonstrating that democracy could not exist in large organizations very easy; if he had considered the group-influence conception of democracy, his task would have been more complicated.

Michels also relied on the assumption that the only effective *group* for achieving democratic results is the fighting revolutionary group. When it becomes bureaucratized and conservatized, however, it loses its fighting qualities and can no longer contribute to the struggle for democracy. This assumption is contained in the following statement:

[When a party begins to compromise with other elements in society], not merely does the party sacrifice its political virginity, by entering into promiscuous relationships with the most heterogeneous political elements, relationships which in many cases have disastrous and enduring consequences, but it exposes itself in addition to the risk of losing its essential character as a party. The term "party" presupposes that among the individual components of the party there should exist a harmonious direction of wills toward identical objectives and practical aims. Where this is lacking, the party becomes a mere "organization" [p. 376].

Linking these two key assumptions, Michels believed that democracy is impossible in large organizations, and as large organizations become undemocratic, they cannot contribute to democracy in the larger society.

I should like to raise the question of whether these two assumptions should be linked in the way that Michels linked them. I shall do so by considering an illustrative example: the history of protest movements among American farmers. In the last three decades of the nineteenth century, American farmers, suffering under great economic hardship, organized themselves into a number of "fighting" organizations, such as the Grange, the Farmer's Alliance, and the Populist movement (though these organizations were not revolutionary in the same sense that European socialist groups were). In this early phase of farmer protest, these groups were burdened with difficulties of recruitment, commitment, and coordination, and they were notoriously ineffective politically. It was only after the American farmer became involved, not in parties, but in organizations—that is, when he sacrificed his political virginity and began dealing in the world of compromise and pressure politics—that he and his organizations really began to influence governmental policy. If democracy is measured by the flow of influence from bottom to top, the mobilization of American farmers into organizations rather than parties clearly increased their effectiveness. The same argument might be made for the history of American labor unions. What I am suggesting by such illustrations is that in many cases Michels' iron law of oligarchy might hold *within* organizations, but that the very development of this kind of leadership might equip those organizations to represent the desires and wishes of their constituents more effectively in the larger society, thus contributing to democracy at another level.

This line of reasoning suggests that in conceptualizing democracy, Michels perhaps considered too few of its aspects. At other times, however, one gains the impression that he fused too many aspects of a phenomenon into a single category. Consider the numerous connotations of the concept of oligarchy, for example. It may suggest a minority giving orders to a majority, with the majority submitting. It may connote that the minority of leaders are the sole source of any significant political action. It may mean that the minority of leaders are free from control by others who hold subsidiary positions in the organization. It may suggest that people in positions of authority pursue their own interests and exploit the others in the organization. Or, finally, it may refer to the tendency for leaders to consolidate their positions of power over long periods of time [Cassenelli 1953].

As Michels developed his argument, he tended to slip back and forth among these several connotations. But surely the causes of the consolidation of an elite over long periods are different from the causes of temporary domination or exploitation. By not discriminating among these different aspects of oligarchy, Michels fell into the difficulty of trying to account for more facets of oligarchy than he could legitimately hope to within his relatively simple analytic framework. If the several aspects of oligarchy had been sorted out from one another analytically, Michels would have been in a better position to account for each aspect by using different combinations of causes.

The Uncertain Status of Psychological Categories, Especially "Ideas"

As indicated, Michels' work falls clearly into that tradition of thought that emphasizes "real factors"—especially economic and political—as the determinants of behavior and minimizes the influence of ideas as determining factors. Michels' repeated assertion that socialist, syndicalist, and anarchist ideologies do not significantly deter oligarchic tendencies within organizations is consistent with this perspective. Also, in summing up his ideas on the origins of oligarchy, Michels concluded that the technical features of organization are a sufficient cause of oligarchic leadership and that the psychological characteristics of the masses and the leaders are only accessory and contributing factors. In all these arguments, psychological variables such as ideas and sentiments are dominated by "objective conditions."

From time to time, however, Michels appeared uncertain about the degree to which he wished to downgrade ideas and sentiments. He entitled an early chapter "The Ethical Embellishment of Social Struggles," which suggests that the moral aspects of conflict are in the nature of unnecessary adornments. Yet in discussing the ethical side of political life, Michels spoke of the need of all political movements to develop an ideology of democracy as "a *necessary* fiction" [p. 15, emphasis added]. "Political parties, however much they may be founded upon narrow class interest and however evidently they may work against the interests of the majority, love to identify themselves with the universe, or at least present themselves as cooperating with all the citizens of the state, and to proclaim that they are fighting in the name of all and for the good of all" [p. 16]. Struggles within parties also involve appeals to ideas. "In the struggle among leaders," Michels noted, "an appeal is often made to loftier motives. When the members of the executive claim the right to intervene in the democratic functions of the individual sections of the organization, they base this claim upon their more comprehensive grasp of all the circumstances of the case, their profounder insight, their superior socialist culture, and their keener socialist sentiment" [p. 172].

In connection with these observations, we might raise a question: why should the struggle for power—which depends in the last analysis on real factors—have to be legitimized by reference to the values or beliefs of the group itself? If the struggle is essentially based on power, why should not the contestants in this struggle feel free to ignore ideological questions? While Michels explicitly minimized ideological factors, his observations indicate that he believed the appeal to ideology to be an important weapon in securing the support of the masses in the drive for power. In short, Michels was ambivalent about the importance of ideas, sometimes treating them as sham and rationalization, at other times recognizing them as important and probably necessary ingredients in the struggles among groups.

A final ambiguity in Michels' discussion of human psychology lies in his treatment of certain psychological forces as both causes and effects. In discussing the "accessory qualities" of leaders, which contribute to their rise to leadership, Michels mentioned the leaders' wider extent of knowledge, their strength of conviction, the force of their ideas, their pride, and their dedication. But elsewhere in his analysis, these same qualities turn out to be the consequences of leadership as well; for example, the longer a leader remains in power, the stronger is his conviction of his own moral correctness, the greater is his self-adulation, the greater is his sense of indispensability.

Certainly it is plausible to organize one's variables into a kind of model whereby a single type of variable becomes first a cause, then an effect generated by the very set of conditions it contributed to causing in the first place. Such a model is often referred to as a "positive feedback" model. Michels made use of such a model—though it is only implicit—in his characterization of the causes of oligarchy. Yet in his own examination of the historical material, he was only able to point to the empirical correlation between the leader's position in an organization and his psychological characteristics. He was powerless to demonstrate the ways in which these psychological characteristics are simultaneously both causes and effects, given the historical data available to him.

The Use of Cultural Differences as a Residual Category

Most of Michels' energies were devoted to eliciting examples of situations that confirm his iron law of oligarchy. In chapters 5–8 of Part One of *Political Parties*, for example, he selected telling examples of the psychological submission of the masses to authorities. Often, however, he noted an apparent exception to the iron law, which he tended to attribute to a specifically national or cultural factor.

For example, in discussing the stability of leadership, Michels ventured the following observation about England:

In international European politics, England has always been regarded as an untrustworthy ally, for her history shows that no other country has ever been able to confide in agreements concluded with England. The reason is to be found in this, that the foreign policy of the United Kingdom is largely dependent upon the party in power, and party changes occur with considerable rapidity. Similarly, the party that changes its leaders too often runs the risk of finding itself unable to contract useful alliances at an opportune moment. The two gravest defects of genuine democracy, its lack of stability . . . and its difficulty of mobilization, are dependent on the recognized right of the sovereign masses to take part in the management of their own affairs [p. 103].

Thus democracy in England appeared to interfere with the conduct of foreign affairs. But England, like all advanced industrial societies, presumably had its share of large organizations, which should have been governed by the iron law of oligarchy as much as other advanced states. If the law were as universal as Michels maintained, the English exception should be an embarrassing instance for his theory. But he merely noted it as a national exception.

Discussing the tendency of leadership to consolidate, Michels made the expected assertion that "with the institution of leadership there simultaneously begins, owing to the long tenure of office, the transformation of the leaders into a closed caste" [p. 156]. Yet in the next paragraph he qualified the assertion: "Unless, as in France, extreme individualism and fanatical political dogmatism stand in the way, the old leaders present themselves to the masses as a compact phalanx—at any rate whenever the masses are so much aroused as to endanger the position of leaders." Here he was identifying something characteristically "French" that made for an exception to the iron law. In another place, he noted the presence of an abundance of Jews among the leaders of the socialist and revolutionary parties and added that "specific racial qualities make the Jew a born leader of the masses, a born organizer and propagandist" [p. 258]. Then he proceeded to detail these specifically Jewish qualities. From Michels' statements it would appear that something distinctively cultural—something associated with Jewishness—would have to do with consolidation of power above and beyond the tendencies inherent in organization itself. Yet Michels tended to leave unanalyzed both these exceptions and the implicit cultural variables that would explain them. These variables surround his theory as convenient categories that are used to add to, or to account for, apparent exceptions to the iron law. This method of proceeding gives his theory an appearance of simplicity and neatness, whereas in reality he was relying on many more variables than were incorporated into his original formulation of the empirical universal.

A Critical But Unexamined Residual Category: Conflict Among Leaders

Let us return for a moment to figure 13, in which the system of technical requisites, psychological factors, accessory qualities, and positive feedback guarantee that oligarchy is the universal consequence of organization. One implication of this explanatory scheme is that if leaders and masses come into conflict with one another, the leaders will win every time, because they command more power; there is nothing in Michels' theory to suggest otherwise. In fact, Michels is explicit: "When there is a struggle between the leaders and the masses, the former are always victorious" [p. 157].

Immediately after this statement, however, Michels added the qualifying phrase "if only they [the leaders] remain united." This suggests the possibility of victory on the part of the masses if their struggle with the leaders coincides with a struggle among the leaders themselves. His qualification further suggests two questions: (1) Why should conflict between leaders occur at all? (2) Does not a victory of the masses in periods of conflict among leaders actually constitute the exercise of democracy? Even more, if conflict among leaders is institutionalized politically, does this not make for a periodic voice of the masses and hence a periodic exercise of democracy, which would thereby qualify, if not contradict, the iron law of oligarchy?

Given the accumulation of independent variables and secondary consequences in Michels' theory, there seems to be no reason why leaders in an organization would ever come into conflict with one another. After all, as leaders they are securely placed, psychologically gratified, possessed of information, cultural accessories, and wealth, and fortified with beliefs in their indispensability. Why endanger these positions by struggling with one another? The only conflicts in Michels' theory would seem to be between those aspiring to power and those holding it, and the cards are so stacked against the aspirants that they would always lose.

Actually, Michels presented a number of reasons why conflicts among leaders arise in organizations. He spoke of "rivalry between established leaders and great outsiders who have established reputations in other fields and then offer their services to socialist parties"; of conflict between age and youth; of conflict between leaders of bourgeois origin and leaders of proletarian origin; of struggles between subdivisions of the organization (between, for example, executive and administrative or local and national); of struggles based on racial (i.e., ethnic) differences (such as the contests between French and German socialists during the Franco-Prussian War of 1870). And, finally, he spoke of struggles based on "objective differences and differences of principle in general philosophical views" [p. 167].

Empirically, these bases for contests among leaders make sense, and it is possible to find illustrations of each from our own knowledge of political conflict. But from a theoretical point of view, *these contests are not a consequence of the major variables in Michels' original theory*. He made no formal use of age, locality, race, ideology, and so on, except occasionally to declare one or another of them irrelevant to the iron law of oligarchy. Thus it appears that in this case, as in others, Michels introduced a number of categories that do not find a place in his original theory, but which he used to develop his argument.

Nevertheless, given *some* basis for conflict among leaders, what are the implications of this conflict for the workings of democracy? Michels did give a certain power to the mass to influence factional struggles. He observed, for example, that "the path of the new aspirants to power is always beset with difficulties, bestrewn with obstacles of all kinds, *which can be overcome only by the favor of the masses*" [p. 177, emphasis added]. Apparently, then, mass support is needed for an emerging leader to overthrow an established one. Having acknowledged this, however, Michels later minimized the importance of this phenomenon by noting that

only in exceptional instances do [overthrows of leaders] signify that the masses have been stronger than the leaders. As a rule, they mean merely that a new leader has entered into conflict with the old, and thanks to the support of the mass, has prevailed in the struggle, and has been able to dispossess and replace the old leader. The profit for democracy of such a substitution is practically nil [pp. 182–183].

Once again, Michels' argument appears to rest on a limited view of democracy. He regarded the *fact* of leadership and followership as antipathetic to democracy. But it is also plausible to regard the overthrow of leaders—which is dependent upon mass support—as evidence of a periodic upward flow of influence. The masses will obviously support the aspiring leader who best represents what they desire. And if he ceases to take their feelings into consideration, they will be inclined to throw their support behind another contending leader.

Furthermore, if conflict among leaders is institutionalized—as in the constitutional provision for free elections involving two or more parties

252

and associated civil liberties and rights—the political system has regularized the struggle among leaders and increased the ability of the masses to express their preferences. This is not to say that the leaders will not consolidate their positions repeatedly, as Michels' analysis suggests that they will do. But it is also possible to institutionalize tendencies that operate to diminish the workings of the iron law of oligarchy. The institutionalization of conflict among political leaders would seem to require a formulation of the law of oligarchy somewhat less rigid than Michels' version.

CHAPTER **14**

Summary and Conclusions

The Character of Theoretical Criticism in Sociology

Academic disciplines may be compared with one another according to their degree of conceptual unification. At the one extreme a discipline may possess a more or less unified paradigm, or set of organizing assumptions, on which there is broad consensus and within which specific theoretical and empirical problems are selected for analysis. Classical physics is an illustration of this extreme. At the other extreme a discipline may possess a number of partially developed paradigms and perspectives that are related to one another only loosely and unsystematically. The study of history is an illustration.

Sociology falls at some middle point between these extremes. On the one hand, there is fairly widespread consensus on the central concepts of the discipline—concepts such as social interaction, role, group, norm, institution, culture, and social structure—and on the canons by which theoretical and empirical knowledge is to be judged. On the other hand, the discipline is also characterized by many debates concerning its fundamental objectives, the most appropriate perspectives around which to organize sociological knowledge, and the nature of sociological knowledge itself. Sociologists debate, for example, whether their field should aim to become an objective science with little regard for practical applications or whether it should be devoted primarily to meeting social crises and to promoting social change. They debate the merits of the integrationist perspective, the conflict perspective, or the symbolic interactionist perspective as the most fruitful organizing paradigm for the field. And they debate the merits of different methods of arriving at sociological truths—by experimentation, by sample survey, by participant observation and emphatic understanding, and so on.

Given this circumstance, it comes as no surprise that theoretical discourse takes a variety of forms in sociology. Sometimes it takes the form of advocating the primacy of a particular moral, political, or epistemological perspective. Durkheim's polemic in favor of positivism as a method of inquiry and in favor of "the social" as an indispensable analytic level are examples of this kind of theoretical statement. Another example is Karl Marx's advocacy of scientific socialism as an intellectual position that is superior to other versions of socialist thought [1848]. Still another example is the contemporary controversy concerning the purposes of sociology, in which some sociologists argue that the field should be made "relevant" and should direct itself toward the eradication of social and political evils; in which others argue for a neutral, scientific posture; and in which still others combine these arguments.

A second form of theoretical discourse involves the analysis of the history of ideas. It places the contributions of a given theorist or school of thought in relation to the dominant intellectual and cultural traditions of the time. The historian of ideas seeks out the dominant positive and negative influences on a theorist; he asks whose ideas were adopted and refashioned and whose ideas were polemically rejected by this theorist. He may also trace the impact of a given theorist or school of thought on subsequent intellectual and social developments.

A third form of theoretical discourse—the one stressed in this essay—involves the critical application of the canons of scientific adequacy to a theory. Using this approach, the theoretical critic asks what problem a given theorist has set for himself, how he organizes concepts to generate explanations relating to this problem, and how he attempts to demonstrate the validity of these explanations. This approach is clearly a normative one, because it asks how well a given theory measures up to the norms of logico-empirical inquiry as these have developed in the social sciences.

Each of these forms of theoretical discourse has a legitimate place in sociology. It is advisable, moreover, to permit each form of discourse to stand or fall on its own merits and not to let one form serve for all. For example, it is illegitimate to conclude from the observation that a theorist has a "Marxist" or a "conservative" perspective that his work is somehow unacceptable scientifically. The scientific adequacy of a work should be established by examining the logical and empirical procedures employed, not by merely identifying a perspective or "bias." Likewise, it is illegitimate to conclude that scientific criticism disposes of all aspects of a theory and that, once its scientific adequacy or inadequacy has been established, no further explorations of the moral, political, or epistemological implications of the theory need be made. These two practices—the first might be called "bias-hunting," the second "scientism"—resemble one another in that each combines several independent types of criticism into a single line of criticism, thereby overextending and overworking it.

257

Furthermore, any given theory may be "important" or "influential" or "good" for a variety of different reasons, of which its scientific adequacy is only one. The theories that we have considered, for example, have attained historical importance because each was a novel, creative, or forceful formulation of the relationships among basic sociological variables, and also because each, in a different way, addressed an especially critical set of social and political issues—issues such as social integration, social control, conflict, social domination, and so on. To undertake the logico-empirical criticism of a theory, then, is to assess not its entire value, but only selected aspects of its value.

Finally, the scientific form of theoretical criticism emphasizes the form of a theory more than its content. It focuses on a theorist's procedures rather than on the substantive implications of his conclusions. Nevertheless, it is possible, even in authors as diverse as the ones we have considered, to note the emergence of common substantive themes. Each, for example, recognized the social importance of committed, organized groups of people pursuing a cause, though each emphasized different aspects of such groups. Durkheim saw them as providing cohesive bonds that counteracted individual tendencies to self-destruction; Parsons regarded them as a setting in which both sides of the ambivalence involved in deviance can be gratified; Marx treated them as revolutionary movements arising from conditions of intolerable exploitation; and Michels likewise regarded them as potentially revolutionary forces but stressed the organizational and psychological forces that tend to undermine their effectiveness. Similarly, not one of the authors analyzed failed to emphasize authority relations as an important variable in their respective schemes, though once again in very different ways—Durkheim as a source of integration, Parsons as crucial ingredients in the processes of social control, Marx as an accessory force in the process of exploitation, and Michels as a force subversive to democracy. My main purpose in this essay, however, was not to focus on these substantive comparisons and contrasts, but rather to ask what place each variable has in the structure of each theory and what procedures the theorist employs in making it part of his explanations.

The Assessment of the Scientific Strengths and Weaknesses of a Theory

To summarize, we have, in this essay, asked a number of questions of several diverse theorists:

What are the central problems that are addressed?

What is the theorist trying to explain?

What are the theorist's basic concepts?

How are the basic concepts identified empirically?

What is the logical structure of the concepts?

How are propositions derived or otherwise generated from the logical structure of the concepts?

How are the propositions made testable?

How are the propositions tested, and what conclusions are drawn?

By asking these questions we have been able to arrive at a number of different comparative assessments of the various theorists. With respect to the specification of an initial problem, Durkheim's theory of suicide appears to possess greater clarity and tidiness than the others, because he selected a relatively identifiable range of data (suicide rates) and asked why groups vary in their suicidal tendencies. Michels' problem—the fate of democracy in organizations—is also relatively simple, but it was clouded by certain ambiguities in the concepts (democracy, organization) that he used to pose the problem. Parsons was clear in specifying the range of data that was of concern to him—behavior that was deviant or nonconforming in relation to normative expectations—but posed few specific problems regarding the differential incidence of each kind of deviant behavior. Finally, while Marx concentrated less on specific problems than on producing a massive conceptual system that would generate invariant laws, he did address himself to a wide range of problems connected with the production and distribution of commodities and with the relations among the social groups under capitalism. In each case it proved possible to identify more or less precisely the central scientific problem or problems associated with the theory, and to develop particular criticisms of each.

With respect to the issue of logical structure, Michels' formal theory of the origins of oligarchy appears at first glance to be the tightest and most economical. On further analysis, however, it proves to be heavily burdened with ambiguities and numerous residual categories that were utilized unsystematically to account for apparent exceptions. Durkheim's structure, involving the paired opposites of egoism-altruism and anomie-fatalism, is also simple in initial formulation, but is likewise fraught with overlapping concepts, with vagueness and ambiguity, with an inconsistent use of variables, and with residual categories. Parsons' classification of the directions of deviance is relatively unambiguous, but the relations between this classification and his more general theoretical concepts are unclear, and the relations among the basic explanatory variables—strain, the structuring of deviance, social control, and so on—are incomplete in a variety of ways. Finally, while the structure of Marx's scheme is remarkable for the systematic transition from one basic set of concepts to the next, some of the basic concepts—such as the components of labor, simple average labor, and socially necessary labor—are couched in so many equivocations that the validity of the entire logical structure is thrown into doubt. In each case, the characteristic flaws in logical structure led us to question whether the basic propositions of any of the theories could be considered to be formally derived from the structure of basic concepts.

With respect to the issue of falsifiability, each theory also contained flaws peculiar to itself. Both Durkheim's and Michels' propositions are stated in sufficiently specific empirical form to permit their falsification in principle, but in both cases the authors' tendency to rely on residual categories makes the theories less falsifiable in practice than in principle. Marx developed a theory that generated specific predictions about the future of capitalism, and these clearly are falsifiable. However, his theory, too, possesses certain elastic or ambiguous categories, such as class consciousness and exploitation, that can lead to the theory's being correct every time, and therefore unfalsifiable. Finally, Parsons' theory also suffers from a lack of falsifiability, but not so much from the presence of residual categories as from its theoretical incompleteness, which leaves the theory relatively unable to generate specific, testable propositions.

Several Cautions in Conclusion

By approaching several theories with a common set of questions in mind, we have been able to assess some characteristic scientific strengths and weaknesses of each. It is hoped, however, that this exercise does not suggest that any theory can be automatically and completely evaluated by the unimaginative application of this particular checklist of questions. While these questions may have a sensitizing function, their rigid application may blind us to other, perhaps more important points of significance about the theory. Furthermore, the theorist's own purposes should in some sense dictate which critical questions should be asked. If a theorist's objective is mainly classificatory rather than explanatory, questions relating to the logical structure of his categories are clearly more salient than questions relating to the empirical validity of his propositions. Theoretical criticism should be tailored in part by the objectives and dominant emphases of the theorist himself.

In addition, the net assessment of the scientific adequacy of any given theory will seldom turn out to be a simple blanket judgment, but rather a mixture of strengths and weaknesses. As the list of criteria indicates, a theory is a multifaceted construction, and many different, independent questions must be asked in assessing it. One type of weakness—for example, an ambiguity in logical structure—does not necessarily mean that the theory will be weak in other respects as well. Moreover, even if one does discover a series of critical weaknesses, one should not necessarily sound the death knell for an entire theory. One of the central propositions of Marx's *Capital* concerned the positive association between technological improvement and the production of relative surplus value. In examining the structure of Marx's theory, we found that the derivation of the concept of surplus value was marred by a number of equivocations and that the predictions about the future of capitalism based on the association between technology and surplus value were questionable. Marx thus appeared to have erred in arriving at the relationship and, in relying on it, to have generated a number of incorrect predictions. Yet the association may still be a sound one, though for reasons different from the ones adduced by Marx; if properly combined with other propositions, it may still prove fruitful in explaining and predicting changes in capitalist societies.

Finally, the discovery of a scientific weakness may indicate not that the theory should be discarded, but that it should be supplemented by further refinement. Some shortcomings of Durkheim's theory of suicide appear to call for a more systematic statement of the relations between social and psychological factors. Some of the explanatory incompleteness of Parsons' theory of deviance calls for the further specification of conditions under which strain gives rise to deviance, deviance excites mechanisms of social control, and so on. And some of the questionable uses of residual categories, such as conflict among leaders, in Michels' theory calls for their more formal incorporation into an expanded theory of the dynamics of power and authority.

A final caution concerns the objective of this essay itself. It has not been ventured as a lesson in the art of intellectual destructiveness. It has been written with the conviction that the best way to learn is to test the critical limits of the knowledge to which we are exposed. My objective has been to assist in developing our critical faculties so that they may be more effectively used in confronting the ideas around us, particularly in assessing our own theories about the social world.

Notes

1. Even this apparently simple distinction opens a number of thorny philosophical problems. For two brief comments on the distinction, see "A Note on the Concept of Fact," pp. 41–42 in Parsons 1937 and pp. 58–59 in Smelser 1968.

2. For a list of typical key concepts in sociology—such as status, role, social distance, and so on—see "The Bearing of Sociological Theory on Empirical Research" in Merton 1968.

3. For Durkheim's own statement on his methodological position, see Chapter 5 of *The Rules of the Sociological Method*, published in 1895, two years before the appearance of *Suicide*.

4. For Durkheim's polemic against Spencer, see Chapter 7 of Book One in *The Division of Labor in Society*; see also pp. 311ff. of Parsons's *The Structure of Social Action*. For an attempt to uncover the relations between the works of Durkheim and Marx, see Zeitlin 1968, Chapter 15.

5. In fact, Durkheim felt that the individual "motives" or "reasons" given for suicide—personal sorrow, economic hardship, and so on— were unhelpful in understanding suicide as a social phenomenon [pp. 148–150]. (The page references in brackets in this section refer to the English edition of *Suicide* [published by The Free Press].)

6. Here Durkheim displayed his "positivistic" preference for identifiable "facts" and his predilection to avoid investigation of inaccessible mental states [p. 43].

7. These arguments are likely to strike us as weak and somewhat quaint. Their weakness lies in Durkheim's relying on the highly unsatisfactory psychological concepts of his day, in his arguing on the basis of very poor data relating to both insanity and suicide, and in his using associations between aggregated social data as evidence for statements about psychological mechanisms.

8. For a brief review of some of the questions that have been raised about suicide statistics, see George Simpson's Introduction to *Suicide* [pp. 17–20].

9. A discussion of the ecological fallacy in *Suicide* is found in Selvin 1958.

10. Whitney Pope [1970] has undertaken a most detailed examination of the statistical basis for the inferences in *Suicide* and has concluded that in some cases Durkheim did not bring to bear on his arguments data that were neutral or disconfirmatory.

11. For an examination of Durkheim's approximations to multivariate analysis, as well as replication, see Selvin 1958.

12. Durkheim himself was aware that the knowledge that death would result is difficult to establish, as his discussion of the relations between pure suicide and the deaths of the heroic soldier, the daredevil, etc., indicate [pp. 45–46].

13. A more detailed examination of the conceptual overlap between egoism and anomie led Barclay Johnson [1965] to conclude that the two concepts should, for all intents and purposes, be treated as identical and therefore as a single variable.

14. For a discussion of the desideratum that a theory should be able to be proved wrong, see the remarks on testing the propositions, in the earlier section entitled "Issues that Arise in Theorizing in the Social Sciences: A General Statement."

15. For a definition of parameters, and a discussion of their place in the logical structure of a theory, see the earlier section on "Issues That Arise in Theorizing in the Social Sciences: A General Statement."

16. For an attempt to contrast the "middle-range" and "grand" styles, compare "On Sociological Theories of the Middle Range [Merton 1968].

264

17. Unless otherwise indicated, the page references in brackets in this section refer to Parsons' *The Social System*.

18. Formal and empirical criticisms of Merton's deviance paradigm are found in Dubin 1959, Cloward 1959, and Cohen 1965. For Merton's commentary on Dubin and Cloward, see Merton 1959.

19. This second level of collective structuring is similar to Merton's concept of rebellion.

20. Without denying the importance of this insight, I should like to suggest that the structuring of individual forms of deviance also gratifies both sides of the ambivalence. Parsons himself mentions the hospital patient who, by virtue of being ill, passively withdraws from the scene; but at the same time, by being a "good patient" living up to all hospital regulations, he is simultaneously a ritualist, a passive conformer as well as a passive withdrawer.

21. In this sense Merton's classification of deviance is more nearly "derived" in that the basic types of deviance are describable in precisely the same terms as his basic categories of social analysis—cultural goals and institutional means. It should be noted, however, that "rebellion" in Merton's scheme constitutes an atypical case, because in this case he permits the introduction of the "±" with respect to both ends and means but does not consider any of the other possibilities raised by this double notation (see Dubin 1959, pp. 147–150).

22. Parsons notes that "another very important phenomenon of reaction to strain is the production of phantasies" [p. 253n]. Anxiety is also mentioned as a typical response, as well as defensive-adjustive mechanisms [p. 485].

23. In practice, however, Durkheim relied on a number of residual categories to reinterpret and accommodate apparently disconfirmatory results.

24. Lewis Coser attempted one kind of reconciliation in *The Functions of Social Conflict*; Ralf Dahrendorf attempted another in *Class and Class Conflict in Industrial Society*.

25. Eric Hobsbawm [1964] has indicated the kinds of distortions that might arise in attempting to analyze Marx piecemeal.

26. Unless otherwise noted, page references in this section are to the Allen & Unwin edition of Marx's *Capital*.

27. For other uses of the argument by elimination, see earlier, p. 163 and later, pp. 244–245.

28. The rate may also be stated in terms of a ratio between surplus labor and the necessary labor, or between surplus produce and necessary produce [pp. 200–213].

29. In discussing simple average labor, Marx reminds the reader that "we are not speaking here of the wages or value that the laborer gets for a given labor-time, but of the value of the commodity in which that labor-time is materialized" [p. 12].

30. For a discussion of this function of conceptual models, see earlier "A Simple Model of Political Behavior."

31. For a discussion of some of the costs of incompleteness in Parsons' theory, see earlier, in the section on "Some Criticisms Regarding the Logic and Testability of Parsons' Theory."

32. For a development of a number of these criticisms, see Dahrendorf 1959, Chap. II.

33. For an elaboration of this and other criticisms of various explanations of British working-class history, see Smelser 1959, Chap. XIV.

34. Unless otherwise indicated, page references in brackets in this section are to Michels' *Political Parties*.

Bibliography

Note: Whenever possible, items are indexed here and in the text according to the year in which they were written or the year in which they were first published. The date that follows the publisher's name below indicates the edition actually used in the preparation of this volume.

Karl Abraham, "A Short Study of the Development of the Libido, Viewed in the Light of Mental Disorders," *Selected Papers on Psychoanalysis*. London: Hogarth, 1924.

Yehoshua Arieli, *Individualism and Nationalism in American Ideology*. Harvard University Press, 1964. Especially Chap. 5.

Raymond Aron, *Main Currents in Sociological Thought*. 2 vols. Trans. Richard Howard and Helen Weaver. Doubleday, 1968, 1970.

Jacques Barzun, *Darwin, Marx, Wagner: Critique of a Heritage*. Little, Brown, 1941.

Carl Becker, *The Heavenly City of the Eighteenth Century Philosophers.* Yale University Press, 1932.

Howard S. Becker, *Outsiders: Studies in the Sociology of Deviance.* The Free Press, 1963.

Robert N. Bellah, "Durkheim and History." *American Sociological Review*, 1959, 24:447–451.

Peter L. Berger and Thomas Luckmann, *The Social Construction of Reality.* Doubleday, 1966.

Peter M. Blau, "Structural Effects." *American Sociological Review,* 1960, 25:178–193.

Eugen von Böhm-Bawerk, *Karl Marx and the Close of His System.* Trans. Paul M. Sweezy. Kelley, 1949.

Phillips Bradley, "A Historical Essay." In Alexis de Tocqueville, *Democracy in America*, Vol. II. Knopf, 1945.

Edmund Burke, *Reflections on the Revolution in France*, 1790. In *Works*, Vol. III. Little, Brown, 1899.

E. H. Carr, *Karl Marx.* London: Dent, 1934.

C. W. Cassenelli, "The Law of Oligarchy." *The American Political Science Review*, 1953, 47:773–784.

Ernst Cassirer, *The Question of Jean-Jacques Rousseau.* Trans. Peter Gay. Indiana University Press, 1963.

Terry Nichols Clark, *Prophets and Patrons: The French University and the Emergence of the Social Sciences.* Harvard University Press, 1973.

Richard A. Cloward, "Illegitimate Means, Anomie, and Deviant Behavior." *American Sociological Review*, 1959, 24:164–176.

Albert K. Cohen, "The Sociology of the Deviant Act: Anomie Theory and Beyond." *American Sociological Review*, 1965, 30:5–14.

Lewis A. Coser, *The Functions of Social Conflict.* The Free Press, 1956.

Lewis A. Coser, *Masters of Sociological Thought.* Harcourt Brace Jovanovich, 1971.

Ralf Dahrendorf, *Class and Class Conflict in Industrial Society.* Stanford University Press, 1959.

Robert Dubin, "Deviant Behavior and Social Structure." *American Sociological Review*, 1959, 24:147–164.

Emile Durkheim, *The Division of Labor in Society*, 1893. Trans. George Simpson. Macmillan, 1933.

Emile Durkheim, *The Rules of Sociological Method*, 1895. Trans. Sarah A. Solovay and John H. Mueller. University of Chicago Press, 1938.

Emile Durkheim, *Suicide*, 1897. Trans. John A. Spaulding and George Simpson. The Free Press, 1951.

Emile Durkheim, "Preface to the Second Edition: Some Notes on Occupational Groups," 1902. In *The Division of Labor in Society*. Trans. George Simpson. Macmillan, 1933.

Emile Durkheim, *The Elementary Forms of the Religious Life*, 1912. Trans. Joseph Ward Swain. London: George Allen and Unwin, 1915.

Sigmund Freud, "Mourning and Melancholia," *Standard Edition*, Vol. 14. London: Hogarth Press and Institute of Psychoanalysis, 1917.

Sigmund Freud, "The Economic Problem of Masochism," *Standard Edition*, Vol. 19. London: Hogarth Press and Institute of Psychoanalysis, 1924.

H. H. Gerth and C. Wright Mills, eds., *From Max Weber: Essays in Sociology*. Oxford, 1946.

Erving Goffman, *Asylums*. Aldine, 1962.

Alvin W. Gouldner, "Anti-Minotaur: The Myth of a Value-Free Sociology." In Irving Louis Horowitz, ed., *The New Sociology*. Oxford, 1964.

Alvin W. Gouldner, *The Coming Crisis of Western Sociology*. Basic, 1970.

Andrew Henry and James F. Short, Jr., *Suicide and Homicide*. The Free Press, 1954. Especially Chap. 2.

Rudolph Hilferding, "Böhm-Bawerk's Criticism of Marx," in Eugen von Böhm-Bawerk, *Karl Marx and the Close of His System*. Trans. Paul M. Sweezy. Kelley, 1949.

Thomas Hobbes, *Leviathan*. London: Crooke, 1651.

Eric Hobsbawm, Introduction to *Pre-Capitalist Economic Formations*. International Publishers, 1964.

Richard Hofstadter, *Social Darwinism in American Thought*. Beacon, 1955.

George C. Homans, "Bringing Men Back In." *American Sociological Review*, 1964, 29:809–818.

Samuel P. Huntington, *Political Order in Changing Societies*. Yale University Press, 1968. Especially Chap. 2.

Barclay D. Johnson, "Durkheim's One Cause of Suicide." *American Sociological Review*, 1965, 30:875–886.

Thomas Kuhn, *The Structure of Scientific Revolutions*, 2d ed. University of Chicago Press, 1970.

Paul F. Lazarsfeld and Anthony R. Oberschall, "Max Weber and Empirical Social Research." *American Sociological Review*, 1965, 30:185–199.

George Lichtheim, *Marxism: An Historical and Critical Study*. Praeger, 1961.

George Lichteim, "Marx and the 'Asiatic Mode of Production.' " *St. Antony's Papers*, 1963, No. 14:86–112.

John Locke, *Two Treatises of Government*. London: Awnsham and Churchill, 1698.

C. B. MacPherson, *The Political Theory of Possessive Individualism*. Clarendon, Oxford University Press, 1962.

Karl Mannheim, *Ideology and Utopia*. Trans. Louis Wirth and Edward Shils. Harcourt Brace Jovanovich, 1936.

Herbert Marcuse, *One-Dimensional Man*. Beacon, 1964.

Karl Marx, "On the Jewish Question," 1843. In *Early Writings*. Trans. T. B. Bottomore. McGraw-Hill, 1964.

Karl Marx, "Contribution to the Critique of Hegel's Philosophy of Right. Introduction," 1844. In *Early Writings*. Trans. T. B. Bottomore. McGraw-Hill, 1964.

Karl Marx, "Theses on Feuerbach," 1845. In Karl Marx and Friedrich Engels, *The German Ideology*. Ed. R. Pascal. International, 1947.

Karl Marx and Friedrich Engels, *The German Ideology*, 1846. Ed. R. Pascal. International, 1947.

Karl Marx and Friedrich Engels, *Manifesto of the Communist Party*, 1848. International, 1948.

Karl Marx, *Grundrisse: Foundations of the Critique of Political Economy*, 1858. Trans. Martin Nicolaus. Random House, 1973.

Karl Marx, *A Contribution to the Critique of Political Economy*, 1859. Trans. N. I. Stone. Kerr, 1904.

Karl Marx, *Capital*, Vol. I, 1867. Trans. Samuel Moore and Edward Aveling. London: George Allen & Unwin, 1949.

Karl Marx, *Capital*, Vol. I, 1867. Trans. Samuel Moore and Edward Aveling. Moscow: Foreign Languages Publishing, 1957.

Karl Marx, *Critique of the Gotha Programme*, 1875. Ed. C. P. Dutt. International, 1938.

Karl Marx, *Capital*, Vol. III, 1894. Ed. F. Engels. Moscow: Foreign Languages Publishing, 1962.

Robert K. Merton, "Conformity, Deviation, and Opportunity-Structures." *American Sociological Review*, 1959, 24:178–189.

Robert K. Merton, *On Theoretical Sociology*. The Free Press, 1967. Especially Chap. 1.

Robert K. Merton, *Social Theory and Social Structure*. The Free Press, 1968.

Robert Michels, *Political Parties*, 1911. Trans. Eden and Cedar Paul. Dover, 1959.

C. Wright Mills, *The Sociological Imagination*. Oxford, 1959.

Arthur Mitzman, *The Iron Cage: An Historical Interpretation of Max Weber*. Knopf, 1970.

Nicholas C. Mullins, *Theories and Theory Groups in Contemporary American Sociology*. Harper & Row, 1973.

Robert A. Nisbet, *The Sociological Tradition.* Basic, 1966.

Anthony R. Oberschall, *The Establishment of Empirical Sociology.* Harper & Row, 1972.

Talcott Parsons, *The Structure of Social Action.* McGraw-Hill, 1937.

Talcott Parsons, *The Social System.* The Free Press, 1951. Especially Chap. VII.

Talcott Parsons, *Societies: Evolutionary and Comparative Perspectives.* Prentice-Hall, 1966.

Talcott Parsons and Edward Shils, eds., *Toward A General Theory of Action.* Harvard University Press, 1951.

Whitney Pope, *Emile Durkheim's Theory of Social Integration.* Unpublished Ph.D. dissertation, University of California, Berkeley, 1970.

Melvin Richter, "Tocqueville's Contributions to the Theory of Revolution." In Carl J. Friedrich, ed., *Revolution.* Atherton, 1966.

Guenther Roth, "Introduction." In Max Weber, *Economy and Society,* Vol. 1. Ed. Guenther Roth and Claus Wittich. Bedminster, 1968.

Jean-Jacques Rousseau, *Discourse on the Origin and Foundations of Inequality,* 1755. In *Miscellaneous Works,* Vol. I. London: Becket and DeHondt, 1767.

Jean-Jacques Rousseau, *Social Contract,* 1762. In *Miscellaneous Works,* Vol. V. London: Becket and DeHondt, 1767.

Hanan C. Selvin, "Durkheim's *Suicide* and Problems of Empirical Research." *American Journal of Sociology,* 1958, 63:607–619.

Hanan C. Selvin, "Durkheim's *Suicide:* Further Thoughts on a Methodological Classic." In Robert A. Nisbet, *Emile Durkheim.* Prentice-Hall, 1965.

Lawrence W. Sherman, "Uses of the Masters." *The American Sociologist,* 1974, 9:176–181.

Edward Shils, "Tradition, Ecology, and Institution in the History of Sociology." *Daedalus,* 1970, 99:760–825.

Neil J. Smelser, *Social Change in the Industrial Revolution.* University of Chicago Press, 1959.

Neil J. Smelser, *Essays in Sociological Explanation.* Prentice-Hall, 1968. Especially pp. 58–59.

Neil J. Smelser, "Alexis de Tocqueville as Comparative Analyst." In Ivan Vallier, ed., *Comparative Methods in Sociology.* University of California Press, 1971.

David Snyder and Charles Tilly, "Hardship and Collective Violence in France, 1830–1960." *American Sociological Review,* 1972, 37:520–532.

Arthur L. Stinchombe, *Constructing Social Theories.* Harcourt Brace Jovanovich, 1968.

Alexis de Tocqueville, *Journeys to England and Ireland,* 1835. Trans. George Lawrence and K. P. Mayer. Doubleday, 1968.

Alexis de Tocqueville, *Democracy in America*, 1840. Trans. Henry Reeves. Barnes, 1851.

272   Alexis de Tocqueville, *The Old Regime and the French Revolution*, 1856. Trans. Stuart Gilbert. Doubleday, 1955.

Jonathan H. Turner, *The Structure of Sociological Theory*. Dorsey, 1974.

Stanley H. Udy, Jr., " 'Bureaucracy' and 'Rationality' in Weber's Organization Theory: An Empirical Study." *American Sociological Review*, 1959, 24:791–795.

Voltaire, "English Commerce," 1733. In *Works*, Vol. XXXIX. Trans. William F. Fleming. Paris: Dumont, 1901.

Voltaire, "Laws," 1757. In *Works*, Vol. XI. Trans. William F. Fleming. Paris: Dumont, 1901.

R. Stephen Warner, "The Role of Religious Ideas and the Use of Models in Max Weber's Comparative Studies of Non-Capitalist Societies." *Journal of Economic History*, 1970a, 30:74–99.

R. Stephen Warner, "Critical or Technical Sociology? A Comment on Somers." *Berkeley Journal of Sociology*, 1970b, 15:64–72.

R. Stephen Warner, "The Methodology of Marx's Comparative Analysis of Modes of Production." In Ivan Vallier, ed., *Comparative Methods in Sociology*. University of California Press, 1971.

Max Weber, " 'Objectivity' in Social Science and Social Policy," 1904. In *The Methodology of the Social Sciences*. Trans. Edward A. Shils and Henry A. Finch. The Free Press, 1949.

Max Weber, *The Protestant Ethic and the Spirit of Capitalism*, 1905. Trans. Talcott Parsons. Scribner, 1958.

Max Weber, "The Social Psychology of the World Religions," 1915. In H. H. Gerth and C. Wright Mills, eds., *From Max Weber: Essays in Sociology*. Oxford, 1946.

Max Weber, *The Religion of India*, 1917. Trans. H. H. Gerth and Don Martindale. The Free Press, 1958.

Max Weber, "Politics as a Vocation," 1919a. In H. H. Gerth and C. Wright Mills, eds., *From Max Weber: Essays in Sociology*. Oxford, 1946.

Max Weber, "Science as a Vocation," 1919b. In H. H. Gerth and C. Wright Mills, eds., *From Max Weber: Essays in Sociology*. Oxford, 1946.

Max Weber, *Economy and Society*, 3 vols., 1922. Ed. Guenther Roth and Claus Wittich. Bedminster, 1968.

Hilde Weiss, "Karl Marx's 'Enquête Ouvrière.' " In Tom Bottomore, ed., *Karl Marx*. Prentice-Hall, 1973.

BIBLIOGRAPHY

Sheldon S. Wolin, "Political Theory as a Vocation." *American Political Science Review*, 1969, 63:1062–1082.

Irving M. Zeitlin, *Ideology and the Development of Sociological Theory*. Prentice-Hall, 1968. Especially Chap. 15.

Irving M. Zeitlin, *Rethinking Sociology*. Appleton-Century-Crofts, 1973.

Index

1 2 3 4 5 6 7 8 9–RJC–82 81 80 79 78 77 76